I0454137

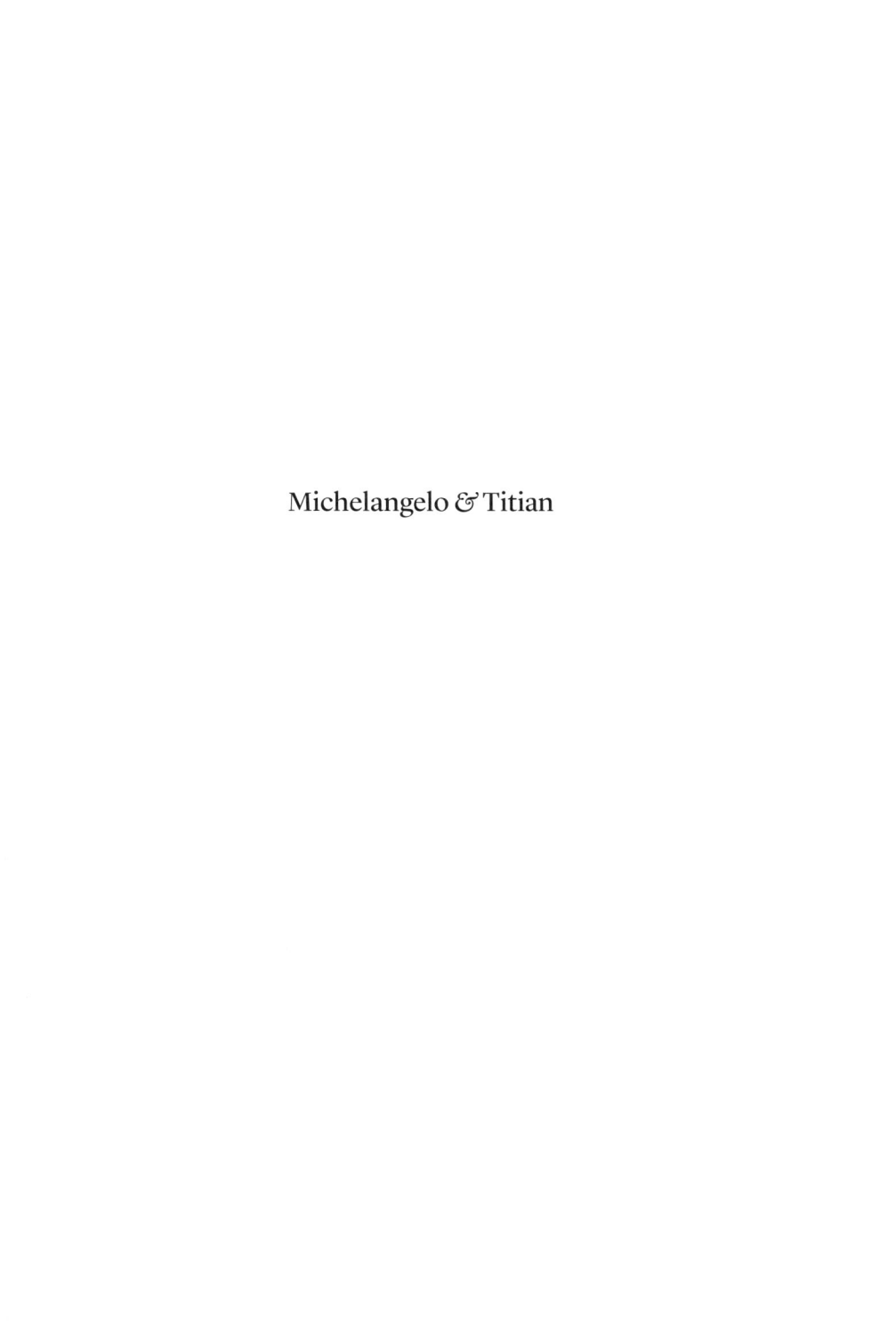

Michelangelo & Titian

Michelangelo & Titian

A TALE OF RIVALRY AND GENIUS

William E. Wallace

PRINCETON UNIVERSITY PRESS
PRINCETON AND OXFORD

Copyright © 2026 by William E. Wallace

Princeton University Press is committed to the protection of copyright and the intellectual property our authors entrust to us. Copyright promotes the progress and integrity of knowledge created by humans. By engaging with an authorized copy of this work, you are supporting creators and the global exchange of ideas. As this work is protected by copyright, any reproduction or distribution of it in any form for any purpose requires permission; permission requests should be sent to permissions@press.princeton.edu. Ingestion of any PUP IP for any AI purposes is strictly prohibited.

Published by Princeton University Press, 41 William Street, Princeton, New Jersey 08540
In the United Kingdom: Princeton University Press, 99 Banbury Road, Oxford OX2 6JX
GPSR Authorized Representative: Easy Access System Europe - Mustamäe tee 50, 10621 Tallinn, Estonia, gpsr.requests@easproject.com

press.princeton.edu

Jacket images: *Michelangelo Buonarroti* (detail), after 1564. Engraving by Giorgio Ghisi, after Marcello Venusti. Engraving on laid paper, 26.8 × 20.1 cm. Rosenwald Collection, NGA, 1964.8.1030. *Titian* (detail), 1587. Engraving by Agostino Carracci, after Titian. Engraving, 32.9 × 23.5 cm. Rosenwald Collection, NGA, 1947.7.14

All Rights Reserved

ISBN 978-0-691-26657-2
ISBN (ebook) 978-0-691-26663-3

Library of Congress Control Number: 2025942881

British Library Cataloging-in-Publication Data is available

Editorial: Michelle Komie and Annie Miller
Production Editorial: Karen Carter
Text Design: Matt Avery (Monograph LLC)
Jacket/Cover Design: Chris Ferrante
Production: Steve Sears
Publicity: Jodi Price
Copyeditor: Lachlan Brooks

This book has been composed in Lyon Text

Printed in the United States of America

1 3 5 7 9 10 8 6 4 2

Contents

Preface

The Emperor Charles V, ruler of half the known world, returns
an accidently fallen brush to Titian, his favored artist (Plate 1).[1]
A golden-haired beauty interrupts her lute playing to watch the
exchange: Titian expresses thanks while his sovereign declares:
"Titian deserves to be served by Caesar."

We are in Titian's Venetian studio in the Ca' del Duca, Venice.
If we open the shutters, we see light sparkling off the Grand Canal.
Titian is dressed in a long silk gown and sports the honorific gold
chain conferred upon him by his illustrious patron. Such a tale of
condescension finds precedence in classical antiquity, mirroring a
story in which Alexander the Great, who frequented the studio of
the famous artist Apelles, declared that he would be painted by no
other artist.[2] Titian, celebrated as the "New Apelles," was accorded
such honors by Emperor Charles V.

A painting in the Casa Buonarroti relates a similar anecdote of
princely condescension toward the Florentine artist Michelangelo
Buonarroti (Plate 2). Fashionably dressed in costly black brocade
with fine leather boots, Michelangelo is seated in a curial chair reserved since Roman times for distinguished personages (Charles V
also is seated in such a chair).[3] Before Michelangelo stands a

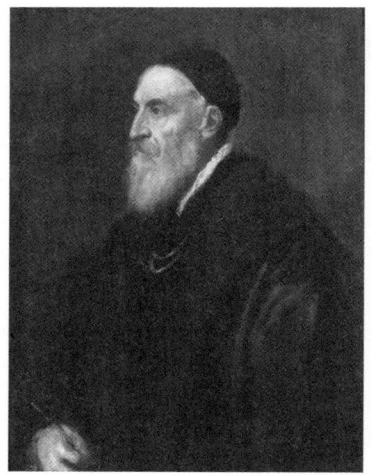

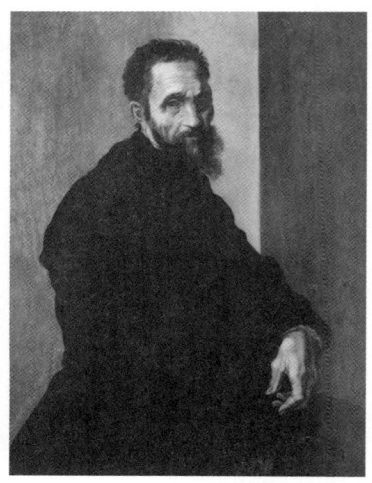

1. Titian Vecellio, *Self-Portrait*, oil on canvas, 34×25.5 in (98.5×65 cm), Museo Nacional del Prado, Madrid, c. 1562.

2. Jacopino del Conte, *Portrait of Michelangelo*, oil on panel, 38.75×26.75 in (98.5×68 cm), Casa Buonarroti, Florence, c. 1540.

deferential prince Francesco, the son of Cosimo de' Medici and the future ruler of Florence and Tuscany. Although seated, Michelangelo enjoys the elevated social position: the artist sits, the young prince stands, Michelangelo speaks, Francesco listens.

These nineteenth century anecdotal paintings celebrate two artists who significantly raised the stature of their profession, from craftsman to genius, from artisan to gentleman. Titian was an artist who became an aristocrat; Michelangelo was an aristocrat who made art. Titian portrays himself in profile, a distinguished gentleman in expensive vestments, proudly sporting his honorific chain (Fig. 1). Jacopino del Conte portrays Michelangelo dressed in similarly expensive, fashionable black attire with no indication of a profession other than that of gentleman (Fig. 2). Both portraits celebrate the artists as aristocrats, geniuses deserving an elevated place in a rigidly hierarchical social world.

Tiziano Vecellio and Michelangelo Buonarroti were the two most esteemed artists of their time. They knew it, and they knew each other. While they met only twice, over the course of more than forty years their lives and art became ever more entwined. They shared a handful of mutual friends, dozens of acquaintances, and the patronage of many of the most important personages of their time. Titian could claim the Holy Roman Emperor Charles V and King Philip of Spain as significant patrons while Michelangelo could counter with a string of a half dozen popes dating back to Julius II. What is surprising is the number of patrons, friends, and acquaintances that they shared and who competed for their services. More than just art bound the two artists. Francesco Sansovino, author of a guide to Venice and son of Jacopo Sansovino (who was a mutual friend of both Michelangelo and Titian), yoked the two together when he wrote: "Titian alone and no other can be considered fit to accompany the divine Michelangelo."[4] For many, the relationship between these two giants has often been described as antagonistic or largely one-sided: what did the younger Titian gain from Michelangelo? Scholars have yet to recognize the extent and importance of what Michelangelo gained from his Venetian contemporary. The relationship was reciprocal and mutually beneficial. The story of their interest and regard, admiration and emulation, and sometimes open competition evolved over half their lifetimes. They grew up, grew famous, and grew old, learning about and from one another, hearing, admiring, envying, criticizing, and competing. Similarly, more than twenty years of mutual attention and admiration inspired Hector Berlioz and Richard Wagner, the two musical giants of their time, to ever greater heights of invention. For twice as long did Titian and Michelangelo nourish and inspire one another, even if they certainly would have denied it. As such, they are the Matisse/Picasso rivalry of their time.

I wish to tell the story of why and how Titian and Michelangelo discovered one another, first met, and maintained an artistic dialogue that persisted to the end of their long lives. How did their interest in one another grow, change, and manifest itself in their respective fields of endeavor? The two artists regarded and challenged one another, sometimes in an open but largely unspoken, slow-burn competition. They were contemporaries but not colleagues, respectfully friendly but not friends. They won fame and exorbitant recognition while doggedly committed to securing social status and lasting legacies for themselves and their families.

This is a story about the lives of two individuals who were more attentive and admiring of one another than either would ever admit. They were the stars on an international stage in which they shared many actors, impresarios, stagehands, and audiences of their time. At first, they were focused on themselves in their different local worlds, but with time and fame came an increasing awareness of one another.

* * *

In a shady, unkempt garden, a young boy gazes dreamily at a statue of the Virgin Mary perched on a thick tree stump (Fig. 3). This is the young Titian who painted with colors as brilliant as the flowers he holds and that are strewn on the ground. Yet, the pages of his sketchbook remain blank. Unlike Florentine artists, for whom drawing (*disegno*) was foundational to their craft, young Titian learned to paint with colors taken entirely from nature, eschewing preparatory drawing. That is precisely the criticism Michelangelo leveled at Titian: "too bad the Venetians never learned to draw." And that is how our story begins.

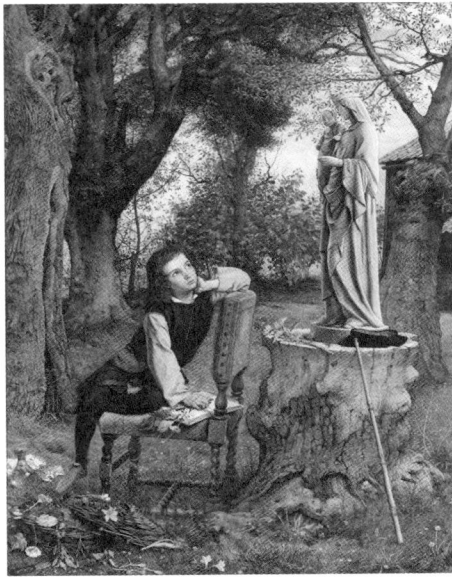

3. William Dyce, *Young Titian in the Garden*, oil on canvas, 41.5 × 31 in (100.5 × 79 cm), Aberdeen Art Gallery, Scotland, 1856–57.

In relating this tale, I am at times attempting to capture unspoken and unwritten history, all that was not said or that was said but not written down. The modern biographer Richard Holmes asks: "Can we catch the sound of their voices across the centuries?" Holmes was after ordinary voices, but my protagonists are among the most notable and best documented subjects of their time. Our difficulty is not a paucity but a surfeit of voices: history and story, archive and anecdote, documents and gossip, biography and hagiography, hearsay, imagination, and fabulation. Gaps in this bountiful record are sometimes narrow enough to bridge with informed imagination, stimulated and underpinned by the plethora of source material. There is more than enough to tell a tale of the two greatest artists of the Italian Renaissance: a tale of genius and rivalry, a tale of Titans.

Michelangelo & Titian

Prologue
A Courtesy Visit

On a damp dreary day—was it January or February of 1546?—Giorgio Vasari stepped over a fresh pile of dung to knock on Michelangelo's door. The street, Macel de' Corvi (slaughterhouse of crows), was crowded with market stalls selling whole and parts of small birds and rodents, fowl and foul meats. Over the busy street loomed a gleaming, hundred-foot marble column, said to be part of a Roman Emperor's palace.

Michelangelo's housemate and general assistant Pietro Urbino welcomed Vasari into the dark entrance hall. The spacious ground floor served as a sculpture studio, airy but cluttered and filled with marble dust. A low portico opened onto the kitchen garden, a stable, and a small forge. A noisy triumphing rooster ruled the yard, along with a few hens and a lamenting cat who took up long-term residency. Toward the rear of the property, fruit trees provided Michelangelo with especially good figs and muscatel grapes, which he enjoyed sharing with his closest friends.

The seventy-year-old Michelangelo greeted young Giorgio familiarly, noted his fine clothes, and smiled at the thought of dandyish Vasari making his perfumed way through the smelly neighborhood. Michelangelo sardonically complained about "piles of excrement around my door, as if there was nowhere else to shit. Dead cats, carrion, filth and slop are my constant companions."[1] Michelangelo slipped on his soft leather boots and was lacing his jerkin when he called out to his servant, "Antonio, bring around *mio ronzinetto piccolo*—my small nag." He and Vasari set off at an ambling pace toward St. Peter's, a thirty-minute ride across wintry Rome. They were to pay a courtesy visit to the Venetian artist, Tiziano Vecellio, recently arrived from Venezia, known as "La Serenissima," the most serene.

In the past weeks, Giorgio Vasari had been serving as companion and formal cicerone, or guide, to Titian who was making his first visit to the Eternal City. Vasari proved the perfect liaison, since Titian, like many of his fellow citizens far from their lagoon city, seemed a fish out of water. Lodged in the Belvedere Palace as a guest of Pope Paul III, Titian was in Rome to paint portraits of the pope and members of his family. Vasari proudly informed Titian that he too was employed by the Farnese, frescoing the large audience hall of Cardinal Alessandro Farnese's Roman palace. To Michelangelo, Vasari boasted, "I finished it in just one hundred days," to which Michelangelo drily replied, "Si vede"—that's evident. Vasari the puffed courtier, Michelangelo the acerbic wit.

On their slow ride across the city, Vasari entertained Michelangelo with inane pleasantries and prattling tidbits about the visiting foreigner. He described having to translate for Titian since Roman shopkeepers and even the Vatican officials struggled to comprehend his Venetian dialect. Vasari chuckled when he told Michelangelo that Titian disliked Roman cuisine. Entrails, eel, and all manner of flying and crawling things appealed little to Titian who preferred the savory taste of fresh fish and the effervescence of a Venetian white wine. Amused, Michelangelo held his tongue.

After crossing the Tiber bridge and entering the teeming Borgo, conversation was interrupted by insistent beggars and loud street vendors selling religious trinkets, paper indulgences, and, more slyly, any sort of sexual services: "We have virgins, young boys . . ." Michelangelo pulled his warm cloak more firmly around his thin frame. Ahead, the massive skeleton of St. Peter's rose into the sky. After forty years of construction, the building still looked more like an ancient ruin than a new church. Having just been appointed papal architect, Michelangelo avoided looking up at the looming hulk. He kept his unhappy thoughts to himself. Vasari chattered on.

Veering north to avoid the muddy building site, the two artists rode alongside the Vatican walls and up the hill to the Belvedere. The Belvedere, "Beautiful View," served as a summer retreat and home to the growing collection of papal antiquities. The little jewel of a palazzetto offered guest quarters for dignitaries and visiting artists. Leonardo da Vinci resided for several months at the Belvedere while he unsuccessfully sought employment from Pope Leo X. Thirty years later, Titian, too, was here to curry papal favor.

Dismounting under a lowering sky, Michelangelo and Vasari relinquished their horses, climbed the stairs, and made their way into airy rooms. A courteous Titian greeted them amid the pungent smell of fresh paint and a wonderful world of color. With a few completed paintings and several more in progress, Michelangelo and Vasari found themselves surrounded by the richly saturated colors of Venetian oil painting, so different from the pale, matte colors of fresco that dominated every inch of Roman wall, including those of the Vatican itself.

Polite but stilted conversation accompanied the inspection of Titian's pictures, some complete, several still in progress. A prominently displayed crimson canvas drew their attention—a triple portrait of the Holy Father and his two grandsons (Plate 3). Dressed in a scarlet cap and a red velvet *mozzetta*, the wily pontiff's dark, intelligent eyes dart from side to side, fully cognizant of the family drama unfolding around him. The elderly pontiff is hunched forward, looking every bit his seventy-eight years, yet also exceptionally alert. With a firm grip on his chair, he turns toward his unctuous twenty-one-year-old grandson, a jutting elbow keeping the young man at bay. Paul's knowing half-smile slips from under a beaky Roman nose; he is fully capable of controlling his contentious family.

Standing in dignified silence behind the pope's chair is the preferred son, twenty-six-year-old Alessandro, dressed in cardinal vestments and bright vermilion *beretta* cap. The scholarly cardinal's dark hair and beard frame pleasant features. His direct gaze fastens upon the viewer, catching us witnessing the tense family encounter.

Suddenly, young Giorgio Vasari burst out: "They appear more alive than painted!" The observation—an ancient topos—was, in this case, true. The admirers of Titian's picture felt the living presence of the most powerful man on earth. As an intimate of Farnese, Michelangelo agreed with Vasari, yet he wondered what the pope might think about this naked revelation of his family. Vasari praised the composition, noting its similarity to Raphael's triple portrait of Leo X and his cardinals.

Looking intently at the unfinished canvas, Michelangelo barely listened as Vasari and Titian chatted about the difficulty (*difficultà*) of creating a speaking picture. Vasari noted the uncomfortable separation of Ottavio from the pope and the contrast with Alessandro, the favored elder son. Ottavio's lupine features, pointy nose, and groveling posture appear to bend under the weight of the heavy maroon curtain. Although a comparatively new member of the Farnese entourage, Titian successfully captured the likenesses and visible strains among the members of the powerful ruling family.

The triple portrait surely encouraged admiration and discussion; however, another picture soon drew the visitors' attention. Propped on a table against the wall was a large painting that Titian was delivering to Cardinal Alessandro: an alluring, lushly colored picture of Danaë (Plate 4). Naked except for a pearl earring, jewel-studded bracelet, and pinky ring, Danaë reclines against a hillock of downy pillows. While gazing dreamily toward Jove who materializes as a shower of golden coins, she sinks further into the soft, disheveled bed. A bit of white sheet prevents us from seeing what Jove spies: her pudenda, revealed as her legs fall open, welcoming the divine copulation. Unconsciously, Danaë grips the rumpled sheets in anticipation of the pain and pleasure of union with the deity.

Somewhat pompously, Titian began describing the Ovidian myth: Danaë, the unfortunate daughter of Acrisius, proud king of Argos, is locked away in a tower . . . to preserve her chastity, of course. But Jove—Lord of Mount Olympus—spies her, is utterly smitten, and penetrates her prison by transforming himself into a golden shower. Attending Cupid turns away in alarm while lovely Danaë yields to divine lovemaking. Titian proudly points to Jove's miraculous metamorphosis and the sparkling *impasto* of the gold coins.

The all-male company leaned close to the canvas, attracted to the life-size, voluptuous nude. Was this a re-creation of an ancient masterpiece, perhaps by Apelles, the most famous painter of classical antiquity? Just as he was aware that contemporaries referred to Michelangelo as "il Divino," the Divine One, so the present company was aware that Titian was celebrated as the "New Apelles."[2] Among general murmurs of admiration, Michelangelo professed, "It pleases me very much" ("dicendo che molto gli piaceva").

Was Michelangelo merely being polite? Can we trust the comment, knowing that it was recorded by Giorgio Vasari some twenty years after the Belvedere meeting?[3] While Vasari may not have remembered Michelangelo's precise words, we can accept the essential veracity of his recollection. An examination of the episode in the context of the characters' long lives will permit us to lend credibility to Vasari's memory. Michelangelo, who stubbornly declared that painting "non è mia arte" ("not my métier"), genuinely admired Titian's *Danaë*. Are we surprised?

As papal architect with significant responsibilities, Michelangelo was under no obligation to extend courtesies to the visiting Venetian. Indeed, following the death of the preceding papal architect, Antonio da Sangallo, in August 1546, Pope Paul charged Michelangelo with taking over the building of New St. Peter's. Objecting mightily but failing to dissuade the stubborn pontiff, the seventy-one-year-old Michelangelo confronted the unimaginably difficult task of organizing the mess of a barely functional worksite and rectifying a myriad of engineering problems. The architect of the largest building on earth could rightly claim to be busy. How and why did Michelangelo find time to visit with a foreign painter from the Veneto, and further, praise him for a work that appears so completely antithetical to his own?

As often as he criticized the art of his contemporaries, Michelangelo also recognized artistic excellence. Moreover, this was not his first encounter with a masterpiece by Titian. By the time the two artists met in the Belvedere, Michelangelo had seen many Titian paintings, first in Ferrara and then when he fled to Venice in 1529. He appreciated his contemporary's skill as a portraitist, a painter of mythologies, a colorist, and perhaps most importantly, as an inventor of dramatic figures engaged in narrative action. Contrary to what we might expect, Michelangelo admired and learned from Titian before openly competing with his Venetian counterpart, including in the latter's preferred medium of paint—an astonishing turn given that the artist declared himself "no painter."

When Michelangelo accompanied Vasari to call on Titian, he partly acted on behalf of his friend and patron, Pope Paul. At the same time, he was returning a favor. Call his visit diplomatic, artistic, or personal: in the Renaissance world of the court and courtier, favors extended were favors reciprocated. Michelangelo had a debt to pay.

In the 1520s, Michelangelo had been busily working for Pope Clement VII at the Medici church of San Lorenzo in Florence. Following the Sack of Rome in 1527, Florence declared itself an independent Republic and expelled their Medici overlords. Despite the pope's efforts to retain him, Michelangelo, a life-long republican, elected to side with his native city, devoting the next two years of his life to the heroic but doomed republican cause. In April 1529, he was appointed Governor and Procurator General of the city's fortifications, tasked with hastily constructing a defensive network to protect the vulnerable city from an impending siege. One day while hard at work on the bastions, Michelangelo received an ominous warning that his life was in danger. Unsettled by the threat, he abruptly abandoned the city, his family, and his critically important post, fleeing to the comparative safety of Venice.

During these unsettled times Michelangelo met Titian. The Venetian government welcomed the fugitive as an official guest of the Republic and delegated Titian to extend courtesy to the renowned artist. It was 1529, and this was the first face-to-face encounter of the two individuals: Michelangelo, the most famous artist in the world—humbled by his current, much reduced circumstances—meeting Titian, preeminent artist of Venice and a rising star in the international firmament. Now, sixteen years later, they met for the second time in Rome. As Michelangelo felt like a stranger in Venice, so Titian felt the same in Rome. And therefore, it was personally and diplomatically appropriate for Michelangelo to extend a complementary courtesy visit to his Venetian counterpart.

In 1546, Michelangelo was seventy-one years old. Tiziano Vecellio was approaching sixty, but like many persons in Renaissance Italy, he was uncertain of his precise age. Michelangelo was the papal favorite and the newly appointed architect of St. Peter's; Titian was the preferred portraitist of the Holy Roman Emperor Charles V, as well as painter to the monarchs, princes, and potentates of Europe. In short, he was the painter of princes and "Prince of Painters." They were the two most famous artists in the world, and they knew it.

Building upon the nascent relationship established in Venice sixteen years earlier, the Roman meeting fertilized a slow-developing reciprocal interest that extended over years. The two artists never met again, but their relationship would continue for another two decades, mostly as a long-distance, unspoken dialogue of mutual if cautious regard. It was a sub-rosa competition between worthy and respectful rivals. Titian and Michelangelo paid attention and learned from one another, followed the other's career, and grew old and famous together. Their relationship was distant and mostly indirect. That does not mean, however, that it was not rich and meaningful, and mutually beneficial. Unexpectedly, almost accidently, the two very different artists and personalities were engaged intermittently with one another for forty years—half of their long lives.

*   *   *

It was time for Michelangelo and Vasari to take their leave. Titian would return to Venice, Michelangelo would turn his full attention to St. Peter's, and Vasari became the self-appointed champion of artists. The meeting had been pleasant and polite, if a bit constrained, as might be expected of the situation and persons involved. Meanwhile, a star-struck Giorgio Vasari—younger by some thirty-five years—was all ears.

Danaë and Company

As Vasari subsequently related, Michelangelo admired the "nude woman, representing *Danaë*, who had in her lap Jove transformed into a rain of gold."[4] Vasari then added the critical nub of this encounter, which is the only thing that most persons remember about the famous meeting. After leaving, Michelangelo and Giorgio began discussing Titian's painting. Buonarroti commended it highly, saying "that his colouring and his style pleased him very much but that it was a shame that in Venice they did not learn to draw well from the beginning."[5]

Of course, this is the famous damnation of Venice by the Tuscan who criticized Titian's drawing even as he admired his painting. Vasari's principal purpose in relating the conversation was to appoint his hero as the spokesperson for the superiority of Tuscan drawing (disegno) versus Venetian color (colorito). Vasari recorded Michelangelo's remark twenty years after the fact, and not until the second edition of his *Le vite de' più eccellenti pittori, scultori e architettori* (1568). Why, we should ask, did Vasari not describe this seemingly momentous encounter in his first edition (1550), just a few years after it occurred, while Michelangelo was still alive to corroborate it? Moreover, it is significant that the anecdote is related only in the life of Titian, but does not appear in the much longer record of Michelangelo's life.

Given Michelangelo's authority, the remark quickly became a rapier-like weapon wielded in an increasingly acrimonious debate regarding drawing versus coloring, morphing into broader discussions of the relative merits of painting versus sculpture and the relationship between the literary and visual arts—the so-called *paragone*, or comparison of the arts.[6]

Like many contemporaries, Vasari was deeply invested in these learned controversies. In relating the anecdote about the *Danaë*,

Vasari took advantage of the encounter between the world's two most famous artists to articulate his own Tuscan bias, which was presumably shared by Michelangelo. We smile and are seduced by a droll story. But, do we imagine that Michelangelo and Titian actually talked about disegno and colorito—the airless oppositional terms of mid-sixteenth-century theoretical discourse? As Michelangelo once said, such academic debates "take up more time than the execution of the figures themselves."[7] He had no time for such disputes. In fact, he expressed his supposed criticism of Titian privately to Vasari, not publicly, and certainly not to Titian himself.

It is, of course, impossible to recover conversation from nearly a half millennium ago, and little of Michelangelo's exchange with Titian is preserved in Vasari's laconic anecdote. Writing more than twenty years after it occurred, Vasari was less interested in narrating history than in composing a literary masterpiece, his *Lives of the Artists*. What he recalled of the conversation was marshaled for his own polemical purpose, setting the two most famous artists in rivalry with one another while explicitly proclaiming the superiority of his hero Michelangelo.

A Long Story

Colored by Vasari's anecdote and Michelangelo's criticism, the relationship between the two artists is often described as antagonistic, and largely one-sided with the younger Titian adapting figures, motives, and ideas from Michelangelo.[8] Scholars have proposed multiple examples of Michelangelo's influence on Titian; they have been less willing to consider what Michelangelo gained from his Venetian contemporary.

The story, as any history between two individuals, is more complex and more interesting, especially as it evolved over half their lifetimes. No matter what we make of the famous meeting in Rome, it occurred in the approximate middle of a prolonged, forty-year acquaintance. There is much to tell before and after that afternoon in the Belvedere studio. Let us escape the confines of Michelangelo's famously clever remark and examine the longue durée.

The forty-year history offers a compelling tale of the two most famous artists of their day, and, almost, of all time. Each was supremely gifted and hugely ambitious. At first, they began and forged careers unaware of one another, largely focused on achieving individual success in their respective and very different worlds of Florence and Venice. Separately, their early successes led to expanded opportunities. Michelangelo's fame spread quickly with the carving of the *Pietà* in Rome and the *David* in Florence. Yet, even as his horizons widened beyond the narrow bounds of Florentine *campanalismo* (local pride) his chauvinistic father reminded him that "honor is worth more in your own country and at home."[9] To Lodovico Buonarroti, fame only mattered in Florence.

So, too, did Venetians measure fame and status by a citizen's contribution to their "Most Serene Republic," La Serenissima. Titian, from provincial Cadore, labored hard to establish his reputation in Venice's highly competitive environment. The two artists therefore first concentrated on their individual lives and local careers. After years of challenges and triumphs, their accomplishments and outsized ambitions eventually led to an awareness of one another. When did this occur? At what point did either artist learn about the other? How did this happen and why? And what came of it?

The story begins with a young and ambitious Titian. Let us listen to what we can of oral culture in early sixteenth-century Italy, including hearsay and "word of mouth." As with most stories, it is best to start at the beginning.

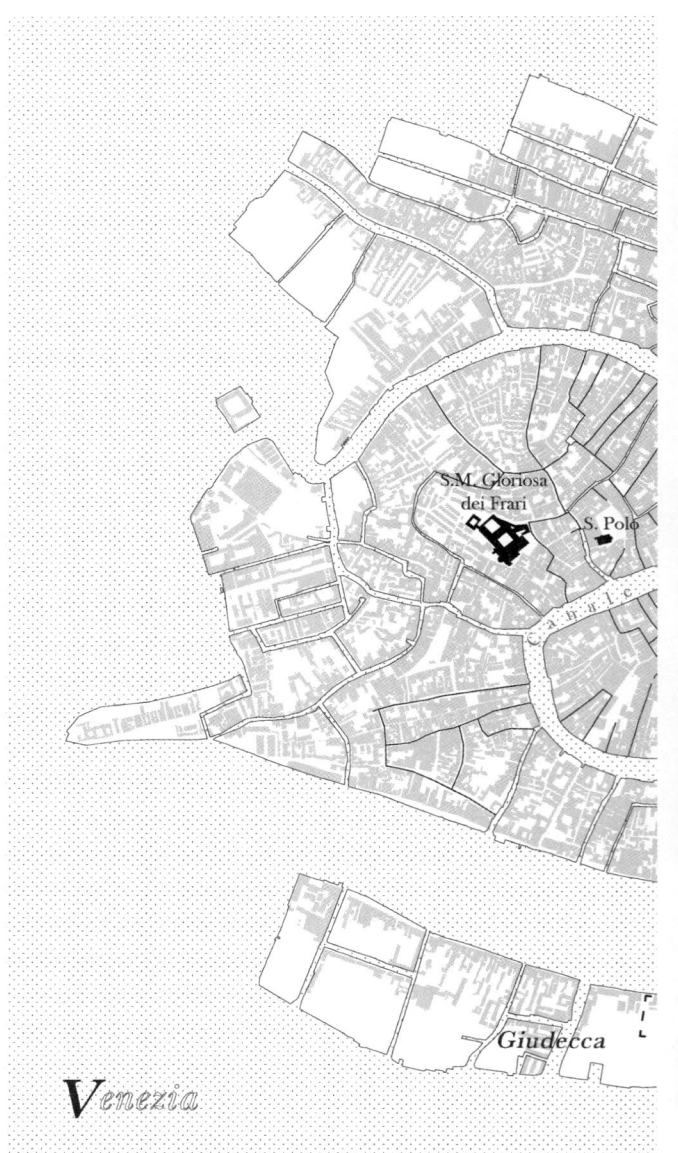

S.M. Gloriosa
dei Frari

S. Polo

Giudecca

Venezia

Map of Venice
(Patrick Hathaway)

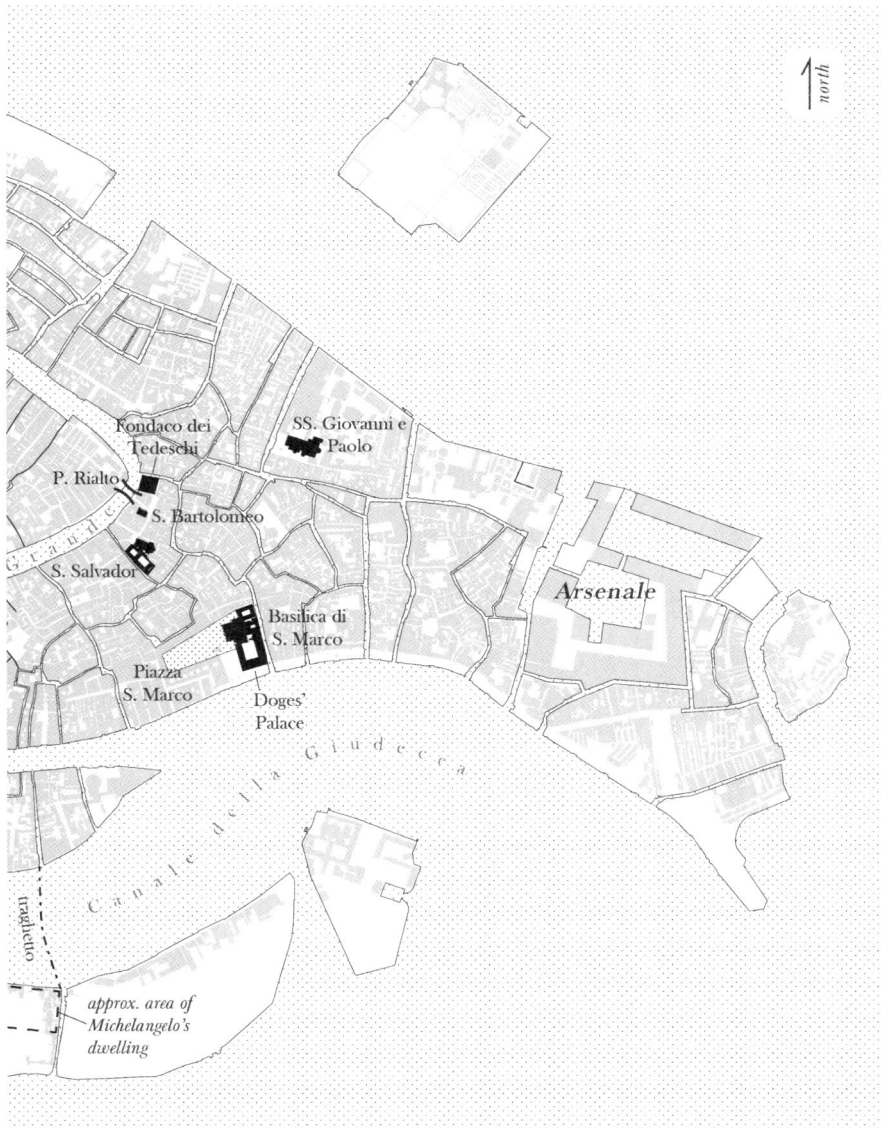

north

Fondaco dei
Tedeschi

SS. Giovanni e
Paolo

P. Rialto

S. Bartolomeo

S. Salvador

Arsenale

Basilica di
S. Marco

Piazza
S. Marco

Doges'
Palace

Canale della Giudecca

traghetto

*approx. area of
Michelangelo's
dwelling*

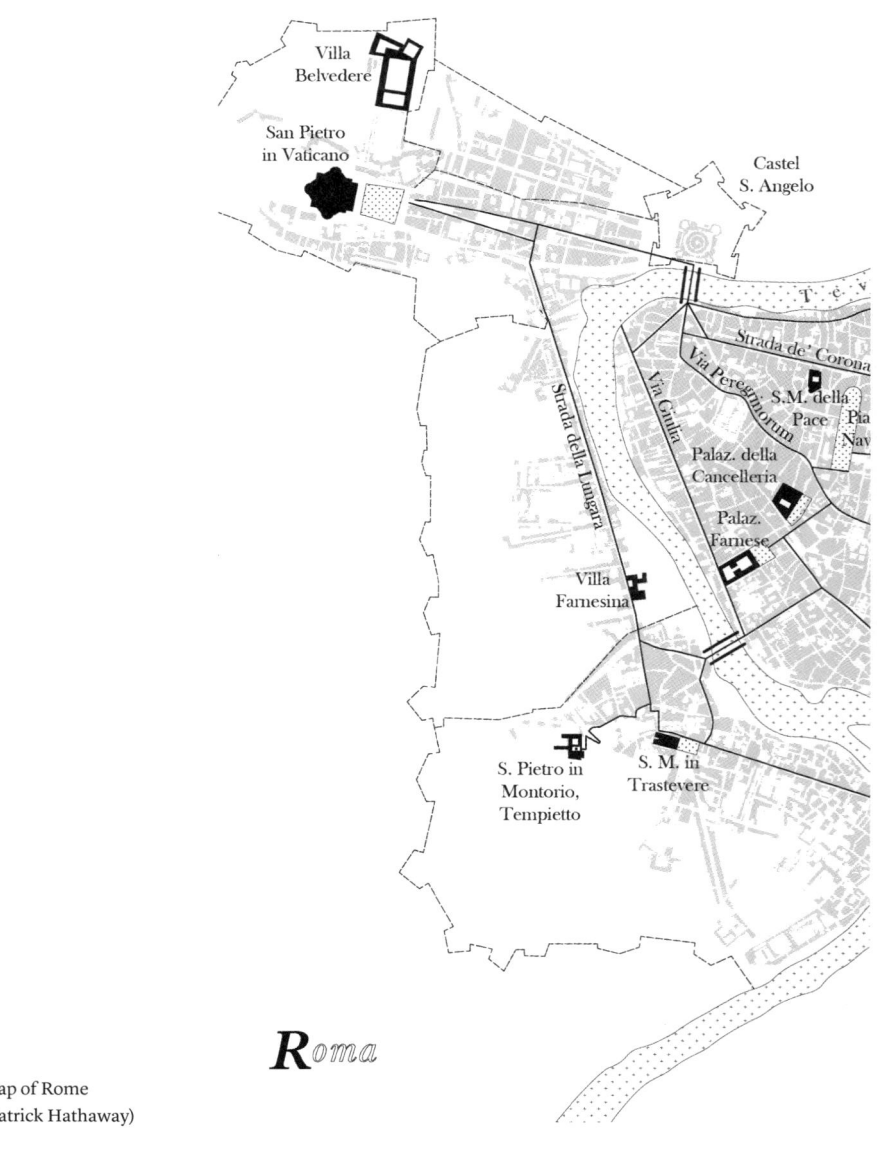

Villa
Belvedere

San Pietro
in Vaticano

Castel
S. Angelo

T e v

Strada de' Corona

Via Peregrinorum

Strada della Lungara

Via Giulia

S.M. della
Pace

Pia
Nav

Palaz. della
Cancelleria

Palaz.
Farnese

Villa
Farnesina

S. Pietro in
Montorio,
Tempietto

S. M. in
Trastevere

*R*oma

Map of Rome
(Patrick Hathaway)

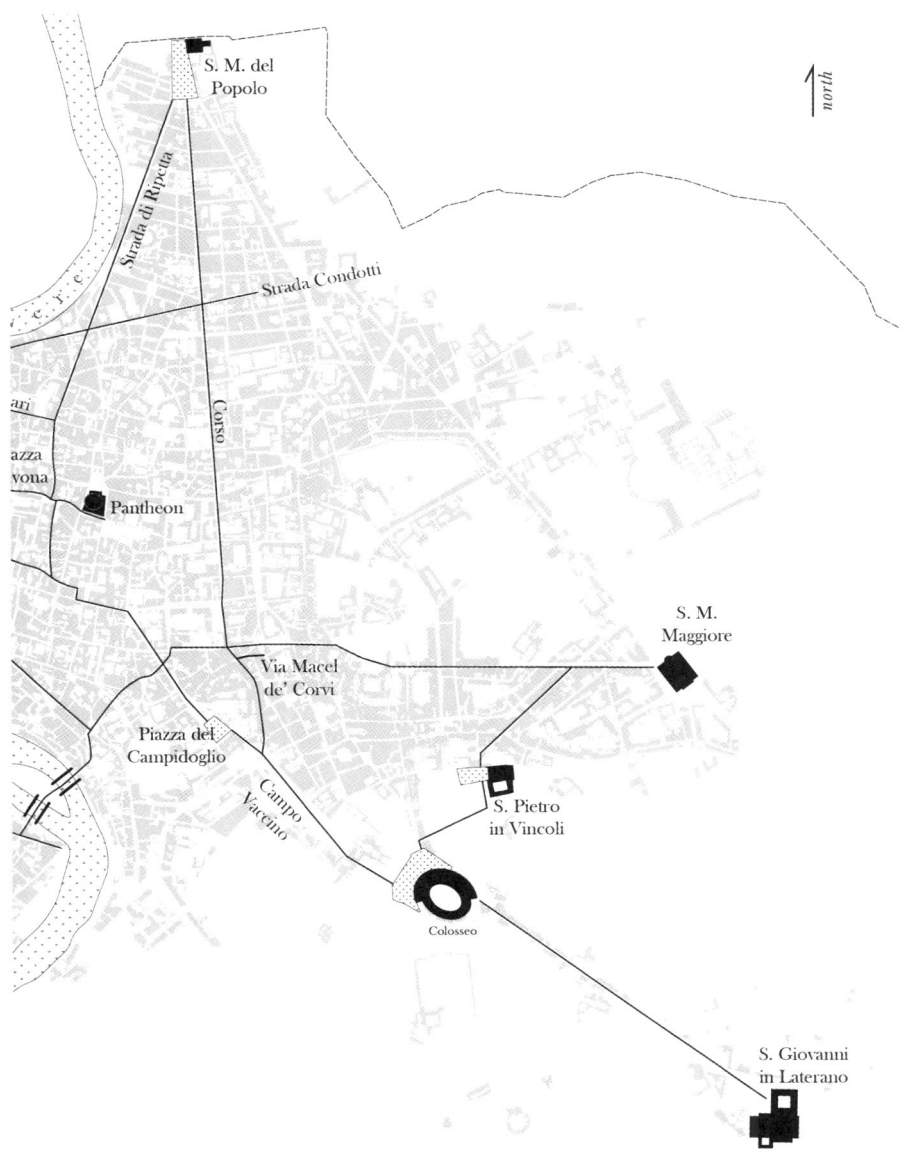

PART I
Rivalry Begins,
1500–1545

In 1500, Venice, Florence, and Rome were separated by more than distance, more than the three to four days it took to ride a horse from Venice to Florence, or the nearly ten days required to travel from Venice to Rome. The cities were different worlds, cultures, and cuisines, and their residents spoke different dialects. Titian and Michelangelo pursued careers in what would have seemed then like two different countries linked by politics, diplomacy, and finance. How did they learn about one another?

Venice Has Ears: "A Bocca"

Rhetoric, one of the seven liberal arts of classical antiquity, is the skill of speaking effectively, usually for political persuasion. Cicero called rhetoric "the Queen of the Arts." It was both an art and a weapon, to be used for positive or nefarious purposes, depending on who wielded it: Cicero or Catalina, Brutus or Mark Anthony. Passed down from the ancients, those living during the Renaissance rediscovered the art and the artifice of rhetoric and sought to speak well and smoothly, with a "silver tongue." Machiavelli, well aware of rhetoric's power, attempted to educate rulers on how to manipulate its potential and remain impervious to its wiles. The English, for example, were constantly wary of Italian diplomats with their well-honed rhetorical skills, invariably distrusting them as "Machiavellian." Whatever one may think about rhetoric and its place in the early modern era, it represents the "high end" of speech. It was the art of speaking well and of oral persuasion. It was rarely accurately recorded.

In the political and diplomatic arenas, spoken communication was widespread and often more effective than writing, because it was performative and could be finessed. The fact that it was not documented made it safer. Although characterized by lengthy dispatches, much diplomatic business was never committed to paper. As it became more sensitive, diplomacy was first carried on in code and then by word of mouth, "a bocca." When, for example, the Florentine Signoria sent Michelangelo to Ferrara in 1529 to negotiate for military assistance from Duke Alfonso d'Este, he was charged with this sensitive mission "di bocca"—orally.[1] In a time of war, avoiding written communication was strategically advisable. An emissary conveying information by word of mouth was less vulnerable to interception. He could elaborate upon whatever written communique was delivered, and could dissemble with impunity. In the personal realm, too, oral expression could be more refined and subtle than written communication. When Michelangelo sent drawings to his new friend of passionate interest, Tommaso de' Cavalieri, he did not entrust his delicate sentiments to paper.[2] Rather, a mutual friend was enlisted to add the most important message "a bocca." Thus, even though Michelangelo was an exceptionally adept writer, we witness him deferring to speech for delicate matters of feeling best expressed by a sympathetic friend.

If the carefully prepared, oftentimes formulaic speeches of diplomats and courtiers were not recorded for posterity, what of the rest of the verbal communication that accompanies, follows, and comments on it?[3] Much of the discussion and chatter among court officials, courtiers, spies, servants, and hangers-on revolved around political or commercial matters. Such discourse carried threads of hearsay, rumors, stories, and gossip. In this way, artists enter the worlds of court and diplomacy through the side door.

Michelangelo in Turchia

Michelangelo *sculptore* or *schultore*. The spelling varied, but not the profession. That is how Michelangelo proudly signed himself for the first three decades of his career. At age twenty-one, he completed the *Pietà*—"the most beautiful work in marble to be found in Rome"—proudly signing with his family name in Latin majuscules: MICHEL ANGELUS BONAROTVS.[4] Four years later he completed the *David*, referred to by awestruck Florentines as "the Giant." These were unique marvels that catapulted Michelangelo's career; he was suddenly the most respected sculptor of his time. Commissions proliferated, as did the beginnings of an international reputation.[5] By age thirty, word of the Florentine sculptor had spread so much that two of the most powerful persons on earth sought his services.

In 1505, Pope Julius II summoned thirty-year-old Michelangelo to Rome, tasking him with creating a monumental marble tomb. The following year the sultan of Turkey—that is, the ruler of the other half of the world—attempted to lure the same young artist to Constantinople. The sultan, Bayezid II (1481–1512), arranged for letters of credit to cover the artist's traveling expenses, and promised that Michelangelo would be met in Ragusa (modern Dubrovnik) and "honorably accompanied" to his court. The fledgling artist was enticed by the sultan's offer. Michelangelo's contemporary and biographer Ascanio Condivi reflected Michelangelo's pride at such an important invitation when he noted: "Such arrangements are not usual, everyday occurrences; they are new and out of the ordinary and they do not happen except in instances of singular, outstanding talent, like that of Homer, for whom many cities contended, each one of them claiming him for its own possession."[6]

The sultan desired to build a bridge across the Golden Horn, a proposition that certainly attracted Michelangelo, in part because Leonardo da Vinci had failed to fulfill a similar invitation some years earlier. Flattered, Michelangelo created a design for the bridge and was still considering making the journey to the infidel court more than ten years later. However, he never left Italy, as Pope Julius II soon commandeered his full-time services.

How did Sultan Bayezid hear about a Florentine sculptor named Michelangelo Buonarroti? There are no letters or contemporary accounts, much less Turkish descriptions of the *Pietà* or *David*. Moreover, written or oral accounts of such works could hardly inspire a Muslim sultan to entrust the most challenging engineering project in the world to a Christian sculptor. While lacking written documentation, we can imaginatively reconstruct the oral culture that was the means by which the sultan, and subsequently Titian, first learned about the ambitious Florentine.

At some point in the early years of the new century, Sultan Bayezid lent a curious ear to a traveler, perhaps a Florentine merchant, a Venetian diplomat, a Turkish agent, or a Genoese spy who described the outsize talent of a young Florentine who had carved a marble giant, "Il Gigante." The sultan was drawn to the report of its colossal size: more than three times as tall as the tallest court Janissary, or elite soldier, and it required more than six elephants to move it . . . like the Colossus of Rhodes! A verbal description would have excited the wonder of a foreign prince, who, because of his religion, favored words more than pictures.

Of course, this is an imagined scene, dependent upon rhetoric. It is actually ekphrasis, a word description so vivid that one sees it in the mind's eye.[7] This means of oral communication, which would be employed to describe the excitement of a work of art, will be of central importance to our story, despite the fact that such verbal traces rarely find their way into documents or archival sources. And importantly, ekphrasis, or, more simply, vivid verbal description, was a natural language among artists.

It was through spoken means that the sultan of the Ottoman Empire and a future doge of Venice first learned of a Florentine with an unusual name, Michael Archangel, and his burgeoning reputation as a creator of marvels. By the first years of the new century, word of Michelangelo's colossal *David* had spread beyond his native city. It likely reached as far as Turkey via the highly developed Venetian trade and diplomatic network in Constantinople, as well as the regular traffic of ambassadors, agents, spies, couriers, and courtiers between Rome, Florence, and Venice. One likely conduit of communication was the Venetian patrician Andrea Gritti, who spent nearly twenty years of his early career in Constantinople. Gritti (1455–1538) was first engaged in mercantile trade until his appointment in 1492 as the Venetian representative to the Ottoman court. He would have returned to service in Venice at the beginning of the new century, as an informed insider.

In October 1505, Gritti was staying in Rome as part of a Venetian delegation sent to negotiate with Pope Julius II. Michelangelo was in Carrara quarrying a mountain of marble for the pope's tomb. While in Rome, Gritti witnessed Julius's ambitions for the artistic renewal of the city. The new construction at St. Peter's, Bramante's Cortile di Belvedere, and the monumental marble mausoleum were unmistakable evidence of Julius's transformation of the dilapidated city. A rapidly rising star in Venetian politics, Gritti shortly afterward became head of the Council of Ten, and in 1523, was elected doge of Venice. Both in Constantinople and Rome, he was well situated to hear murmurings of the Florentine sculptor now working on a megalomaniac papal project. Gritti is only one of dozens of figures—but perhaps the earliest—who directly and indirectly connect Titian and Michelangelo. We will meet him again—as doge—when Michelangelo visits Venice in 1529 (see Plate 40).

Word of artists traveled within this oral culture, along the margins of diplomacy and barely above the level of gossip. And artists thrive on gossip, especially about one another. Thus, it was through such means that Titian first heard about a Florentine artist working in Rome, who, it was rumored, was invited to Constantinople by the sultan. Long before Titian met or saw a single work by Michelangelo, he was aware of the Florentine master through word of mouth, "a bocca." Titian's ambitions and competitive spirit were stimulated by such descriptions. As he listened, what more might he have heard?

Michelangelo in Rome, 1505

In 1505, Michelangelo was summoned to Rome by Pope Julius, whose papal name signaled his ambition to create an imperial Rome in emulation of Julius Caesar. Julius was known as the "warrior pope" for he led troops into battle in a campaign to re-establish hegemony over the Papal States. He was headstrong, displayed a fierce temper, and brooked no opposition. Contemporaries referred to him as *terribilità*—frightful even dreadful—a strong-willed and often difficult individual. At the same time, he was a brilliant manager of his equally difficult and headstrong artist. Michelangelo was thirty years old, short in stature but giant in ambition. Thus, he was—along with Donato Bramante and subsequently Raphael—a perfect partner to help Julius realize his ambitious program of artistic and urban renewal.

Recognizing their mutually outsized ambitions, Julius and Michelangelo imagined creating a magnificent papal mausoleum, an imposing work on the scale of a Roman emperor. In July 1505, Michelangelo, entrusted with a thousand ducats, departed for the quarries of Carrara to extract hundreds of marble blocks for the giant tomb. He remained six months. Through the hot summer and the cool weather of fall, Michelangelo searched for marble, increasingly in the grip of his grandiose vision: a three-story monument with forty life-size figures, replete with ornament, including bronze reliefs. It would take years to complete. Forty years! There, among the sublime peaks of the Apuan Alps, Michelangelo's soul soared and his imagination was unleashed. While looking at the scarred mountain face, he imagined using the entire peak as raw material to carve a colossal figure. "And he certainly would have done it," Condivi confidently asserted, "if he had had enough time."[8] Like Alexander the Great's sculptor Dinocrates who carved a colossus from Mount Athos, Michelangelo imagined doing the same. His enthusiasm transcended the realm of the possible, yet word of this colossal enterprise circulated "a bocca," long before Condivi wrote it down.

Soon, blocks of marble began arriving at the Ripa Grande, the riverport of Rome. A growing number of gawking citizens watched the laboring workmen (*facchini*) who unloaded the unwieldy blocks as barges deposited a seemingly infinite quantity of freshly quarried Luna marble. Gossip on the street became rampant; the pope was building an imperial monument to himself!

It must have been exciting to witness the pope's frenetic building activity across Rome. The papal architect Bramante was busy designing a three-tiered garden court enclosed by long corridors connecting St. Peter's to the Belvedere Villa. He was also supervising the building of a circular Tempietto over the place of Peter's crucifixion on the Janiculum Hill. And Michelangelo was moving a mountain of marble from Carrara to Rome. But suddenly the pope's attention turned elsewhere, to a scheme to have Bramante replace the venerable Constantinian basilica of St. Peter's with a new church. At the same time, Julius redirected the energies of a resistant Michelangelo to a different and seemingly unsuitable project for a sculptor: the painting of the ceiling of the Sistine Chapel. What and when did Titian hear about what was transpiring in Rome?

Titian in Padua, 1510–11

Titian's breakout moment came not in Venice but in its subject city of Padua. In December of 1510, he contributed to a cycle of frescoes relating the life and miracles of St. Anthony, patron saint of Padua. The paintings lined the walls of the Scuola del Santo, a lay confraternity dedicated to children and the poor. Among the works he painted in the Scuola was an audacious composition of a husband murdering his innocent wife (Plate 5).[9] In a tour de force of dramatic narrative, an insanely jealous, knife-wielding husband looms over his sprawling wife who turns back toward him in a desperate but failed appeal for mercy. Deeply repentant of his crime, the husband will be forgiven by Anthony, as we see in the background vignette.

In a posthumously published lecture delivered more than fifty years ago, the great Michelangelo scholar Johannes Wilde made

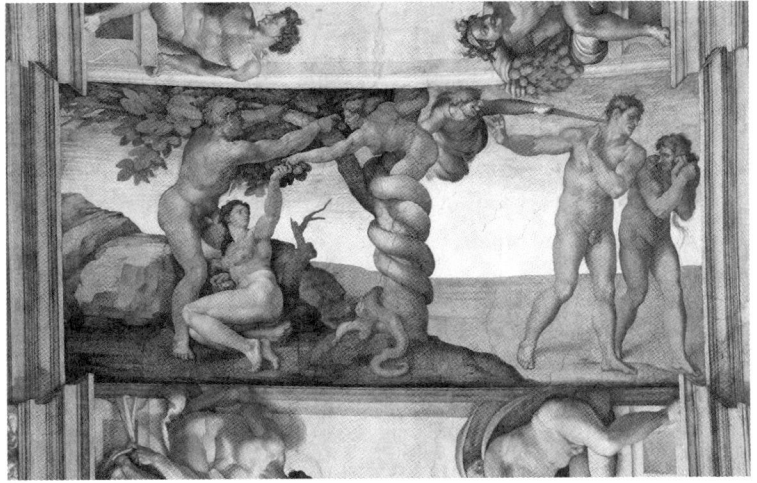

4. Michelangelo, det. *Fall of Man*, fresco, Sistine Chapel, Vatican, 1508–12.

a passing observation. The entwined poses of husband and wife appeared similar—in reverse—to Adam and Eve from Michelangelo's *Fall of Man* on the Sistine ceiling (Fig. 4). The observation has been repeated frequently despite Wilde's cautionary query: "You will rightly ask: how could he [Titian] know Michelangelo's fresco which was unveiled on 15 August 1511?"[10] That is, how might Titian, who did not visit Rome until 1545, know what Michelangelo was painting at the same moment in the mostly shuttered Sistine Chapel? A more difficult follow-up question not asked or answered by Wilde is: by whom and by what means would Titian in Padua have been alerted to Michelangelo's frescoed ceiling?

Scholars have confronted Wilde's challenge by attempting to explain that Titian may have been informed via drawings or an engraving, thereby explaining the reversal of the pose.[11] However, no such drawings or engravings exist; moreover, one is still left explaining who was responsible for transmitting the information from Rome to Padua, and exactly how. This supposed connection between Titian and Michelangelo at a time when they were working simultaneously, more than three hundred miles distant from one another, quickly becomes more convoluted than likely. It is also unnecessary.

Interesting suggestions over time have a tendency, through repetition, to crystalize into facts.[12] The relationship of Titian's *Jealous Husband* to Michelangelo's *Fall of Man* in the Sistine has been repeated so often as to have become a generally accepted truism—an early instance of Titian adopting a figural invention from the older master. I would like to suggest another way to benefit from Wilde's insight, by placing it in the longue durée history that is our subject.

Wilde made a purely formal comparison. In following him, we are allowing formal analysis to occlude subject and significance. Let us ask instead: what are the subjects of the respective frescoes; what and how are they narrating those subjects, and how different in action and meaning are the poses and gestures?

Michelangelo's *Fall of Man*—the guile of temptation and the impending tragic fall from grace—is a subject radically different in character, magnitude, and significance from Titian's murderous scene (see Plate 5). Titian painted a swarthy, bearded, and bedraggled husband violently yanking the hair of his collapsed and pleading wife, exposing her neck and half-naked breast to the long dagger that he is about to plunge into her innocent flesh. The rust-red stripes of the husband's belted tunic anticipate the streams of blood that are beginning to stain his wife's white chemise and lemon-ochre dress. In her vain appeal, she raises a hand to deflect the brutal final thrust.

Titian painted a vivid, violent, and rapidly unfolding narrative of murder, quite the opposite of Michelangelo's slow-moving, intimately entwined figures facing temptation. Eve, Michelangelo's artless ingenue, gazes with open lustrous eyes at the pleasantly florid face of a seemingly congeneric creature. Eve's fixed attention and raised arm prevent her from recognizing that her interlocutor is actually a monstrous serpent wound tightly around the tree. Having been lured to temptation, Eve pays no attention to Adam and his coeval fall from grace. Equally distracted from his consort, Adam willfully transgresses God's commandment by assertively plucking fruit from the forbidden tree.

In Michelangelo's rendition of the *Fall of Man*, the traditional Christian subject is presented as an alluring double entrapment. As spectators, we are drawn into temptation, ultimately realizing that we inherit Adam's and Eve's fallen state. It is a very different experience from Titian whose rapidly unfolding narrative action nonetheless allows us to remain detached witnesses to the violently murderous scene.

Rather than connecting Titian's figural pose to Michelangelo, it is more fruitful to consider the younger Venetian artist ambitiously and successfully experimenting within a genre of dramatic narrative. The *Jealous Husband* is an outlier among the Paduan frescoes. All the other scenes in the cycle lack a similar level of action; rather, they are stilted, tableau compositions belonging to a conservative Venetian idiom and style. As an experiment in action painting, the *Jealous Husband* marks a significant advance over another painting by Titian in the fresco cycle, *The Miracle of the Speaking Infant* (Fig. 5). This work, like the others in the Paduan Scuola, is an artificially posed, planar composition lacking the sudden and shocking drama of the murder scene.[13] For Titian to make this artistic evolution—probably within weeks, if not days—did not require Michelangelo, and certainly not the *Fall of Man*, a subject diametrically different in every respect, except for the limited formal similarity recognized by Wilde.

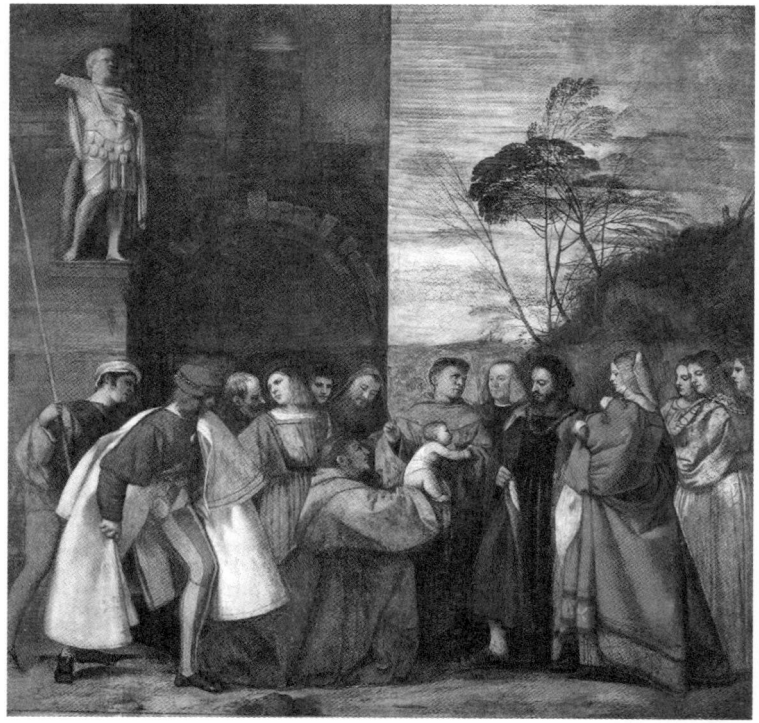

5. Titian Vecellio, *Miracle of the Speaking Infant*, fresco, 11 × 11.5 ft (340 × 355 cm), Scuola del Santo, Padua, 1511.

Let us imagine a more likely scenario, taking greater account of the circulating oral culture of the early modern period. As an ambitious upcoming artist, Titian had his ear to the ground. He did not need an engraving or drawn copy of Michelangelo's contemporaneous creation to invent the *Jealous Husband*. By mid-1511, there was a pervasive murmuring about Pope Julius and the bevy of artists whom he brought to Rome, including the much talked about master from Florence now painting in the papal chapel. Titian may have heard rumors of Michelangelo's ambitious undertaking, thereby piquing his competitive interest, but these did little to assist his own specific invention.

Thanks to diplomats, ecclesiastics, artists, friends, visitors, and pilgrims, certain foreign names were circulating in the contemporary media-sphere, most prominently those of Donato Bramante and his young compatriot Raphael. Conversations possibly also included talk of Leonardo da Vinci. Venetians knew about Leonardo as he had passed through the city in 1500 and was one of the most discussed artists of the day. However, by the beginning of the second decade of the sixteenth century, Leonardo had disappeared to Milan, and talk turned to his compatriot, a Florentine sculptor named Michelangelo. By 1511, even Titian would have heard something of the marble colossus called "il Gigante," and maybe—through the Venetian grapevine, the sculptor's invitation to the court of Sultan Bayezid II. That would be news of interest to any Venetian!

So why, Titian might have asked himself, was a Florentine sculptor in Rome painting in the pope's chapel? He has heard little more than vague gossip, even if gossip can be enormously stimulating to a young and ambitious Titian. As of yet, however, he was inventing *on his own*.

Muscular Nudes

Following the completion of the Scuola del Santo frescoes in Padua, Titian painted several pictures that featured seminude figures: the *Baptism of Christ* and a *Noli me Tangere* (Fig. 6).[14] His altarpiece for the church of Santo Spirito on the island of Isola, included a scantily clad St. Sebastian standing in a relaxed, contrapposto pose (Fig. 7). We see a near twin of this figure in the San Niccolò altarpiece, now in the Vatican Museum (Fig. 8).[15] Given the

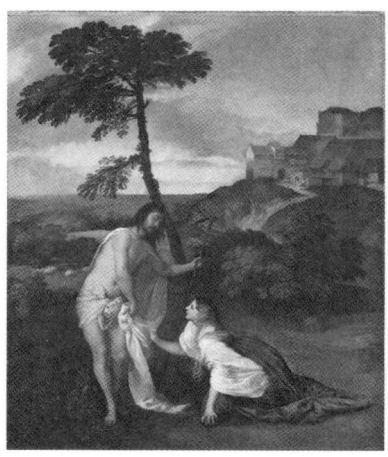

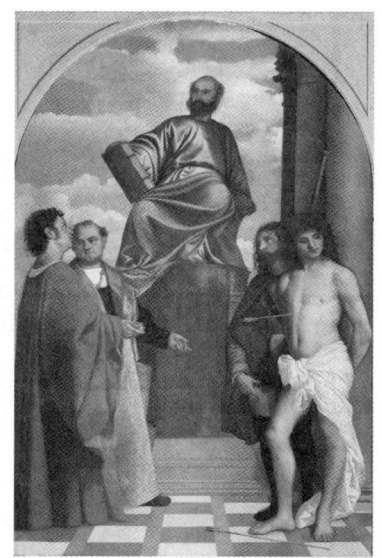

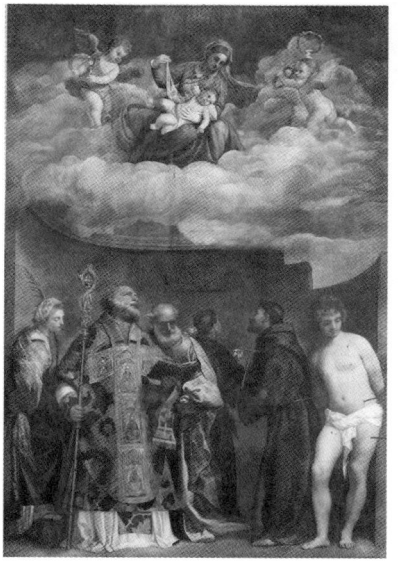

6. *(top left)* Titian Vecellio, *Noli me Tangere*, oil on canvas, 43.5 × 36 in (110.5 × 91.9 cm), The National Gallery, London, c. 1513–14.

7. *(top)* Titian Vecellio, *San Marco altarpiece*, oil on panel, 7.5 × 4.75 ft (230 × 149 cm), Santa Maria della Salute, Venice, c. 1511–12.

8. *(left)* Titian Vecellio, *San Niccolò altarpiece*, oil on panel (transferred to canvas), 13.75 × 9.5 ft (420 × 290 cm), Pinacoteca Vaticana, Vatican City, c. 1520–25.

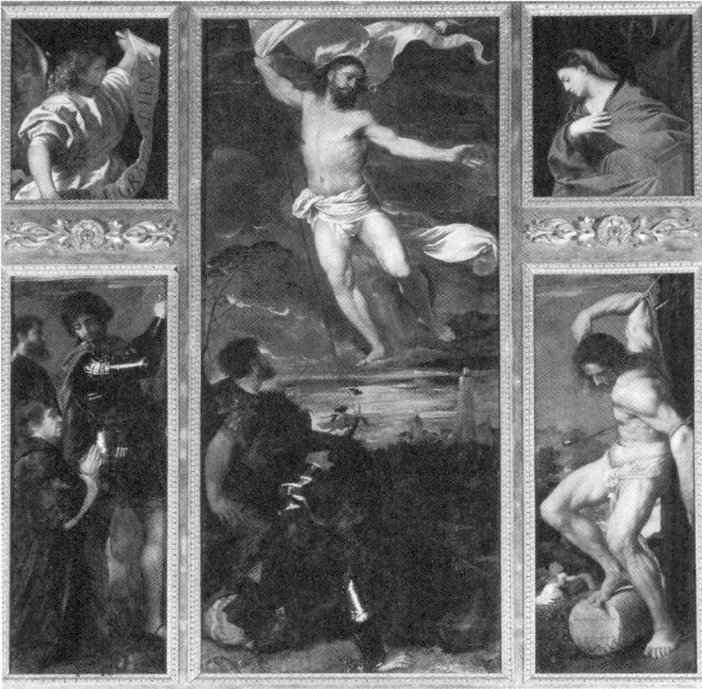

9. Titian Vecellio, *Resurrection polyptych*, oil on panel, 9 × 4 ft (278 × 122 cm), SS. Nazaro e Celso, Brescia, 1519–22.

repeated appearance of these muscular, nude figures in Titian's art in the first two decades of the sixteenth century, one might ask, as scholars have, if Michelangelo was a source of inspiration.

For an important commission in Brescia, Titian painted a multi-panel altarpiece of the *Resurrection*, which includes a bound, arrow-pierced St. Sebastian hanging from rope restraints (Fig. 9).[16] This figure is more muscular and energetic than any of Titian's previous nudes and is widely thought to have been inspired by Michelangelo's *Rebellious Slave* (Fig. 10). But was it? When did Titian first see this or any work by Michelangelo?

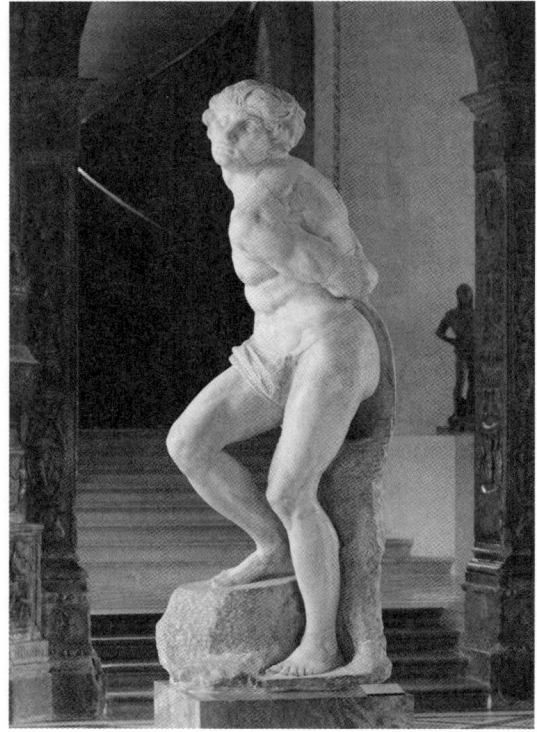

10. Michelangelo,
Rebellious Slave,
marble, h. 7 ft (215 cm),
Musée du Louvre,
Paris, c. 1513.

A drawing in Frankfurt attributed to Titian is the key piece of evidence in this investigation (Fig. 11). When Titian's drawing is put alongside Michelangelo's *Rebellious Slave*, a relationship seems evident (compare Figs. 10 and 11). As the cataloguer of Titian's drawings baldly stated, Titian's drawing of St. Sebastian "is *based directly on* Michelangelo's *Rebellious Slave*"[17] (my emphasis). Yet, the obvious but often skirted question is: how could Titian have known Michelangelo's sculpture? Michelangelo carved the *Rebellious Slave* in his Roman workshop where it was seen by few people, and only by those who enjoyed privileged access. Michelangelo

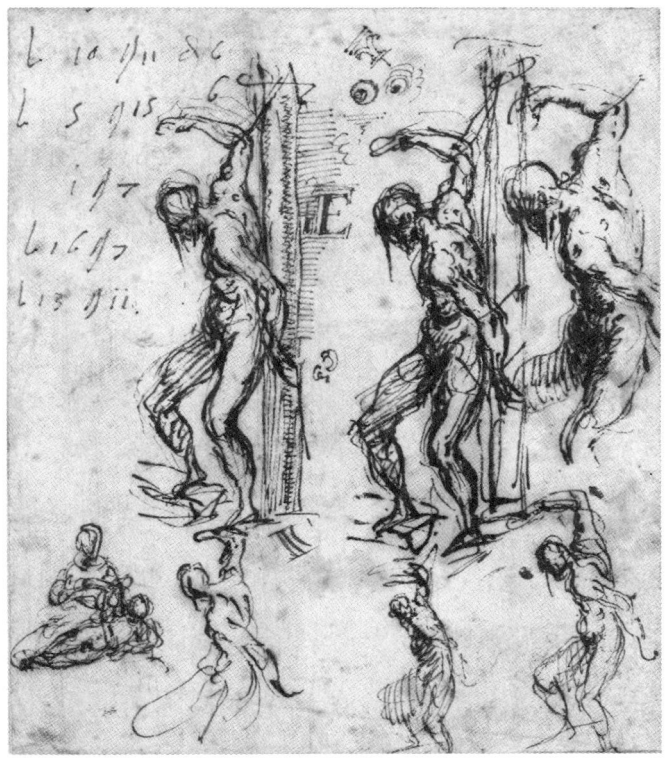

11. Titian Vecellio, *St. Sebastian*, pen, ink, and brush, 6.25 × 5.25 in (162 × 136 mm), Staatliche Museen, Kupferstichkabinett (Inv. K.d.Z. no. 5962), Berlin, c. 1518.

was so reticent about the sculpture that even informed persons close to the artist knew little about it.[18] How could Titian draw this sheet *directly* from Michelangelo's statue, given that his first visit to Rome only occurred in 1545? And if Titian didn't see the statue, who may have transmitted knowledge—visual or verbal—to him in Brescia? How precisely did such an unlikely communication take place? More importantly, did Titian require such a model and inspiration?

Titian was more likely influenced by well-regarded paintings of St. Sebastian created by contemporary Venetian masters, such as Giovanni Bellini and Andrea Mantegna. Or we might simply consider Titian's nude as an example of his ability to paint naturalistic figures "who seem alive . . . lifelike . . . composed of real flesh."[19] That is how the biographer of Venetian artists Carlo Ridolfi described Titian's St. Sebastian, painted "delicately" and "with a certain grace," which are scarcely terms to describe Michelangelo's contorted marble slave.

It is time to cut the Gordian knot. Titian, having already painted several fleshy nude figures in contrapposto, did not need Michelangelo's sculpture to paint a three-dimensional, muscular nude. Moreover, a more critical comparison of the *Rebellious Slave* with Titian's scratchy preparatory drawing reveals that they share only a meager and superficial resemblance. In short, we are comparing apples and oranges. Titian has not yet seen Michelangelo's work, and certainly *not* the *Rebellious Slave*. He is possibly *hearing* about the Florentine artist and the monumental tomb now underway for the pope with its many nude figures, some in exaggerated contrapposto poses. But Titian has already and independently embarked on a similar path of invention (*invenzione*). Titian forged his own path to artistic success. We need not trace every nude to Michelangelo.

*   *   *

In 1525, Michelangelo turned fifty, and Titian was approaching forty. Both were in the prime of their careers and had created a number of early masterpieces that helped establish their artistic preeminence: Michelangelo's *Pietà*, *David*, and the Sistine ceiling; Titian's paintings in Padua, Brescia, and Venice. Each had a strong reputation at home and increasing fame, but they inhabited separate worlds. Their lives and careers had advanced without either artist having seen a single work by the other. Titian may have been "listening" more attentively than Michelangelo, although the latter would soon become interested thanks to his first encounter with Venice and Venetian art. It is time to visit Venice, asking when Michelangelo first traveled to the lagoon city and what he saw there.

Michelangelo in Bologna, 1494–95

During the two years following the death of Lorenzo de' Medici in 1492, hostility to Florence's premiere family mounted, especially as Lorenzo's haughty and politically inept son, Piero de' Medici, squandered the public trust. When the Medici were expelled from Florence in 1494, Michelangelo, who had been nurtured in their household, found himself in urgent and suddenly unsettled circumstances, without secure patronage or proper employment. Hoping to maintain relations with his only source of support, Michelangelo followed his Medici benefactors north to Bologna.

He remained in Bologna for nearly a year. Thanks to his Medici connections, he was welcomed into the household of Giovan Francesco Aldrovandi, a Bolognese nobleman and Medici sympathizer. For nearly a year, Michelangelo lived a mostly desultory life, making the most of his nascent courtier-like skills honed within the Medici entourage. In turn, the Bolognese gentleman arranged for Michelangelo to carve some figures for the tomb of Saint Dominic, Bologna's most important pilgrimage site.

Meanwhile, most of the Medici family and entourage moved on to Venice, where they had important banking and commercial interests. Given that he was not overly busy carving three or four modestly sized marble sculptures, it is possible that Michelangelo went to Venice sometime during his year-long sojourn.[20] If so, this would be the twenty-year-old's first exposure to Venice and Venetian art. As scholars have suggested, an encounter with Tullio Lombardo's nude marble *Adam* may have inspired Michelangelo when, a half dozen years later, he carved the *Bacchus* and then an unexpectedly nude *David*.[21] However, the primary purpose of such a trip would have been to maintain contact with his faltering patronage network. In any case, Michelangelo would not have heard anything of a young Titian growing up in provincial Pieve di Cadore.

Bologna, 1506–8: A Venetian Sojourn?

Another opportunity for Michelangelo to visit Venice occurred during his second, fifteen-month residence in Bologna between November 1506 and February 1508. Following Pope Julius's reconquest of Bologna, Michelangelo—having abandoned Rome and the Julius tomb—traveled north to repair relations with the pope. Hoping to renew his interrupted work on the Julius tomb project, Michelangelo was instead charged with casting a larger-than-life-size bronze statue of the pope. The marble sculptor was profoundly unhappy with his circumstances in Bologna but could not say "no" to "Papa terribile." We know much about this episode thanks to a regular stream of letters that Michelangelo exchanged with his family in Florence, complaining about unreliable assistants, the envious Bolognese, and the city's wine, which was "expensive and as bad as it could be." Moreover, he had to sleep with three assistants in a single bed "in a terrible room."[22]

While a resident in Bologna and struggling with the manifold problems of casting the Julius statue, Michelangelo may once again—or, for the first time—have traveled to Venice. As with the first supposed Venetian trip of 1494/95, this hypothesized visit sometime in 1506–8 has no documentary foundation. Despite the lack of evidence, and overlooking what would have been Michelangelo's significant preoccupation with casting the bronze statue of Pope Julius, scholars nonetheless have widely embraced the notion of a possible Venetian sojourn. It is a hypothesis that has been repeated so frequently that it too has become a widely accepted fact.[23] The supposed visit is again based purely on visual connections made between works in Venice and some that Michelangelo subsequently carried out in Rome. Let us momentarily consider the implications of this generally accepted trip to Venice.

Michelangelo may have been impressed, as many visitors still are, by the giant, multi-tiered tombs in many Venetian churches, such as the Niccolò Tron monument in the Frari and the recently installed tomb of Doge Pietro Mocenigo in San Giovanni e Paolo (Fig. 12). It has been suggested that the monumental scale and sculptural abundance of these wall tombs might have inspired Michelangelo in designing a three-tier, multi-figure tomb for Pope Julius II.[24]

Had Michelangelo visited Venice, he undoubtedly would have passed through the commercial heart of the city encountering the Fondaco dei Tedeschi, the "German" warehouse and community center at the Rialto bridgehead. In 1508, Giorgione was busily frescoing a series of large-scale figures on two principal facades of the building. Famous for his inventive, avant-garde approach to style and subject matter manifested in mostly small, exquisitely painted "cabinet" pictures, Giorgione was perhaps an inappropriate choice to paint large-scale frescoes on the exterior of a prominent public building. Nonetheless, he painted a series of large-scale figures in the heart of commercial Venice. The frescoes garnered much attention, even if contemporaries were unable to discern their subject. Giorgio Vasari admired the "very finely painted and vivaciously

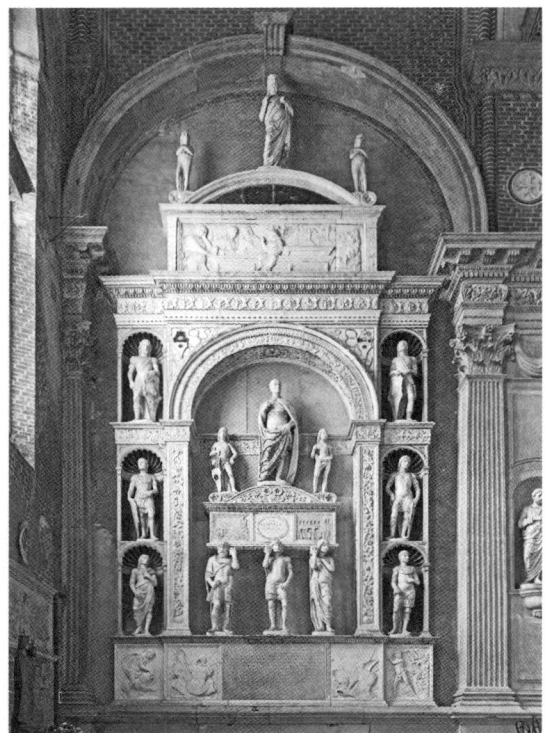

12. Pietro Lombardo,
*Tomb of Doge
Mocenigo*, SS.
Giovanni e Paolo,
Venice, 1481.

coloured" figures, but was "not able to interpret the meaning" even
after consulting knowledgeable Venetians.[25]

   Because of their exposure to the damp conditions in Venice, the
frescos rapidly deteriorated. A selection of fragments and a series
of engravings made by A. M. Zanetti in the eighteenth century
provide an idea of some of the imposing figures, including a few
sometimes attributed to Giorgione's young assistant, Titian (e.g.,
Fig. 13). Although we have only a dim view of these frescoes, they
were a novel and highly public decoration that may well have attracted the attention of Michelangelo.

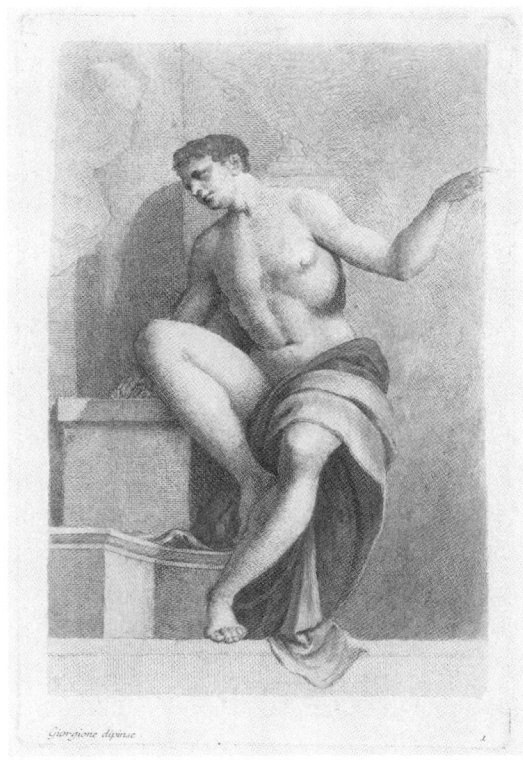

13. Antonio Maria
Zanetti, figure from
the facade of the
Fondaco dei Tedeschi,
engraving, 8.5 × 5.5 in
(217 × 140 mm), c. 1760.

Did Michelangelo see the fresco decorations on the Fondaco
dei Tedeschi sometime before the spring of 1508, when he is documented as having been in Rome preparing to undertake the painting of the ceiling of the Sistine Chapel? Are they, as some scholars
have suggested, a generative inspiration for his large-scale prophets and sibyls? An alternative scenario has also been advanced:
might Giorgione have profited from Michelangelo—either from his
concurrent work in the Sistine Chapel, or possibly from the artist's
celebrated *Battle of Cascina* cartoon?[26] But, as with the Wilde hypothesis, one must ask how.

The relationship between Giorgione and Michelangelo must remain in the arena of learned conjecture, especially because Michelangelo's visits to Venice in either 1494 or sometime between 1506 and 1508 are undocumented hypotheses. Thus, despite repeated assertion by scholars, we are left with speculation based purely on formal comparisons of figures and poses. What is certain, however, is of central importance to our story: even if Michelangelo went to Venice, he would not have known anything of Giorgione's young assistant. To Michelangelo, Titian, as yet, was an unknown figure.

Sebastiano Veneziano: "A Meeting of Minds"

Sebastiano del Piombo (1485–1547) was the important catalyst and earliest intermediary between Titian and Michelangelo.[27] Trained in the studio of Giovanni Bellini and attracted to the art of Giorgione, Sebastiano enjoyed a brief but successful career in Venice before moving permanently to Rome. He was painting monumental organ shutters for the church of San Bartolommeo di Rialto at the same time Giorgione and Titian were painting exterior frescoes on the nearby Fondaco de' Tedeschi. Like Titian, Sebastiano may have completed some of Giorgione's pictures when the latter died prematurely in 1510. Thus, he and Titian were well acquainted by the time the fabulously wealthy banker Agostino Chigi lured Sebastiano to Rome in 1511. Chigi provided entrée to Roman society and commissioned Sebastiano to help decorate his love-nest villa on the Tiber River (subsequently known as the Villa Farnesina), which we will visit shortly.

In one of his first paintings made in Rome, Sebastiano combined a Venetian setting in luminous color with figures inspired by Michelangelo and ancient sculpture (Plate 6). We don't know how they first met, but Sebastiano and Michelangelo became fast, albeit seemingly unlikely friends. Was it the Venetian's brushwork and brilliant color that attracted the Florentine sculptor, or was it his humor and cheeky manners? Sebastiano was proud, vain, and convinced of his superior painting abilities. Incredibly witty, he delighted Michelangelo with his ribald and irreverent badinage—a welcome relief to the simpering sycophants and bureaucrats who sullied the papal court.

Michelangelo especially appreciated Sebastiano's special brand of humor. We can almost hear the two friends chuckling, especially when reading each other's salty letters. "I know you will laugh at my chatter," wrote Sebastiano in one long letter that included a dig at the money-pinching, irritating duke of Urbino "who will have to take medicine in order to shell out 8,000 ducats" (for the tomb of Julius II).[28]

Sebastiano and Michelangelo were wildly dissimilar personalities—one worldly, lazy, and certainly impious, the other taciturn and increasingly concerned with his aristocratic status—and due to these differences, they eventually drifted apart. But, for some years they were "dearest colleagues" who enjoyed a creative partnership—the first true collaboration in Michelangelo's career. Moreover, Sebastiano quickly established himself as a Vatican insider, providing Michelangelo with eyes and ears in Rome when the latter was working in Florence between 1513 and 1534. Sebastiano was a faithful proponent of Michelangelo's interests, which proved an invaluable asset in the slanderous and competitive papal court. Michelangelo remained sincerely grateful to his friend, even agreeing to stand as godfather to Sebastiano's son.[29]

Indeed, Sebastiano not only represented Michelangelo's interests, he helped relieve the artist's multiple anxieties, once by teasing him that the bailiff's ugly hag "is in love with you." The unnamed wife cared for Michelangelo's house while the artist was absent from Rome. Sebastiano intimated that, "she made an offer of the beds, the furniture, and everything in the house, even the hens. I didn't want to accept anything without your permission."[30] Another time he reminded the officious functionaries at the papal court who were carping about the artist's reticent manner: "You should be glad for what you have, because it does not rain Michelangelos."[31] The two friends took huge delight in the fact that the unholy Venetian was required to take holy orders prior to accepting the lucrative office of *Piombatore*—the Keeper of the Papal Seal—for which Sebastiano received a lifelong sinecure, a paid position with few responsibilities. Sebastiano joked about his new peacock-like attire: "If you saw me I'm sure you would laugh. I am the handsomest friar in Rome."[32]

Michelangelo played well at this bantering game. After all, he was a Tuscan with an acerbic, often cutting wit, which manifested itself both verbally and visually.[33] For example, on the verso of an exquisite drawing of the Resurrected Christ (Fig. 14) made to assist Sebastiano in painting an altarpiece for Santa Maria della Pace, Michelangelo drew an amusing doodle completely at odds with the serious character of the sheet's recto (Fig. 15).[34] Responding to Sebastiano's self-deprecating comment that he had been forced to take priestly orders to become a papal functionary—the office of Piombatore, a functionary stamping and sealing papal documents—Michelangelo drew a ridiculous animal weighed down with two engorged, lead-like breasts. Michelangelo was cleverly alluding to an old Venetian expression, "tette di piombini"—that is "breasts of lead"—thereby poking fun at his friend who was now weighed down as the keeper of large lead papal seals. Thus, while helping his friend paint an important sacred altarpiece, Michelangelo simultaneously indulged in a private joke on the sheet's verso. An inclination to humor—sometimes playful, sometimes

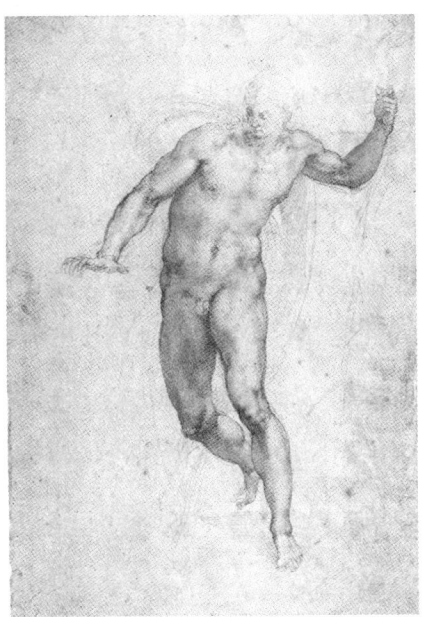

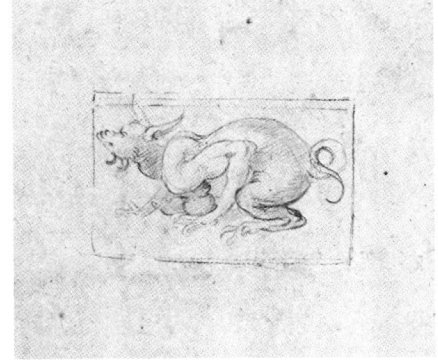

14. *(left)* Michelangelo, *Risen Christ*, black chalk on paper, 13 × 7.75 in (330 × 198 mm), Casa Buonarroti 66F recto, Florence, 1520s.

15. *(right)* Michelangelo, *Joke sketch (scherzo)*, black chalk on paper, 13 × 7.75 in (330 × 198 mm), det. Casa Buonarroti 66F verso, Florence, 1520s.

bawdy, mostly verbal but sometimes visual—was something that Michelangelo, Sebastiano, and Titian all shared. We will have reason to reconsider Sebastiano's unfulfilled commission for Santa Maria della Pace when Titian arrives in Rome.

Amid this idle chatter and low-level whimsy, Michelangelo was befriending an exceptionally skilled artist who expanded his artistic horizons, primarily by fostering his interest in painting and color. Michelangelo enjoyed Sebastiano's Venetian patois and admired his versatile brush. For the first time in his life, and contrary to his tendency to do everything himself, Michelangelo elected to collaborate with a painter, and significantly with a Venetian colorist. Recognizing Sebastiano's exceptional talent, Michelangelo willingly furnished his friend with drawings. Their partnership was short-lived but remarkably fruitful. It was a meeting of two artists with special and complementary talents—Michelangelo's drawing (disegno) and Sebastiano's color (colorito). If relatively brief, it proved to be one of the most important collaborations in the history of art, resulting in several notable masterpieces, including a large painted *Pietà* for Viterbo, the monumental altarpiece, the *Raising of Lazarus*, painted in competition with Raphael (see Fig. 26), and the Borgherini Chapel in San Pietro in Montorio (Plate 7), which Sebastiano would proudly show to Titian when the latter came to Rome in 1545-6.

It is somewhat sad to observe the gradual demise of Michelangelo's and Sebastiano's once lively friendship and fruitful collaboration. Michelangelo was generous in providing his friend with drawings; Sebastiano returned the favor by giving unwanted and unhelpful ideas about how to go about painting the *Last Judgment*. The friendship faltered on the shoals of their very different personalities; however, it is important to emphasize that, for a brief period, Michelangelo benefitted from his first, truly collaborative relationship. It exposed him to Venetian painting and demonstrated what *could be* achieved by working with the talents of other artists. It opened Michelangelo to a much wider receptivity to the art of painting, especially Venetian color, and, somewhat surprisingly, given his well-known disparagement of the genre, to portraiture, an arena in which both Sebastiano and Titian excelled. In a warm letter to Sebastiano, Michelangelo lauded the Venetian's abilities as a portrait painter as "unique in the world" ("unicho al mondo").[35] And, perhaps most importantly for our story, it was from his garrulous friend that Michelangelo first learned of Titian. Sebastiano, who was well acquainted with his Venetian contemporary, prepared fertile ground for Michelangelo's first and transformative encounter with Titian.

The Die Is Cast: Ferrara, 1529

From the accession of Pope Clement VII in November of 1523, Michelangelo worked like a demon on Medici commissions associated with San Lorenzo, the family's parish church in Florence. The newly elected pontiff (Fig. 16) charged Michelangelo with a succession of architectural and sculptural projects that included completing the Medici burial chapel and designing the Laurentian Library. Responsible for hiring and managing hundreds of workers, Michelangelo was designer, architect, sculptor, engineer, project manager, personnel coordinator, site supervisor, and overall chief executive responsible for every facet of the multiple and massively complicated endeavors. Unfortunately, he could not avoid the intrusion of contemporary politics.

Clement was a generous and understanding Maecenas but an unfortunate, vacillating politician who stood on the brink of a European conflict. He attempted to juggle the contending powers of the Holy Roman emperor and the king of France, to contain the bickering and villainous behavior of the various Italian states, and to stem the tide of defection from the Catholic Church. He failed, and catastrophe lay on the near horizon. Meanwhile, Michelangelo remained focused on his work despite a significant curtailment of funds available for Medici projects. Characteristically myopic to politics, Michelangelo inquired of Pope Clement whether his salary would be continued, given "that the times are unfavorable to this art of mine."[36] On the verge of an international crisis, Michelangelo worried about funding for his projects, oblivious to the ancient proverb: "In arma silent artes" ("during war, the arts fall silent").

Intrigue and hesitation brought Clement face-to-face with disaster. In May 1527, for the first time in more than a thousand years, Rome was sacked by the unpaid, unruly soldiers of the imperial

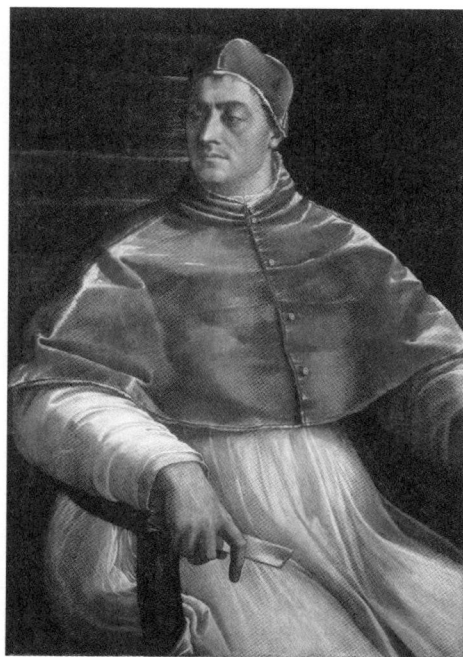

16. Sebastiano del Piombo, *Pope Clement VII*, oil on canvas, 57 × 43.25 in (145 × 110 cm), Gallerie Nazionali di Capodimonte, Naples, 1526.

army of the Holy Roman Emperor Charles V. The defeat dealt a devastating blow to papal prestige with far-reaching consequences for Florence. Soon, Michelangelo was caught up in circumstances beyond his control.

Shortly after the Sack of Rome, the Florentines expelled the governing Medici and instituted an independent Republic. Betrayed by his native city, Clement worked tirelessly to reestablish his family's hegemony over rebellious Florence. The Treaty of Barcelona, signed by Pope Clement and Charles V in June of 1529, sealed Florence's fate, as the two potentates agreed to a restoration of Medici power. Every Florentine citizen suddenly faced a difficult choice: flee the city or face the superior forces of a hostile army.

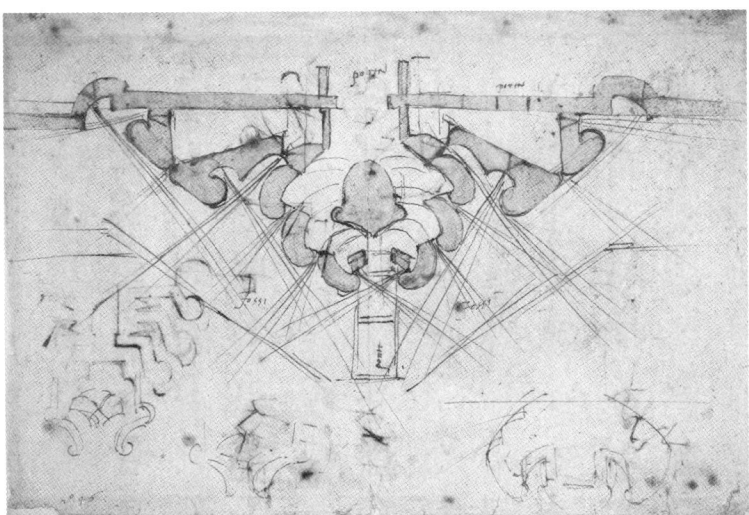

17. Michelangelo, *Fortification design*, pen and brush ink on paper, 11.5 × 16.5 in (293 × 412 mm), Casa Buonarroti 22A recto, Florence, 1528/29.

Despite Clement's efforts to dissuade him, Michelangelo elected to side with his native city. Above all, he was a Florentine with deeply republican sympathies. In Florence's hour of need, Michelangelo committed himself to the doomed Republic, thereby defying the very man who was a boyhood acquaintance and his current patron, pope, and loyal supporter.

Florence was ill-prepared for war. The city had no standing army and her defenses were woefully inadequate. Michelangelo offered his services to a government in dire straits. Quipping that he knew little about painting and sculpture but considered himself an expert on fortifications, Michelangelo drafted a number of designs to strengthen the medieval walls in anticipation of an impending siege (e.g., Fig. 17).[37] The three years of Florence's Last Republic (1527–1530) ultimately brought disaster to the city and hugely disrupted Michelangelo's life. Yet, these are the circumstances that led to his initial encounters with Titian, first in Ferrara and then in Venice.

In Alfonso's Web

In January of 1529, Michelangelo was elected to the *Nove della Milizia*, the Florentine Nine of Military Affairs (overseers of the Florentine militia), and on April 6, he was appointed Governor and Procurator General of fortifications with the generous salary of one florin per day (enough to feed a family of four for a month). The government dispatched him to inspect defenses in the Florentine territories, including Pisa, Livorno, and Arezzo. In July, the Signoria sent Michelangelo to Ferrara, as the fortifications of that city were the most advanced in Italy and Duke Alfonso d'Este was a potential ally with a much-coveted arsenal of cannon. The duke cordially received Michelangelo as an artist-cum-diplomat, freely offered advice, and dangled the prospect of military assistance. Alfonso accompanied Michelangelo on an inspection of Ferrara's walls, showing the artist "all the relevant items and more, from bastions to artillery."[38]

Alfonso, who owed his tenuous position as duke to Emperor Charles V, proved wary of becoming entangled in Florence's messy politics. Throughout the day with Michelangelo, Alfonso redirected discussion from military to artistic matters. He demonstrated evident respect for his guest by showing Michelangelo "everything with his own hands, notably some works of painting and portraits of his ancestors."[39] Among "everything" was the remarkable suite of pictures that adorned Alfonso's private *studiolo* known as the Camerino d'Alabastro, including Giovanni Bellini's *Feast of the Gods*, and three of Titian's greatest mythological pictures:

The Worship of Venus, *Bacchanal of the Andrians*, and *Bacchus and Ariadne* (Plates 8–11). Michelangelo had never seen anything like it. The walls sparkled with sumptuous color, bright oil paintings on canvas, seductive mythological tales. It was Michelangelo's first encounter with Titian, a bounteous immersion in color and inventive picture making.

Imagine it: You are with an expansive Duke Alfonso and several of his sweet-smelling courtiers and sycophantic retainers, possibly including Alfonso's court poet, Ludovico Ariosto. You are dressed in leather jerkin and riding boots, still smelling of sweat and horses. The duke conducts you to a small, low-ceilinged room where he proudly shows you ancient coins and a rare Turkish powder horn sent from distant Trebizond. The duke is especially excited about his recent acquisition of a suite of erotic prints—*I modi*—graphic depictions of sexual positions accompanied by scandalously pornographic sonnets penned by Titian's saucy friend Pietro Aretino.[40] While Alfonso lingers over the most lascivious images, Michelangelo's attention is drawn to the magnificent paintings glowing with gem-like color on the studiolo walls (Plate 12). The surrounding suite of works is a visual feast. Michelangelo did not necessarily recognize the artists or many of the recondite subjects, but the sheer beauty of the richly decorated room surely impressed him. Noting Michelangelo's interest, the duke brashly proclaimed his pictures superior to those owned by his sister Isabella d'Este. While Alfonso waxed loquacious, Michelangelo struggled to return the conversation to the ostensible purpose of his visit—a diplomatic mission on behalf of a desperately needy Florence.

Alfonso is loud, officious, domineering. The duke fills the room with his outsize personality and equally outsize figure. The time Michelangelo spent among these masterpieces was limited and he was constantly distracted by Alfonso's garrulous chatter, which included a bawdy recounting of the recent performance of Ariosto's play *La Lena*—as prurient as some of his risqué paintings.[41] Thanks to his years spent in the Medici entourage, Michelangelo could make sense of Alfonso's messy recounting of Ovidian myths. While he may not have grasped the sophisticated literary conceits that lay behind many of the pictures, he would remember certain figures, the bountiful inventions, the vivid color and overall *magnificenza* of the studiolo.[42] It was an eye-opening experience, cut short by an impatient duke.

How much time was Michelangelo given to absorb this first encounter with the art of his Venetian contemporary? Five minutes? Fifteen? Did he and Duke Alfonso speak about the relative merits of disegno and colorito? This is highly doubtful. More likely, the duke talked and Michelangelo listened, all the while trying to remain focused on his principal reason for being in Ferrara.

Before leaving the studiolo, the duke and Michelangelo paused before Titian's portrait of Alfonso d'Este (Fig. 18). As a good diplomat anxious to flatter the duke, Michelangelo "enthusiastically praised" the picture.[43] Was Michelangelo merely being polite or was there another reason the portrait attracted his attention? Titian portrayed Alfonso with his hand resting on the polygonal barrel of a "great piece of artillery"—a fearsome giant among contemporary ordinance. The duke jokingly referred to his cannon as "La Giulia," as it had been cast from remnants of a bronze sculpture of Pope Julius II that once lorded over Bologna's Piazza Maggiore. The cannon was cast from Michelangelo's melted-down sculpture.

In 1506–8, Michelangelo had spent two miserable years in Bologna casting and chasing the monumental statue of Julius II. Less than three years later, an unruly mob pulled the statue down, smashing it to pieces. Duke Alfonso acquired enough of the valuable bronze to create the cannon that he caresses in Titian's

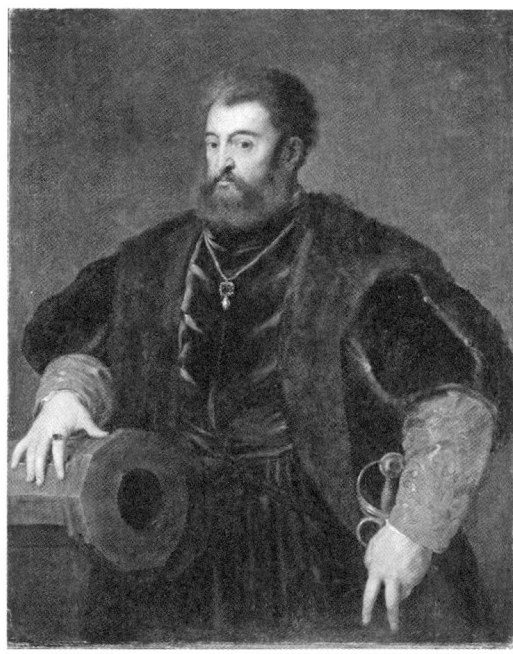

18. Titian Vecellio,
Alfonso d'Este, oil on
canvas, 50 × 38.75 in
(127 × 98.4 cm),
Metropolitan Museum of
Art, New York, c. 1525.

portrait. Alfonso was certainly cognizant of this history, as was Michelangelo. While Michelangelo praised Titian's portrait, he stifled his real feelings, inevitably reminded of two years of life and labor squandered. Here was his Julius statue reincarnated as one of Alfonso's proudest possessions, a cannon that Florence desperately needed to bolster its paltry arsenal. Alfonso undoubtedly enjoyed the delicious irony of the moment. Did Michelangelo? Was Titian aware that he had painted a double portrait: the martial duke and his infernal machine, created from an important bronze sculpture by the much-touted Florentine marble sculptor? Thus, before Michelangelo and Titian ever met, their lives had become inadvertently entwined by a manipulative duke and his infamous cannon.

A Prisoner's Challenge

Michelangelo was no ordinary diplomat, as both the Florentine Signoria and Alfonso were fully aware. His stature as a famous artist added to the hope of diplomatic success. Fully cognizant of Florence's weak position, Alfonso took advantage of the current situation. In sharing his artistic treasures with Michelangelo, Alfonso did not merely act as courteous host to the representative of an ostensible ally; he was pursuing his own agenda. As Michelangelo prepared to depart Ferrara, Alfonso became jocular, thus forcibly reestablishing the social gap between a duke and a pleading diplomat without title, money, or much to offer.

"Michelangelo, you are my prisoner. If you want me to let you go free, I want you to promise me to make me something by your own hand."[44] Of course, Michelangelo was probably prepared for this gambit, partly because it was the very reason the Florentine Signoria elected to send an inexperienced diplomat on such an important mission. Before Michelangelo answered, Alfonso condescendingly offered the artist complete freedom to choose the subject and medium, stating only that he longed to have "something by your own hand, as suits you, just as you wish, sculpture or painting."

Art had long been used as a tool to oil diplomatic machinery. From the mid-fifteenth century, the Medici repeatedly employed art and artists to further their political agendas. For example, Lorenzo de' Medici curried favor with the king of Naples by sending him a bronze equine head (then attributed to Donatello), and subsequently sent both Donatello and Andrea del Verrocchio to cultivate relations with Venice by creating equestrian monuments in Venice and their subject city of Padua. Michelangelo seemed the ideal diplomatic agent to Ferrara since he had met Alfonso many years previously when Alfonso d'Este was in Rome mired in difficult negotiations with Pope Julius II.

Alfonso was one of the few persons granted access to the Sistine Chapel while Michelangelo was still painting the ceiling. The unique encounter was described at length by the Mantuan ambassador in Rome writing to Alfonso's sister, Isabella d'Este:

> His Excellency desired greatly to see the vault of the great chapel which Michelangelo is painting . . . and the Lord Duke went up on the vault with several persons; at last everyone little by little came down from the vault and the Duke remained up there with Michelangelo for he could not see enough of those figures, he flattered him copiously, and in the end His Lordship requested that he should make him a painting, and he made him discuss it, he offered him money, and he extracted a promise to do it.[45]

That was 1512. Now, seventeen years later, Alfonso had Michelangelo in his clutches with an unfulfilled promise. Thus, Alfonso effectively deflected the request for military assistance by repeating, in a more insistent fashion, his desire for a work from the master. Alfonso had "copiously flattered" Michelangelo and granted him privileged access to his collection of artistic treasures. Not only because he was Alfonso's "prisoner," but because he was a diplomat acting on behalf of Florence, Michelangelo agreed to satisfy the duke's request for something "by his hand." What would that be: sculpture or painting?

Although Alfonso supposedly gave Michelangelo a "free hand," he most likely wanted a painting—especially a mythological subject that would complement the pictures already adorning his studiolo. Despite the brevity of the visit, Michelangelo astutely divined the situation and Alfonso's tastes. Michelangelo knew how to satisfy a patron who warranted gratifying.

Once he returned to Florence, Michelangelo set about creating a work that would greatly please Duke Alfonso and fit well within his suite of masterpieces. This moment deserves emphasis: in the face of an impending siege, the chief military engineer of the Republic of Florence and a self-proclaimed marble sculptor began work on a large painting, "un quadro grande." Considering his many concurrent obligations, it is noteworthy that Michelangelo created a painting, as well as one with a mythological subject, something he had not done since carving the *Bacchus* more than thirty years earlier. Alfonso was the catalyst, Titian the challenge, *Leda* the result (Plate 13).

Leda and the Duke

Let us momentarily return to Michelangelo's visit to Alfonso's studiolo. Aside from Titian's portrait of Alfonso, there were many pictures that might have attracted the artist's attention. The duke's voluble discourse did not permit much time to discuss individual paintings, but Michelangelo required little assistance in admiring another artist's work. He could be ungenerous with praise, but he recognized genius. What certainly struck Michelangelo was the brilliant color of oil paints, so different from the matte palette of fresco and most Florentine tempera painting. Especially startling were the crimson reds and ultramarine blues, rare and expensive pigments more readily available in Venice than in Michelangelo's native city. Also surprising were the many figures in active poses and convincing movement. The pictures teemed with life! Botticelli, Pollaiuolo, Verrocchio, not even his own teacher Ghirlandaio had ever invented such living, mobile figures. It was wonderful and disconcertingly new.

Michelangelo was suddenly confronted by a talented and worthy rival who, despite their very different fields of endeavor, awakened the Florentine's naturally competitive instincts. Did Michelangelo recall a verse from his beloved Dante in which the famous Cimabue, once considered the best of painters, was suddenly overshadowed by the younger Giotto: "Credette Cimabue ne la pittura / tener lo campo, e ora ha Giotto il grido": "In painting Cimabue thought he held the field, and now Giotto has the cry [acclaim]" (Dante, *Purgatorio* XI:94–96)? Having surpassed all his predecessors, did Michelangelo perceive Titian as a rival to supplant him? Michelangelo now entered the lists; he would show who could "tener lo campo," that is, be best in the field, overshadowing all rivals.

Titian's *Bacchus and Ariadne* was one of those pictures that stimulated Michelangelo's interest (see Plate 11). Smitten by the beautiful and understandably startled Ariadne, Bacchus leaps from his cheetah-drawn chariot while performing a nearly impossible mid-air pirouette. Equally astonishing is the naked Laocoön-like figure struggling to escape entwining snakes. Such figures riveted Michelangelo's attention. The duke, however, insisted on directing the artist to the voluptuous, full-length nude languidly reclining in the foreground of Titian's *Bacchanal* (see Plate 10). The duke maintained that it was far more alluring—and lusciously desirable—than the similarly disposed figure in Bellini's *Feast of the Gods* (see Plate 8).

Months later, when he began a picture for Alfonso, Michelangelo would recall Titian's startlingly original and colorful inventions, including the duke's conspicuous attraction to the full-length nude in Titian's *Bacchanal*. Thus, in choosing Leda and the Swan as a subject, Michelangelo was directly confronting Titian's nude as well as the Venetian's prowess as a painter and inventor of sensuous mythological pictures. In contrast to earlier moments in his career when Michelangelo claimed that painting "non è mia arte," the self-described sculptor was willing to make a painting, albeit in the more readily available and familiar medium of tempera.

In painting the *Leda*, Michelangelo created the most erotic picture of his entire career: Olympian Jove, metamorphosed into a snow-white swan, coupling with an acquiescent Leda (see Plate 13). Nude except for a pearl and gilt-bronze diadem, Leda slumps into the luxuriant red drapery that suggests and envelops their lustful passion. The downy-smooth swan slithers across Leda's ample belly and rises between nipple-erect breasts. She tilts her head and willing lips to meet Jove's horny beak, eyes fastening, a slender smile inviting consummation. Leda's left arm drapes over her pillowed couch, long fingers dangling, tingling in anticipation. The index finger of her equally languid right arm—a secular counterpart to Adam's receptive gesture on the Sistine ceiling—directs our attention to the titillating foreplay taking place in the shadowed area of Leda's pudenda. A soft, feathery wing brushes her fleshy thigh and expansive bottom prompting Leda to wrap her leg around the soft, fluttering wing, assisting and encouraging Jove's penetration. Despite the lovers' intercourse, an overall lassitude permeates the picture.

While Michelangelo's *Leda* is a celebration of flesh and passionate desire, the painting has the chiseled quality of a solid figure carved from stone—a two-dimensional translation of his sculpted *Night* (Fig. 19). At the same time, *Leda* is a striking and purposeful contrast to Titian's enticing nude. The picture, however, can be somewhat off-putting for the modern viewer. Its bestial subject and Leda's ungainly, masculinized body composed of masses of solid flesh are unsettling. Perhaps our chilly reaction is due to the fact that we only know the original from its many

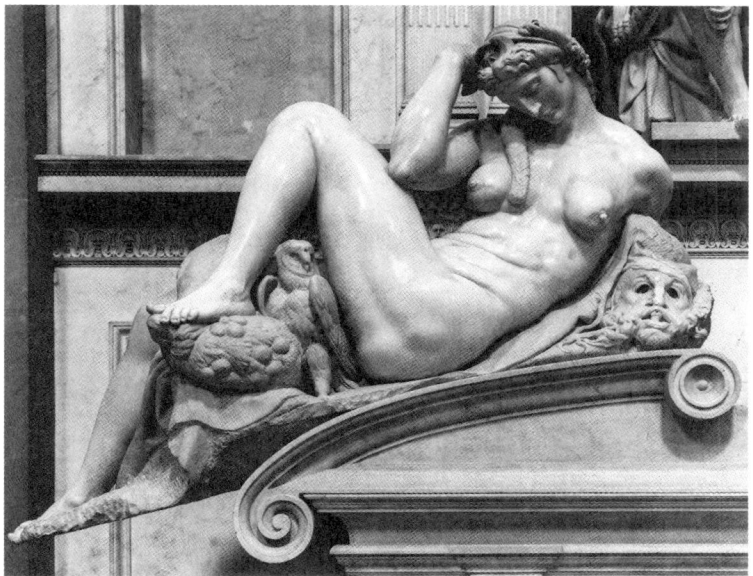

19. Michelangelo, *Notte*, marble, l. 6.33 ft (194 cm), Medici Chapel, Florence, 1524/26.

copies, the best of which is generally attributed to the very fine painter Rosso Fiorentino, who saw the original when it arrived in France (see Plate 13).

Let us consider Michelangelo's preliminary drawing in the attractive, flesh-like medium of red chalk on woven cream paper (Plate 14). The drawing of an aristocratically demure, full-lipped beauty suggests that Michelangelo began his Leda in a similar sensuous modality as Titian. In the final analysis, however, when it came to portraying sexuality in paint, Titian's brush was the more versatile instrument. No matter what we currently make of Michelangelo's unsettling painting, it is certain that libidinous Alfonso d'Este lusted after the picture. But, as we will see, the duke's political dithering cost him the painting.

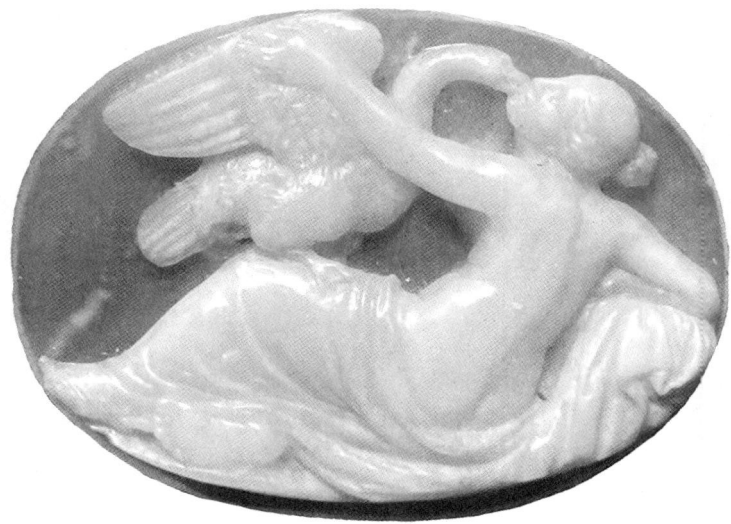

20. Anon., Roman Cameo of *Leda*, c. 5 cm, Bargello Museum, Florence, second to third century CE.

Leda was the opening gambit in what would become Michelangelo's increasingly competitive dialogue with Titian. At the same time, *Leda* was a sophisticated picture appealing on multiple levels to a learned patron. Although painted, Michelangelo created a sculptural figure that Alfonso would recognize as a painted counterpart to Michelangelo's own sculpture of *Night* (see Fig. 19), which, in turn, was based on an ancient cameo (Fig. 20). A politician and collector who emulated his Florentine counterparts, Alfonso was familiar with Michelangelo's sculpture and the famous cameo. Thus, Michelangelo's *Leda* was simultaneously modern and antique with the sort of multiple allusions that appealed to the sophisticated collector.

Michelangelo's purposeful entwining of past and present contained further resonances intended to appeal to Alfonso's family history and dynastic pretensions. Like many Renaissance princes who imagined and constructed fanciful genealogies, the Este claimed descent from the Trojans.[46] It was family lore confirmed by frequent assertion in the art, poetry, and local histories of Ferrara. Of course, Leda and the Swan is a story intimately bound up with Trojan history, as two of her offspring—Helen and Clytemnestra— were central to the fame and fall of Troy. The infamous twins initiate a history that leads from Troy to the founding of Rome and the eventual rise of the Este family. Whether selected by the artist or patron or by the two in conversation, the *Leda* cleverly and intelligently appealed to Alfonso's robust sexuality, family history, and intellectual acumen.

At the same time, the picture would stand apart, triumphing over all others in Alfonso's collection. In comparison to the multifigure canvases adorning the studiolo, the large figure of Leda fills Michelangelo's canvas. The elegant curl of the swan's neck, the gentle kiss of beak against pursed lips, and the feather that softly strokes Leda's ample bottom draw our concupiscent attention. Had the *Leda* ever joined its Venetian counterparts, it would fit perfectly into the greatest ensemble of modern mythological pictures in Italy, while simultaneously declaring itself the boldest and most sexually explicit of Alfonso's paintings. Altogether, the *Leda* was a magnet of attention and an artistic gauntlet thrown down before a contemporary rival. Learning of the picture, an equally competitive Titian would respond in kind, but first the two artists would meet in person.

* * *

Michelangelo began the *Leda* shortly after his visit to Ferrara in July 1529. Because work at San Lorenzo was largely suspended due to the impending siege, Michelangelo had time to devote to Alfonso's picture, especially during the comparatively inactive winter months of 1529–30. By beginning work on the large and ambitious painting, Michelangelo fulfilled his end of the unwritten bargain for Alfonso's military assistance. Meanwhile, Alfonso dithered, setting "considerations of state ahead of fidelity," in the words of historian Francesco Guicciardini.[47]

In the end, Alfonso never came to Florence's aid. Realizing that the city could not withstand the forces arrayed against her, Alfonso refused to be drawn into a conflict that would compromise his tenuous hold on his duchy. He equivocated, made promises, but ultimately did little to help his erstwhile Florentine allies. Rather, he remained loyal to the one person—the Holy Roman Emperor Charles V—who guaranteed his position as ruler of Ferrara.

Alfonso's strategic neutrality secured his duchy but lost him the *Leda*. His failure to assist Florence resulted in a severance of Michelangelo's obligation. Instead, after the fall of Florence in 1530, Michelangelo gave the painting to his pupil Antonio Mini who carried it off to France where it proved a sensation. Sometime in the seventeenth century the picture was destroyed for being too prurient. But it survived via the multiple drawn and painted copies as well as in manifold engravings (e.g., Fig. 21), which is how we know it today.[48]

Titian learned of the *Leda*, first as a diplomatic episode involving his best patron, and shortly afterward via widely circulating engravings. He did not need to see the original painting to know Michelangelo's *Leda*. He had good reason to be interested in the picture and to pay attention to a formidable and unexpected rival. The die was cast.

* * *

Before we allow Michelangelo to leave Ferrara, let us revisit one picture in Alfonso's studiolo that certainly attracted the artist's

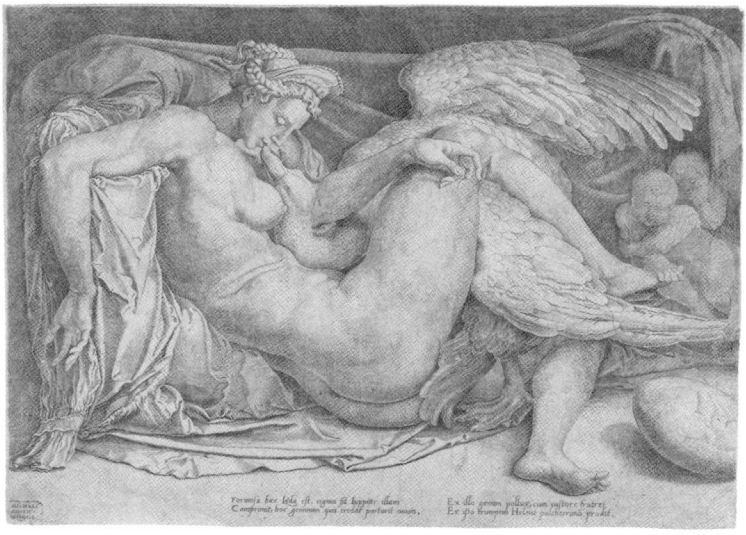

21. Cornelius Bos after Michelangelo's *Leda*, engraving, 13 × 17.75 in (334 × 450 mm),
Metropolitan Museum of Art, New York, late 1530s.

attention. Although brilliant color and landscape are ostensibly
foreign to Michelangelo's art and sensibility, Titian's *Bacchus
and Ariadne* (see Plate 11) remained in Michelangelo's vice-like
memory and later found resonance in his art. The *Bacchus* is Titian at his most inventive and audacious. A raucous entourage
accompanies the love-besotted god who, on spying the beautiful
Ariadne, leaps from his chariot and nearly out of the picture. This
is narrative painting coming to life in a surprising and engaging
fashion—a sixteenth-century anticipation of cinema. Such a picture is far removed from anything Michelangelo had ever seen or
created; however, this would soon change.

Michelangelo never forgot Titian's leaping Bacchus. It rooted in
the artist's fertile imagination and thanks to a thorough process of
assimilation, the figure eventually became his own. As yet, it was

merely a surprising invention, a seedling that would be fertilized by further encounters with Titian's art. A catalyst for this unexpected germination was the artist's unplanned visit to Venice in 1529, and his first face-to-face meeting with Titian.

Winds of War

Abandoned by its supposed allies, the Republic of Florence braced for war. As an imperial army approached Florence in the early fall of 1529, Michelangelo feverishly directed some three thousand laborers to strengthen the defenses of the city. Hastily constructed dirt bastions, reinforced with brick and rubble, sprung up at strategic points to protect the thin medieval walls from the destructive power of modern cannon. As the crisis mounted, those with money and property fled the city. Florence was left with a motley assemblage of hastily trained and impressed citizen-soldiers.

One day, while supervising work on the bastions, a friend warned Michelangelo of treachery afoot in Florence. The unnamed person was likely the Florentine aristocrat Rinaldo Corsini, who persuaded Michelangelo that their lives were in danger. Over dinner, Corsini offered to accompany the artist if he agreed to flee Florence.[49] They would travel in company with Michelangelo's household companion and sometimes pupil, Antonio Mini, and the goldsmith Giovanni Piloto, a friend and collaborator in the Medici Chapel. On September 21, the quartet of mounted companions escaped through the Porta al Prato and rode north on the Via Bolognese. Outside the gate, a hired soldier joined them, mainly as protection in crossing the brigand-infested Apennines.

As the broad plain of the Po River valley opened before them, the refugees skirted east to avoid papal Bologna and continued on to Ferrara where Rinaldo Corsini left their company. A change of horses and days of hard riding brought Michelangelo and his two remaining companions to the river Brenta, where they relinquished their mounts and hired a boatman to ferry them across the lagoon to Venice. The vibrant city, the most serene Republic—longer-lived than the Roman Republic—offered asylum to many Florentine refugees.

The fifty-four-year-old Michelangelo arrived in Venice in a fearful and disordered state. He rented modest lodgings on the Giudecca island across from San Marco. The Giudecca, so named because it was one the first areas of Venice that accommodated the influx of Jewish exiles from Spain, was a poor neighborhood where fugitive Michelangelo could find temporary and anonymous asylum. The outlying island—like the Jews themselves—looked both ways at once: toward a grudgingly welcoming city where Jews could be tailors, used clothes merchants, money lenders, and sometimes doctors and tutors to rich patrician families. At the same time, the community faced outward to the formidable sea, never knowing when they would be exiled again. In his current straitened circumstances, Michelangelo may have felt some empathy for their diasporic existence. Several days after arriving in Venice, he found a moment of calm to write his friend Battista della Palla in Florence:

Battista, dearest friend—I left Florence, as I believe you know, and intended to go to France, but when I reached Venice and made enquiries about the route I was told that going from here one has to pass through German territory which is difficult and dangerous . . . I left without taking leave of any of my friends and in a very haphazard fashion . . . On Tuesday morning, the twenty-first day of September, someone came out from the San Niccolò gate to the bastions where I was, and whispered in my ear that to remain any longer would be to risk my life. And, he came home with me, where we had dinner, and he brought me mounts and never left me till he got me out of Florence, assuring me that this was for my good. Whether he were god or devil I know not.[50]

Michelangelo had departed Florence in such haste—"molto disordinatamente"—that he scarcely had a change of clothes. Shortly after arriving in Venice, he listed his recent expenses: ten lire for the armed soldier who accompanied the travelers across the Apennines; three ducats to the boatman who ferried them across to Venice, and five ducats to Messer Loredon for lodging on the Giudecca. Michelangelo recorded the purchase of a table, two stools, and straw bedding for his Spartan accommodations. He purchased a pair of shoes for Piloto, stockings and a pair of boots for Antonio, and a pair of shoes, two shirts, and a hat for himself. Altogether, the expenses amounted to nearly forty ducats, a substantial sum. Michelangelo had just abandoned a salary that paid him handsomely: a gold florin per day, which is how much Antonio's new boots cost. Michelangelo wrote out these various expenses in a disordered and uncharacteristically messy hand (Fig. 22).[51] He mistook the proper date and twice recorded differing costs for the rented horses. An agitated Michelangelo found himself in temporary accommodations in a foreign city without an income, a well-defined plan, or much of a future. Guilt at having abandoned family, city, and his post as director of fortifications, are poignantly revealed on this messy scrap of paper.

By taking modest lodgings on the Giudecca, Michelangelo clearly wished to remain incognito. His half-formulated idea was to accept a long-standing invitation from King Francis I to join the French court, as had Leonardo da Vinci, Andrea del Sarto, and

22. Michelangelo, *Ricordo*, Archivio Buonarroti I, n. 69 recto, Casa Buonarroti, Florence, September 10, 1529.

Rosso Fiorentino before him. He also might find refuge among the large Florentine community in Lyons. However, as he mentioned in his letter to Battista della Palla, he had been warned about the difficulty of an Alpine crossing and the dangers of a long journey through Germanic lands. He felt at loose ends, and uncertain of his future.

Scarcely a week after he fled Florence, Michelangelo and twelve other prominent citizens were declared rebels by the Florentine

Signoria.[52] Michelangelo had impulsively abandoned his official post and was especially fearful of government reprisal. The entire Buonarroti family faced confiscation of their property and possible exile. During the weeks he spent in Venice, the consequences of his precipitate actions weighed heavily on the artist.

Battista della Palla pleaded for the artist's return to Florence in order to "preserve you, your friends, your honor and your possessions."[53] Michelangelo's honor and self-interest were at stake—*onore* and *utile* were sacred possessions that no Florentine willingly sacrificed. However, having been branded a rebel, Michelangelo was terrified of returning to the city. Further letters from Florence kept Michelangelo in a state of desperate indecision.

Despite his desire to maintain a low profile, there were no secrets from the ever-vigilant Venetian police state. Pleased to accommodate an illustrious visitor, the Venetian government extended an invitation for Michelangelo to be an official guest of the city. Michelangelo's purchase of shoes, shirts, and a cap may have been in preparation for his meeting with Venetian officials, and subsequently with Doge Andrea Gritti. Unlike most artists of his day, Michelangelo was supremely conscious of his family's noble lineage, dressing and comporting himself in a manner appropriate to his social station. Once, for example, Michelangelo had not ventured out of his house until a tailor furnished him with proper clothes, including an expensive doublet.[54] Despite being a stateless exile, he still observed social protocol.

Tiziano Vecellio, then in his mid-forties and the official painter to the Republic of Venice, was among the small delegation sent to welcome the artist, and in late September or early October of 1529, the two artists met for the first time. This is a critical moment in our story, but it must be largely reconstructed from scant documentation.[55]

An Imagined Exchange

The Venetian delegation is expected to arrive shortly. Michelangelo is conscious of the extreme deference: the all-powerful Venetian Republic extending a welcome to a renowned artist, albeit a foreigner in exile. Titian arrives with a small entourage, including one or two state officials, one of his sons—Pomponio or Orazio—and perhaps a workshop assistant. As a close friend of Titian and sometimes friend of Michelangelo, it is likely that the Florentine sculptor / architect Jacopo Sansovino was also present. Despite having exchanged angry words regarding the San Lorenzo facade commission a dozen years earlier, Sansovino, as a state employee of Venice and a Florentine acquaintance, was an obvious choice as intermediary.[56] Attending Michelangelo were his companions from Florence, Giovanni Piloto and Antonio Mini.

After diplomatic niceties, the tenor of the meeting might have devolved from formal and diplomatic to more particular and personal. Michelangelo is invited to be a guest of the Venetian state and to accept more dignified lodgings. He is also offered a prestigious commission: to design a new Rialto bridge. This latter invitation originated from widespread knowledge that many years earlier both Leonardo da Vinci and Michelangelo had been invited by the Turkish sultan to design a bridge to cross the Golden Horn of Constantinople—a commission of such prestige that it had reached international ears. Venice now saw a welcome opportunity to exploit Michelangelo's presence to build, or at least design, a stone bridge across their own Bosporus, the narrow elbow of the Grand Canal. The invitation surely flattered Michelangelo, although he returned to Florence before the project came to fruition.

It is difficult resisting the wish to be a fly on the wall. Did Titian and Michelangelo speak of the Florentine's recent visit to Ferrara and his admiration of Titian's pictures? Did they exchange gossip about Alfonso d'Este? Did the conversation include mention of Michelangelo's promised *Leda* or Titian's portrait of Alfonso with his notorious cannon, "La Giulia"? All topics of mutual interest, but the two artists probably talked less than we might like to imagine. However, a polite rapport was established, providing groundwork for an acquaintance that continued over the next three decades. The two artists would meet only once again, in Rome, sixteen years later.

*   *   *

Some fifty years after Michelangelo's death, the artist's grand-nephew Michelangelo Buonarroti the Younger (1568–1646) commissioned a series of paintings to celebrate the life of his illustrious ancestor. These pictures decorate a gallery in the family's home, the Casa Buonarroti in Florence. A Florentine artist, Valerio Marucelli, painted the Venetian episode: *Michelangelo Received by Doge Andrea Gritti* (Fig. 23). A subsequent Buonarroti scion, Michelangiolo di Leonardo di Buonarroto Buonarroti, described the painting: "Michelangelo, going to Venice, is received and visited by Doge Andrea Gritti and many gentlemen; he is offered a salary if he resolves to live there; who, being exempt from any obligation, made for Gritti the design of the Rialto bridge."[57]

Of course, the painting and its narrated story belong to family lore, but that does not render it completely fictitious. Given that he had departed Florence in haste and without a proper wardrobe to meet the doge, the manner in which Michelangelo is dressed in Marucelli's picture—in brocaded burgundy doublet, crimson hose, and long, black serge over-cloak—is obviously exaggerated. Nor did he yet own the expensive felt hat that he extends in his

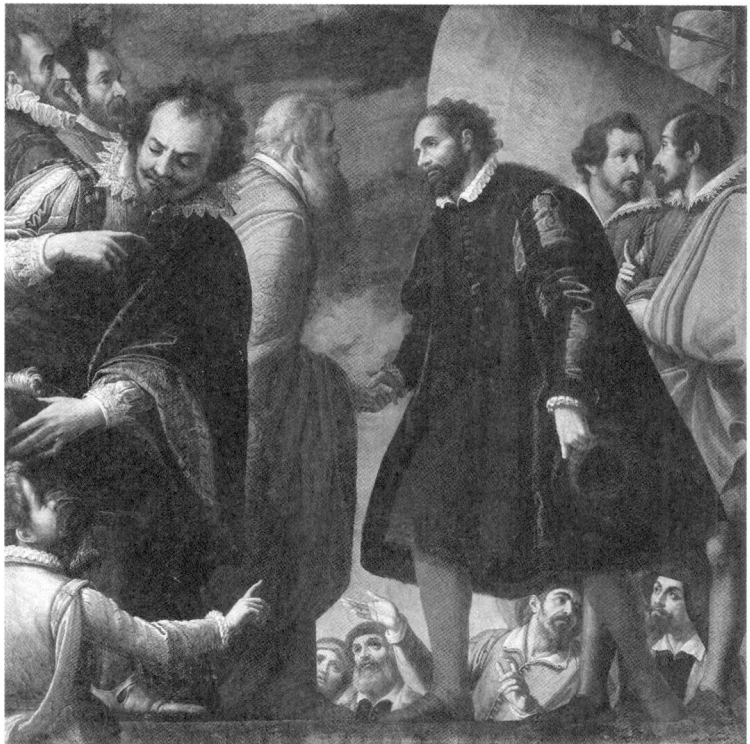

23. Valerio Marucelli, *Michelangelo Received by Doge Andrea Gritti*, oil on canvas, 57 × 55.5 in (145 × 141 cm), Casa Buonarroti, Florence, 1616–18.

left hand, a favorite and expensive sartorial accoutrement of his elderly years.

Note that we are examining a picture painted nearly one hundred years after the supposed encounter between Michelangelo and Doge Gritti in Venice. The painting is hagiography, presenting Michelangelo as the equal in stature and dress to the doge of Venice. This is Florence portraying Venice, and a pictorial celebration of Michelangelo as principal protagonist. Yet, aside from the hagiographic intent, the picture helps confirm contemporary accounts that the Venetian state indeed warmly welcomed Michelangelo and invited him to design a new Rialto bridge. This is the same Andrea Gritti, now doge, who lived in Constantinople for nearly twenty years, serving as Venetian representative to the Ottoman court. Thanks to Gritti's famously prodigious memory, he would have recalled the sultan's still active desire to span the Golden Horn. Thus, oral, written, and pictorial tradition, including both Vasari and Condivi, all attest to Michelangelo having produced a design and a model for the Rialto bridge. As Michelangelo's friend and assistant Tiberio Calcagni subsequently recounted: "He told me that this is true and that he had made a model."[58] Over the next six weeks, Michelangelo surely spent time at Rialto imagining how to replace the rickety wooden bridge with a new stone span. He had plenty of time to see much else in Venice, including paintings by his new acquaintance, Titian.

Michelangelo, Tourist in Venice

Even if Michelangelo visited Venice in 1494 and/or 1506/8, this was by far his longest stay in the city. Six weeks does not seem long considering the full span of Michelangelo's nearly eighty-nine years, yet six weeks is more than most persons devote to a trip abroad or to a summer vacation. Moreover, the effects of an extended stay in one place can prove catalytic and long-lasting, especially in a city as rich and cosmopolitan as Venice. Properly dressed yet grumbling at the high *traghetto* fee to cross by gondola from the Giudecca to Dorsoduro and San Marco, Michelangelo had plenty of time, according to a contemporary chronicler, to see the "admirable works by the Cavaliere Tiziano, who excels in painting and in portraits."[59] As a friend and fellow Florentine, Jacopo

Sansovino likely accompanied Michelangelo around Venice, as did Michelangelo's companion in exile, the goldsmith Giovanni Piloto, who was already familiar with the city. Moreover, Piloto was a "most entertaining and facetious fellow" who could lighten Michelangelo's currently dark mood.[60]

When Michelangelo met Andrea Gritti in the doge's palace, he passed through state rooms decorated with acres of large-scale propagandistic canvases relating a thousand years of Venetian history. Like many first-time visitors, he would have had little interest in most of these pictures; moreover, his mind was on meeting the doge. He might have seen a large fresco of St. Christopher, but would he have recognized—or been told—that it was by Titian?

After his audience, Michelangelo's companions led him into San Marco and around the piazza that would shortly be transformed thanks to the architectural interventions of Jacopo Sansovino. When Michelangelo passed through Rialto, he likely stopped in San Bartolomeo to see the majestic organ shutters painted by his friend Sebastiano del Piombo.[61] Not far from Rialto was the prominent church of Santa Maria Glorioso dei Frari. Michelangelo gravitated to the church as he had a lifelong predisposition toward Franciscans: his mother was Francesca; he was born close to La Verna where St. Francis received the stigmata; he grew up in the neighborhood of Florence dominated by the Franciscan church of Santa Croce; and, early in his career, he was commissioned to paint a St. Francis for San Pietro in Montorio in Rome. The Frari housed the polychromed wood statue of St. John by Donatello, the sculptor most admired by Michelangelo (Fig. 24), and the church was replete with masterpieces by the best contemporary painters of Venice, including Giovanni Bellini and Titian. It is impossible not to be impressed by the vast basilica and its high altar adorned with Titian's masterpiece, the *Assunta*, painted a dozen years earlier (Plate 15).

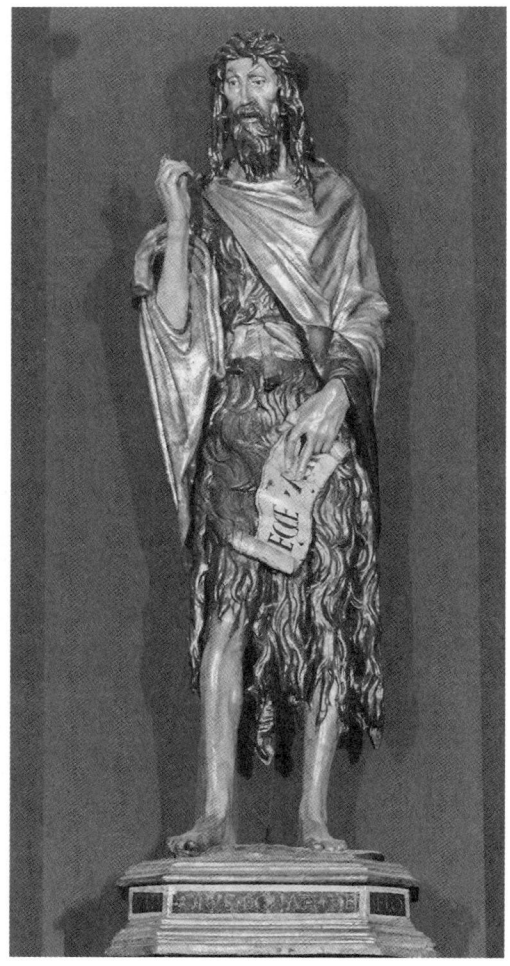

24. Donatello, *St. John the Baptist*, polychrome wood, h. 4.6 ft (141 cm), Santa Maria Glorioso dei Frari, Venice, 1452–53.

Titian's *Assunta* dominates the enormous hall-like church, and was by far the largest panel painting Michelangelo had ever seen.[62] Light pours through the floor to ceiling windows of the gothic apse, virtually blinding a spectator. Normally such *contraluce* (looking directly into light) would render the altarpiece extremely difficult

to see; however, Titian's effulgent reds, blues, and gold successfully compete with the natural light. The tall vertical composition,
divided into three easily discernible zones, draws our attention to
the central figure of the Virgin in a vermilion dress and azurite
cloak framed by a halo of glowing golden light. Barely discernible
as individual figures, a host of cherubic angels surround the as-
cending Virgin while the crowd of larger-than-life-size apostles—
spectators like us—turn their gazes and gestures heavenward.

The painting dates from precisely the same time that Raphael
and Sebastiano del Piombo were creating their respective altarpieces in Rome, the *Transfiguration* and *Raising of Lazarus* (Figs. 25,
26). Michelangelo had furnished drawings for Sebastiano's *Lazarus*,
a work equivalent in size and ambition to Titian's masterpiece.
The grand scale and animated gestures of Titian's earthbound
apostles—often described by scholars as "michelangelesque"—
would naturally attract Michelangelo's attention. In fact, a contemporary described these figures as possessing "the grandeur and
awesomeness of Michelangelo."[63] As he studied the row of monumental figures, one can easily imagine the Florentine seeing his
own inventions come to colorful life.

There was more for the artist to see and admire. Titian's recently completed *Pesaro Madonna*—on an altar in the nave's
left aisle—also called for attention. Did Michelangelo note how
the oblique view of the painting took advantage of the viewer's
movement, helping to animate the unfolding composition as one
proceeds toward the high altar (Plate 16)?[64] Unlike any Florentine
Madonna or *sacra conversazione* that Michelangelo had ever seen,
the off-center, diagonal composition effectively unites the space
of the picture with that of the church itself. As one walks down
the nave, the diagonal composition draws one into its fictive yet
convincing extension of the majestically columned space of the

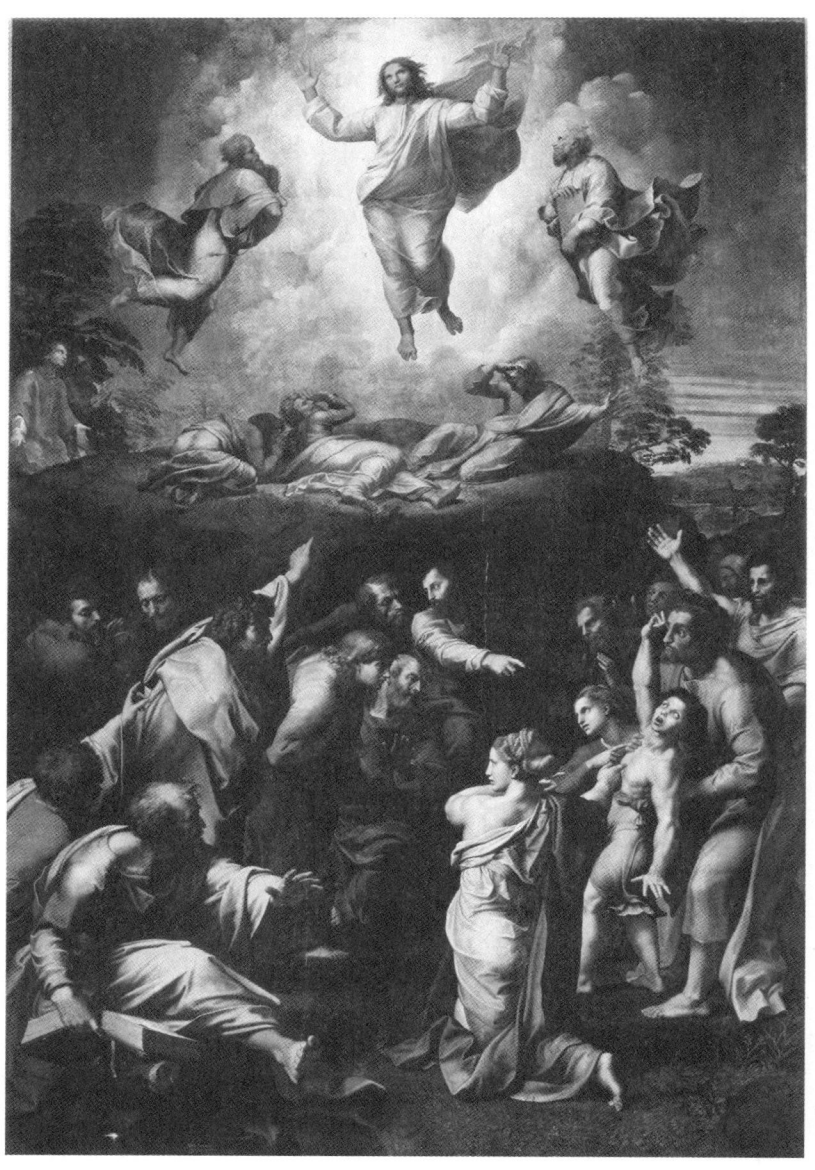

25. Raphael, *Transfiguration*, oil on wood, 13.33 × 9 ft (405 × 278 cm), Pinacoteca Vaticana, Vatican City, c. 1518/20.

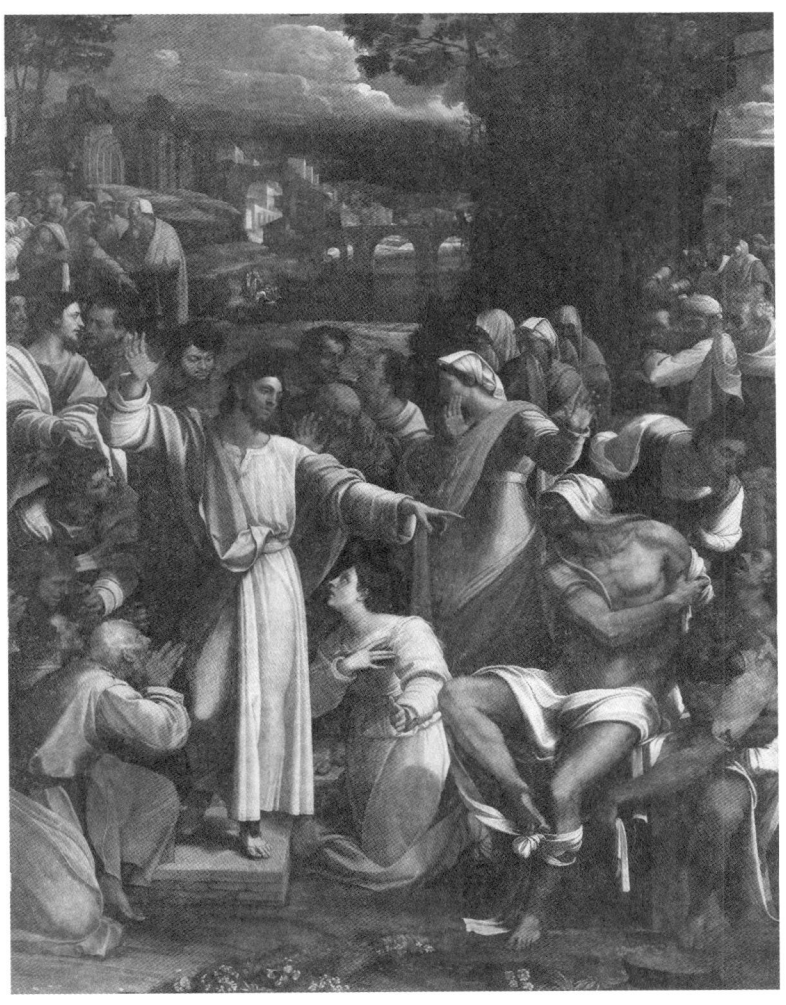

26. Sebastiano del Piombo, *The Raising of Lazarus*, oil on canvas, 12.5 × 9 ft (381 × 289 cm), The National Gallery, London, 1517–19.

church. One is lured by pictorial illusion, a melding of real and fictional space, art and life joining to relate sacred history. Titian was inventing altarpieces as unfolding drama.

Titian's Masterpiece

The Frari had lured Michelangelo, yet for multiple reasons he also would have visited the Dominican church of San Giovanni e Paolo. In many respects, San Zanipolo (as it is known to Venetians) was the most important church in Venice since it was the preferred burial place of Venetian doges. Andrea del Verrocchio's equestrian statue of Bartolomeo Colleoni commanded the piazza. A significant "foreign" monument, the larger-than-life-size bronze could spark Michelangelo's Florentine pride and motivate him, many years later, when he designed his own equestrian monument for King Henry II of France. Titian was currently painting a major altarpiece for the church, having secured the commission in competition with his contemporaries Palma il Vecchio and Pordenone. After recently meeting Titian, Michelangelo was repaying a courtesy visit.

The *Death of St. Peter Martyr* (Fig. 27), long considered Titian's most famous painting, was described by Michelangelo's Florentine friend Niccolò Tribolo as "the most beautiful work in all Italy."[65] Vasari concurred when he wrote that it was "the most finished, the most celebrated, the greatest and the best conceived and executed."[66] Centuries later, John Constable considered it the birth of landscape art, despite the fact that he mainly knew the picture from the widely disseminated black-and-white engraving by Martino Rota (Fig. 28). The painting achieved such fame that when a fire destroyed it in 1867, it was immediately replaced by the copy painted in 1691 by Johan Carl Loth, which we currently see in situ (Plate 17).

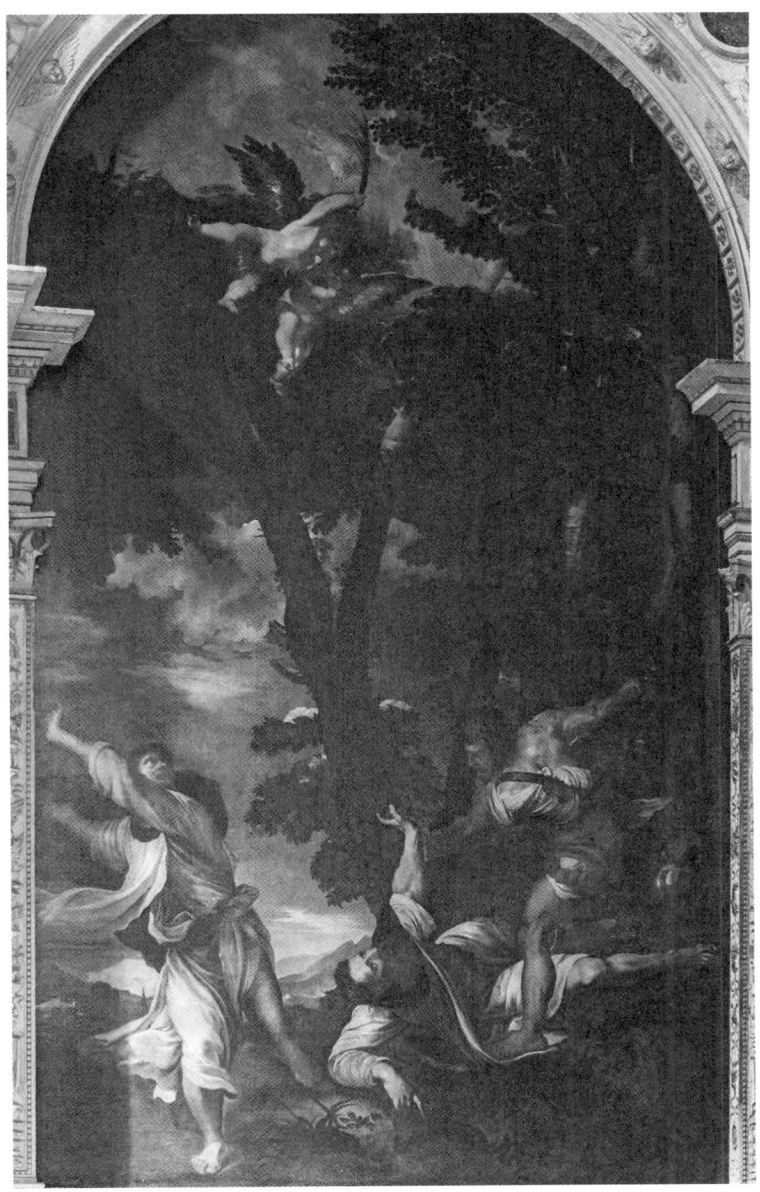

27. Copy of Titian Vecellio, *The Death of St. Peter Martyr* (Carlo Loth, 1691), oil on canvas, 17 × 10 ft (515 × 308 cm), SS. Giovanni e Paolo, Venice, 1529/30.

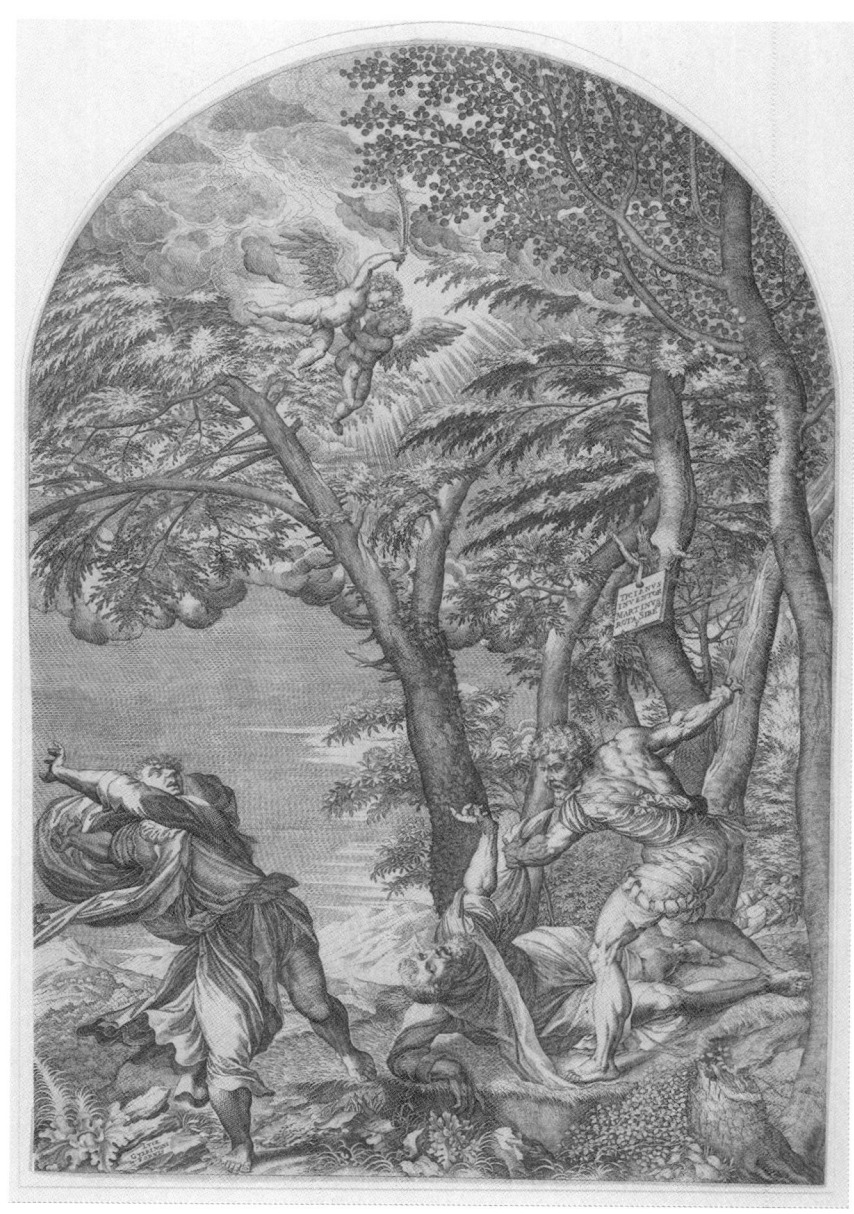

28. Martino Rota after Titian, *The Death of St. Peter Martyr*, engraving, 15.8×10.6 in (40.1×27.2 cm), Metropolitan Museum of Art, New York, c. 1560.

Michelangelo was among the very first people to see Titian's picture in person and still in progress. It was a revelation: a church altarpiece transformed into a startling narrative of murder, mayhem, and martyrdom, described by a contemporary as so alive that we are "hearing a shriek."[67] The whispering quiet of a forested mountain path suddenly erupts in shocking violence and barbarous action: stumbling, falling, stabbing, fleeing, terrifying; rushing wind, swaying trees, roiling sky, and scudding clouds; plangent cries and pungent odors, dirt, stones, sweat, fear, and spilled blood.

Emerging from a darkened wood, the famously intolerant preacher against heresy, Peter of Verona, is brutally attacked. The Dominican friar falls under the first blows of a muscular, swarthy assassin poised to deliver a final, ferocious thrust of his murderous blade. Although mortally wounded, Peter manages to write a bloody "credo"—I believe—in the soil. He turns to gaze toward two descending cherubs bearing a martyr's palm. The tall trees split open to permit their aerial descent amid a resplendent flood of golden light—the promise of Peter's victory over cruel death. Peter's terrified companion, pervaded by "the whiteness of cowardice and the pallor of fear," rushes down the steep mountain path, his black-and-white Dominican habit flapping wildly.[68] Protectively throwing up his arms, he looks back, not to the murderous scene but to the descent of God's angelic messengers.

As one walks toward the high altar of San Giovanni e Paolo, the *Peter Martyr* is seen obliquely on the nave's left wall (see Plate 17). As he did in the Pesaro altarpiece, Titian effectively exploited this diagonal view. The life-size Dominican brother bolts from the murderous scene, escaping the picture and into the church. One wonders about a priest saying mass before such a cruel episode that threatens to erupt into his space and violently disrupt the

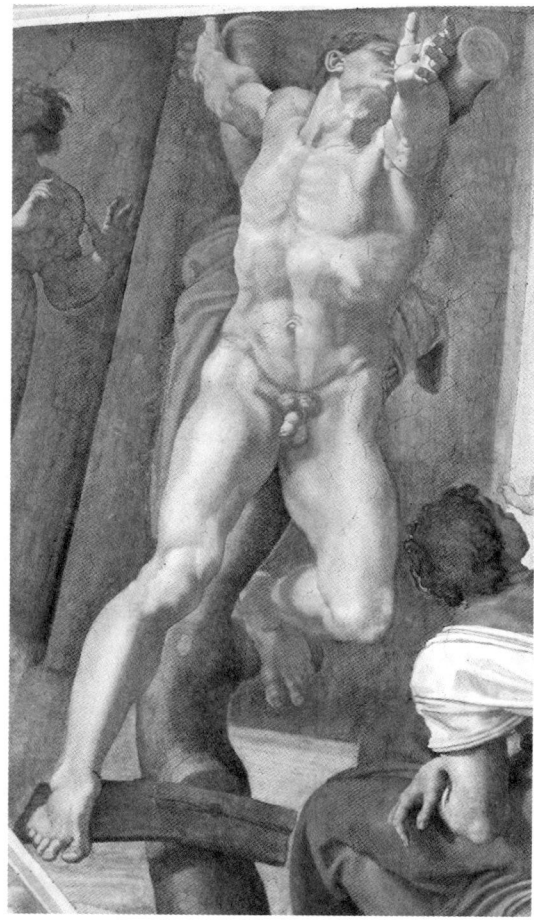

29. Michelangelo, det. *Haman*, fresco, Sistine Chapel, Vatican City, 1508–12.

sanctity of the altar. Imagine a parishioner attempting to pray before such a horrific spectacle. Imagine Michelangelo witnessing it.

Michelangelo had invented similarly twisting contrapposto figures for his *Battle of Cascina* cartoon, and an even more violent *sforzato* figure of Haman for the Sistine ceiling (Fig. 29). However, those individualized, mostly artificial poses lacked the convincing movement of Titian's narrative action and his Aristotelian unity of time, place, and action. Michelangelo would not forget this painting.

*   *   *

Never before had the iconic and sacred purpose of the altarpiece been so radically transformed into hair-raising theatrical drama barely contained by the picture's frame. Michelangelo's encounter with Titian's paintings in Ferrara prepared him for the master's inventions in Venice. Yet, the Venetian's works were especially surprising given that Titian was painting public altarpieces, not secular pictures for private consumption. In the *Assunta*, *Pesaro Madonna*, and especially the *Peter Martyr*, Michelangelo witnessed a revolution in altarpiece design. He saw his Venetian counterpart at his dramatic best, using color, setting, and life-size figures in bold action, creating a living art, blurring distinctions between real and fictive space. According to a knowledgeable contemporary, Titian was "a source of astonishment" for Michelangelo.[69] The experience proved catalytic, and the Florentine responded in his own highly personal manner.

Return to Florence

After six weeks in Venice, Michelangelo felt safe enough to return to Florence. Thanks to the repeated urgings of his friends who were concerned about his exile status and the compromised position of his family, Michelangelo finally acquiesced to leaving the safe haven of Venice. His good friend Battista della Palla promised to meet him in Lucca and accompany him safely to Florence.[70]

Michelangelo nervously slipped into a now tense and fearful city. He appeared before the Eight of War, the *Otto di Guardia*,

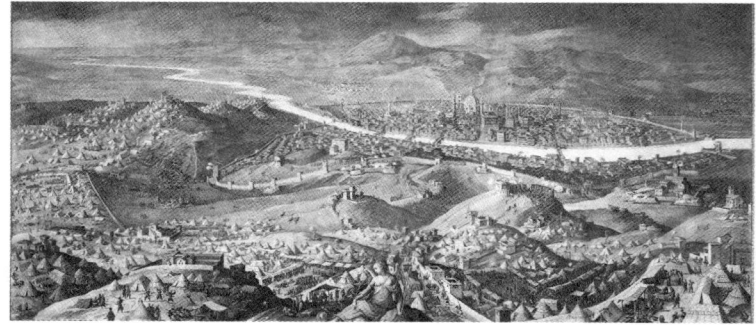

30. Giorgio Vasari, *The Siege of Florence*, fresco, Palazzo Pubblico, Florence, 1558.

and exonerated himself by once again taking up his position as director of fortifications. Manned by brave citizen soldiers, Michelangelo's defensive works proved successful in keeping the besieging army at bay (Fig. 30). But, after months of siege, a tightening cordon had left Florence in dire straits. The starving population was reduced to eating vermin, as all meat and grain had been requisitioned. Toward the end, starvation claimed some fifty persons a day. Even well-to-do families such as the Buonarroti family found themselves "in great want for bread; there is none." Michelangelo's brother Gismondo, who managed the family farm properties, declared, "There is still nothing to eat or drink."[71] The misery was compounded by torrential rains that the family attributed to "the universal judgment of God." Michelangelo's younger brother Giovansimone offered a more profane description: "There is nothing in abundance except mud and shit" ("Non ci è dovizia se non di fango e di merda").[72] After holding off a grueling ten-month siege, Florence was betrayed by insiders. On August 12, 1530, the enemy army swept into the city, seeking revenge and exacting retribution. All were in jeopardy. Many citizens were executed or exiled.

Knowing his life to be in danger, Michelangelo sought the protection of influential friends. Imaginative historians have him hiding for weeks in the San Niccolò gate tower, or spending months in a basement room below the Medici Chapel. He was, however, a prominent citizen, and more likely found refuge with well-placed clerical friends, such as the Prior of San Lorenzo or the canon of the Florentine Cathedral.

It is something of a miracle that Michelangelo survived the chaotic aftermath of the Republic. Pope Clement, true to his name and in honor of his longtime friendship with Michelangelo, forgave the artist for his ill-advised defection. Even more astonishing, in December of 1530, Michelangelo's regular salary was restored and he resumed his work at San Lorenzo. Once again, he was managing and directing hundreds of workers in an accelerated effort—encouraged by the pope—to complete the Medici funerary chapel and the new Laurentian Library. Michelangelo immersed himself in work, although his sympathetic biographer, Ascanio Condivi, wrote that he was "driven more by fear than by love."[73] It would take some months for Michelangelo to adjust from being a political rebel to once again being an artist beholden to the man responsible for the demise of the Florentine Republic.

The effects of six weeks in Venice eventually would manifest themselves, but Michelangelo's immediate concern was the safety of his family and his multiple obligations, first and foremost to his magnanimous papal patron. However, in the aftermath of the Republic, Michelangelo found himself inundated by requests for work, many of which—given his comprised position—he could not refuse. Federico Gonzaga Marquis of Mantua, Cardinal Innocenzo Cibo, Cardinal Antonio Pucci, Cardinal Giovanni Salviati, the Bolognese aristocrat Matteo Malvezzi, Alessandro de' Medici of Florence, King Francis I, and the widow of the Prince of Orange all pressed Michelangelo for something: a sculpture, a painting, a design. Everyone, it seemed, wanted something "by his hand" ("di sua mano"). The most immediate and insistent demand came from Alfonso d'Este of Ferrara who aggressively sought the delivery of the *Leda*.

Less than two months after the fall of the Republic, Alfonso sent an envoy to Florence to collect the *Leda*, "fearing he might lose this treasure in the disturbances."[74] Vasari tells us what happened next: "When the man arrived in Florence he sought Michelangelo out and presented his letters of introduction. Michelangelo made him welcome and showed him the picture of Leda embracing the swan, with Castor and Pollux coming forth from the egg, which he had painted very rapidly in tempera. The duke's go-between, mindful of what he knew of Michelangelo's great reputation and being unable to perceive the excellence and artistry of the picture, said to him: 'Oh, but this just a trifle.'"[75]

Affronted by the tactless comment and the man's condescending behavior, Michelangelo sent him away empty-handed. But Duke Alfonso was not so easily dissuaded. Employing a degree of tact, but also exercising the prerogative of a prince, Alfonso wrote directly to the artist:

Dearest friend, I am extremely pleased to receive from messer Alessandro Guarino, formerly my representative in Florence, the message you sent regarding the picture you have made for me. And this is because I have long desired to have in my house some work of yours, as I have told you myself. Waiting

to see it, every hour seems like a year. I am sending my servant Pisanello, the bearer of this letter, and I pray that you
will kindly have him bring it to me, giving him advice and
direction as to how he should transport it safely.[76]

Given the duke's notorious equivocation, Michelangelo no longer felt obliged to satisfy Alfonso. Rather, Michelangelo welcomed
the ready excuse provided by the ill-mannered courtier to refuse
Alfonso. The duke made a final effort to obtain *his* "treasure," by
appealing directly to Pope Clement.[77] It had been more than a
year since Michelangelo first declined to relinquish the picture,
yet within one day—if not the very day—that he received word of
Clement's inquiry regarding the painting, Michelangelo gave the
Leda to his pupil, Antonio Mini, who—ever so conveniently—was
just then departing for France. Thus, the *Leda*, once a personal
and diplomatic pawn in negotiations with Ferrara, instead went to
France where it was acquired by Michelangelo's longtime admirer,
King Francis I. Although Titian never saw the painting, the *Leda*
nonetheless would play an important role in the nascent relationship and rivalry of the two artists.

In the aftermath of the siege of Florence, Michelangelo suddenly found himself engaged in several simultaneous painting
projects. While completing the *Leda*, another strong-willed
Alfonso—Alfonso d'Avalos, the general of the victorious imperial forces—pressed Michelangelo for a painting. As with Duke
Alfonso d'Este, Michelangelo was given remarkable freedom to
choose the subject, manner ("a vostro modo"), and technique—
whether on canvas or panel: "con vostro comodità . . . in pano o
in tavola, a vostro modo." Michelangelo drew a design (*cartone*)
for a *Noli me Tangere* and selected Jacopo Pontormo—the most
brilliant colorist in Florence—to paint the picture (Plate 18).[78]

This was the beginning of a brief but fruitful collaboration with Pontormo, in which Michelangelo's disegno was melded with Pontormo's colorito.

Instead of the more common representation of Magdalene falling at the feet of the Risen Christ, Michelangelo invented a standing buxom figure lunging at her Lord such that his arresting extended fingers nearly brush her protuberant breasts. It is an engagement with a female subject, heightened by a startlingly erotic frisson wholly original and unexpected in Michelangelo's art. Was Michelangelo consciously or unconsciously channeling Titian, even as he and Pontormo painted a picture that may have had strong political resonance? Following his city's bitter defeat, the picture's subject—"Touch me not"—might be seen as Michelangelo's personal and political *cri de coeur* against the harsh subjugation of Florence.

Even more surprising, Michelangelo elected to furnish a painting for his close friend and banker Bartolomeo Bettini. Once again, Michelangelo drew a full-size cartoon that Pontormo rendered into a much admired and frequently copied *Venus and Cupid* (Plate 19).[79] As with the *Leda*, a modern viewer may find the twisting, heavy-set body of Venus off-putting, more like a masculinized river god than the soft sensuous beauty one reasonably expects of the goddess of love. Her broad chest, bulbous breasts, generously sagging belly, and thickset thighs are thrust forward while her left arm bends in unnatural torsion. Venus turns to meet the inelegant advance and proffered kiss of an improbably contorted Cupid whose left leg awkwardly steps across her abdomen and pudenda. If *Leda* sparked a sense of bestiality, the *Venus and Cupid* prompts a cold shudder of incest. In both cases, Michelangelo has recast Titian's soft, sensual approach to nudity into his own sculptural, *all'antica*, psychologically fraught language of disegno.

As with the *Leda*, Titian never saw Michelangelo's *Venus and Cupid*, but he knew both pictures from painted replicas that Giorgio Vasari sold in Venice.[80] For nine months in 1541/42, Vasari was in Venice "to see the works of Tiziano" and collect information on Venetian artists for his *Lives of the Artists*. He was a guest of his fellow Aretine, Pietro Aretino, who, along with another Tuscan, Jacopo Sansovino, were Titian's closest friends—the so-called "Triumvirate."[81] Previously, Vasari had sent Aretino a *modello* of one of Michelangelo's Medici Chapel figures, most likely crafted from wax or terracotta. Aretino gushed his thanks and showed the model to his friends "as a relic" ("come reliquia").[82] Vasari, Aretino, and Sansovino proved to be magnets pulling Titian and Michelangelo into an ever-tightening clutch even if their opposing poles kept them at a respectful distance. Little by little and then emphatically, Titian became aware that Michelangelo was painting erotized mythological pictures, which the Venetian could rightly claim as his "campo," *his* field of expertise.

One might explain Michelangelo's willingness to paint and design pictures as an expedient means to fulfill multiple obligations during an especially busy time. Yet, it is noteworthy that this burst of pictorial activity took place immediately after Michelangelo's encounter with Titian, first in Ferrara and then in Venice. This was no brief episode in the life of Italy's most famous sculptor. Rather, Michelangelo regularly took up painting over the next thirty years of his career, including the creation of three large and innovative masterpieces of pictorial invention: the *Last Judgment* and two frescoes in the Pauline Chapel. At the same time, he regularly furnished drawings to younger artists including Marcello Venusti and Daniele da Volterra, who each rendered his designs into glowing color. Michelangelo proved to be a brilliant practitioner of painting and an inventive designer of paintings executed by others. This frequent and deepened engagement with the pictorial arts must in part be credited to the challenge posed by Titian.

Recollections of Venice

Now back in Florence and once again confronting his unfinished projects for San Lorenzo, Michelangelo considered adding painted decorations to complement the architectural and sculptural ensemble of the Medici Chapel. In the early 1530s, Michelangelo made a number of drawings for a Resurrection of Christ. These are not preparatory drawings for sculpture but dynamic, multi-figure compositions that suggest narrative movement beyond the pictorial field—something altogether new in Michelangelo's artistic imagination and graphic oeuvre.[83] A small, red chalk drawing in the Musée du Louvre (Plate 20) and a related yet more fully developed drawing for the same subject in Windsor Castle (Plate 21) offer unmistakable evidence of Michelangelo's new interest in multi-figure, pictorial designs. Why did he make such drawings, given that he rarely made such fully developed compositions?

Michelangelo generally drew to solve problems. For the most part, his figural drawings are specific and focused, concentrating on single figures and details. We seldom encounter fully realized multi-figure compositions. Even his cartoon for the *Battle of Cascina* (1504), supposedly a large history painting, was composed of individual studies with little consideration for suggesting the figures' setting, narrative, or unified action.[84] As a result, subsequent artists felt little compunction about cutting the cartoon into individual figure studies, which is how it was studied, copied, and largely survived . . . piecemeal. Therefore, in the rare instances that Michelangelo makes a compositional design—especially in the more "painterly" medium of red and/or black chalk versus pen and ink (as he preferred earlier in his career)—we should pay attention and ask why he did so.

Although small, the Louvre sheet (see Plate 20) is barely capable of containing the explosive energy of more than a half dozen figures in violent motion. Christ abruptly steps from the tomb, thrusting arms and head heavenward as he vigorously rises from the dead. The conception is radically different from most precedents, such as the somnambulant Christ in Piero della Francesca's *Resurrection* (Fig. 31). Does Michelangelo's design have its origins in Titian's dramatic paintings?

The general composition of the figures, and, in particular, Michelangelo's dynamically moving Christ echoes the figure of the fleeing Dominican friar in Titian's *St. Peter Martyr* altarpiece (Fig. 32). But Michelangelo has absorbed more than a single, impressive figure. The violent dynamism of his composition also recalls Titian's masterpiece: active figures quickly moving along diverging diagonals, leaving a recumbent figure to fill the voided central foreground.

Michelangelo did not draw the Louvre sheet while looking at Titian's *Peter Martyr*, but instead recalled the central idea weeks or months after his return from Venice. Michelangelo's experience of Titian's paintings in Ferrara in 1529—especially the mid-air leap of the god Bacchus—prepared him to appreciate the figural inventions and energetic composition of the *Peter Martyr* that he saw just three months later. In reworking Titian's dramatic pictorial compositions, Michelangelo condensed more action into this tiny sheet than almost any previous drawing of his oeuvre. In this small drawing, we are witness to Michelangelo's retentive memory and his process of artistic assimilation. In a brilliant metamorphosis, he transformed Titian's composition and fleeing figure into a dynamic Resurrection, the very antithesis of a brutal murder.

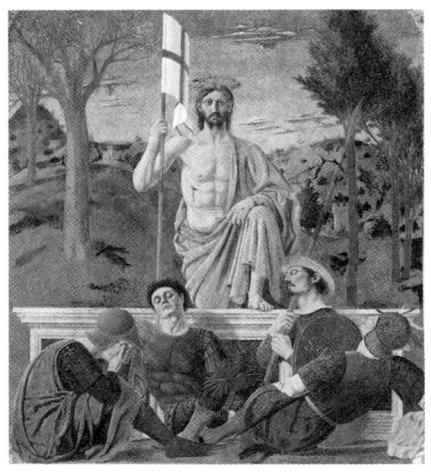

31. *(left)* Piero della Francesca, *Resurrection*, fresco and tempera, 7.25 × 6.5 ft (225 × 200 cm), Pinacoteca Communale, Sansepolcro, 1463–65.

32. *(below)* Comparison, Titian, (det. left) *Peter Martyr*, and (det. right) Michelangelo, Musée du Louvre (691recto).

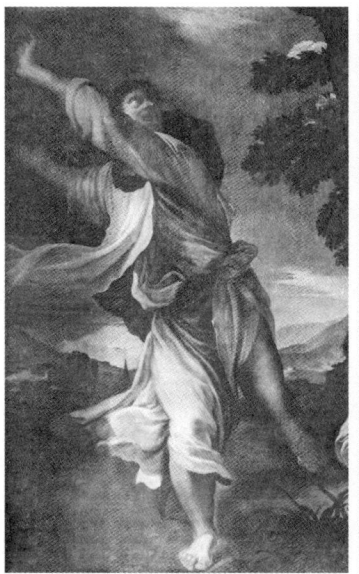

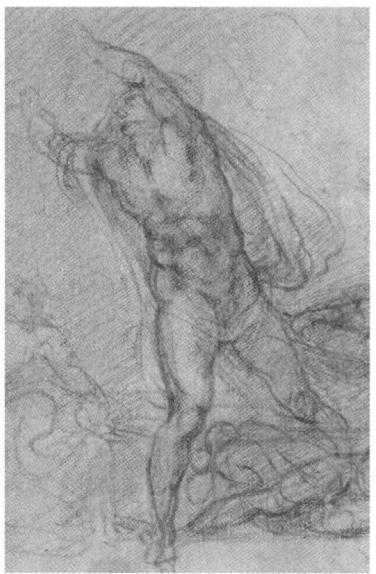

As is characteristic of Michelangelo, who drew as much inspiration from his own inventions as from others, the quick sketch in the Louvre generated another and another until we arrive at what might be considered an "original idea." Michelangelo was so successful in assimilating and transforming the ideas of other artists that we sometimes fail to recognize their origins. Thus, a probable source of inspiration rapidly becomes nearly unrecognizable as Michelangelo begins to work an idea for his own purposes. This is precisely what occurred in a subsequent drawing, created shortly if not minutes after his initial design.

Michelangelo developed the small Louvre composition in the larger, black chalk drawing now in Windsor Castle (see Plate 21). The essential compositional motive—figures moving on diverging diagonals—has been retained, although this sheet reveals its origins as much in Michelangelo's own preceding red chalk drawing as in Titian's paintings. In the more developed, richly pictorial Windsor drawing, the resurrected Christ erupts from the tomb and rises toward heaven. A nude soldier, seen from the rear, bending to the right, counterbalances the leftward-inclining figure of Christ. More than a dozen figures are reacting—or will shortly—to the figure that emerges from the shadowy depths of the rock-cut tomb.

It should be evident that the dynamic, split-open composition of the Windsor Resurrection is rooted in Titian's *Peter Martyr*, yet in the course of an afternoon, the idea has become Michelangelo's own. Rather than being merely challenged by Titian, as was the case with *Leda*, this is an instance in which Titian genuinely inspired Michelangelo. The Venetian provided a rich lode of source material: startling figures, imaginative tragic-drama narrative action, and brilliant color. Michelangelo's vast catalog of figural poses had just received an animating infusion.

The Windsor drawing is one of the most fully developed, most complete pictorial designs in all of Michelangelo's extensive graphic oeuvre, a rare multi-figure composition replete with dynamic figures acting in a richly articulated ambiance of lights and darks. The graphic pictorialism of the sheet is unusual; it both suggests its inspiration in painting and successfully anticipates a painting. But one must ask why—at this moment of personal disruption and multiple demands upon Michelangelo's time—is he designing such a complicated, painterly, multi-figure, narrative composition?

Michelangelo conceived the Medici Chapel as a seamless integration of architecture and sculpture. After his return to Florence in 1530, he unexpectedly—and without specific direction from his patron, Pope Clement—added painted decorations to his integrated ensemble. This was partly motivated by Clement's suggestion that Michelangelo could accelerate completion of the chapel by assigning more work to his many talented assistants. With Titian in mind and Jacopo Pontormo as his collaborator, Michelangelo implemented his patron's directive by adding painted decorations to the chapel.

For the semicircular lunette over the principal Medici tomb, Michelangelo drew a half dozen or more ideas for a Resurrection of Christ, an apposite subject given the chapel's dedication to the Resurrection. As suggested by scholar Anny E. Popp more than a century ago, Michelangelo's drawn design fits comfortably within the semicircular lunette over the tomb (Fig. 33).[85] With the light falling from the lantern above, the *pietra serena* architectural molding casts a shadow that enhances the sense that the lunette frames a three-dimensional rock-cut tomb. Christ emerges from the painted darkness and rises toward the light of the cupola, the only source of illumination in the tenebrous funerary chapel. It is a stunning fusion of fictive and real space, a painted design uniting with the architecture of the chapel to create a dynamic, theatrically convincing, and

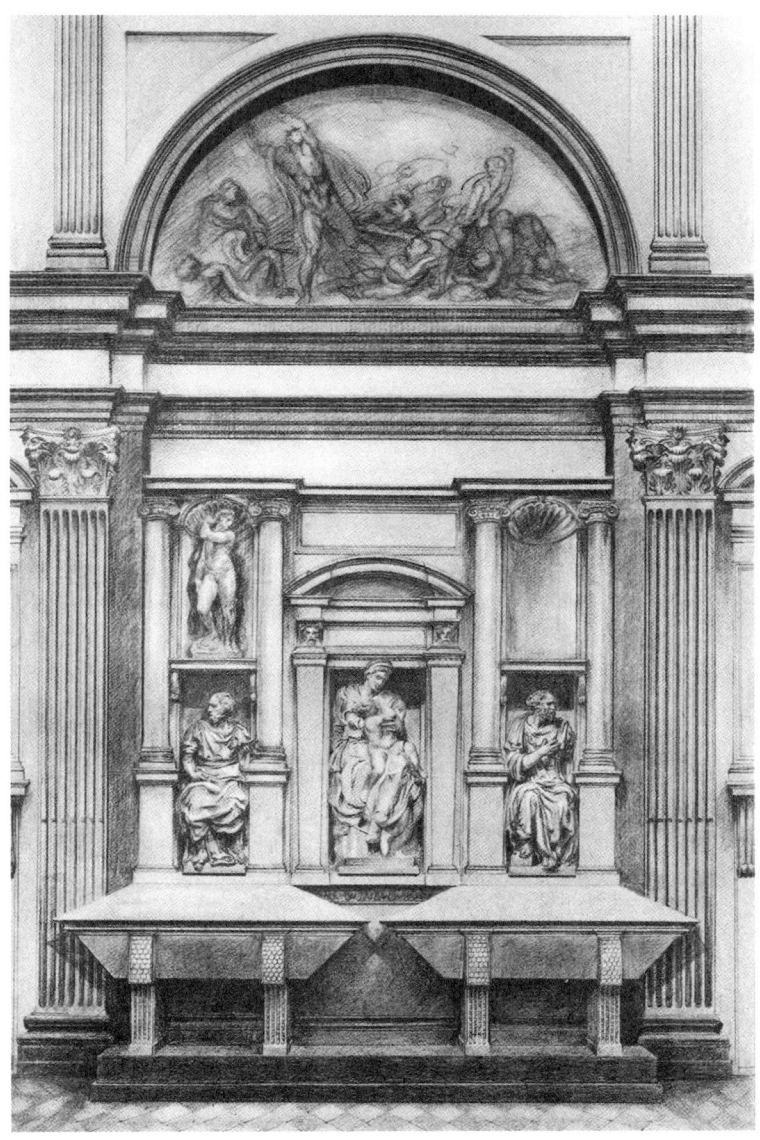

33. Photomontage of principal Medici Chapel tomb, from A. E Popp, *Die Medici-Kapelle Michelangelos* (Munich, 1922), pl. 9.

theologically appropriate *Gesamtkunstwerk*, anticipating and perhaps inspiring the inventions of Gianlorenzo Bernini (1598–1680), Michelangelo's worthy successor in the following century.

*   *   *

For most of his career, Michelangelo, the self-proclaimed sculptor, declared that "painting is not my art." Following his extended exposure to Titian in Ferrara and Venice, however, Michelangelo became increasingly active in the Venetian's field of expertise, his campo. Michelangelo's contemporaries praised his tenacious memory, claiming he never forgot what he saw, whether antique sculpture or works by his contemporaries. Michelangelo's memories of Titian's paintings in Ferrara and Venice "astonished" and inspired him, thereby reawakening an interest in painting and narrative art. Although painting was supposedly anathema to the Florentine artist, Michelangelo's encounter with Titian gave him a means and a creative stimulus during a particularly fallow period in his life—the result of unavoidable personal and historical circumstances.

Titian should be particularly credited with reanimating Michelangelo's interest in mythological subject matter, dormant since he carved the *Bacchus* some thirty years earlier (Fig. 34). The *Leda* was a first foray, immediately followed by the *Venus and Cupid*, and shortly thereafter by a stunning suite of passionate mythological drawings that the artist gifted to his new friend Tommaso de' Cavalieri. Working within his preferred medium of drawing, Michelangelo also created highly finished, pictorial images for Vittoria Colonna, who praised these precious sheets as "ben dipinta" and "perfettamente depinto."[86] Although the drawings for Tommaso de' Cavalieri and Vittoria Colonna were created as private expressions of friendship, they quickly, almost instantly, became public,

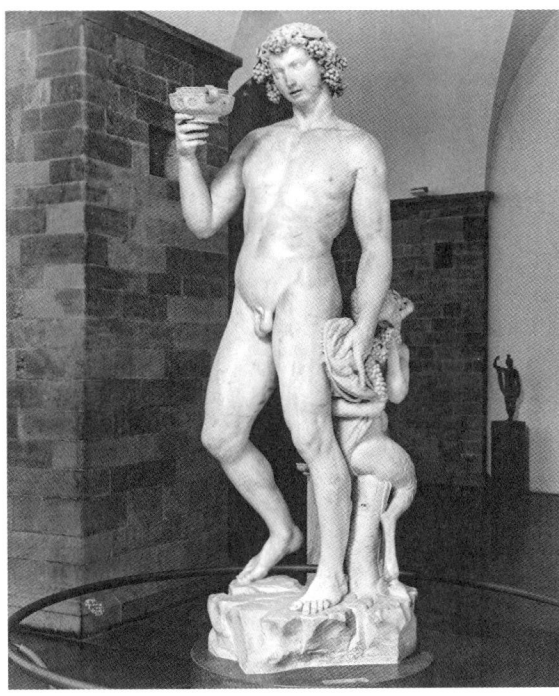

34. Michelangelo, *Bacchus*, marble, h. 6.16 ft (190 cm), Bargello Museum, Florence, 1496–97.

disseminated through a wide variety of precious, painted, and engraved media.[87] Although at first resistant, Michelangelo gradually realized that drawing and *invenzione* could be his surrogate means of satisfying an overwhelming demand as well as a means of multiplying and extending himself into the public sphere, so successfully exploited by Raphael and Titian. At the same time, Michelangelo continued his achievements as a painter, wielding his inventive brush and personal color palette to paint the important frescoes that culminate his career: the *Last Judgment* and the Pauline Chapel frescoes.

When he began work on the *Last Judgment*, he recalled Titian's brilliant blue color, and went to unusual lengths and expense to obtain ultramarine pigments from Venice and ten pounds of azurite (*azuro tedescho*) from Ferrara, the cities where he had been exposed to Titian's use of such precious and vibrant colors.[88]

Looking ahead, Michelangelo might have created very different paintings for the Pauline Chapel had he not learned so much about narrative and pictorial design from Titian. As Titian did in the *Pesaro Madonna* and the *Peter Martyr*, Michelangelo exploited the oblique viewing angles to compose dramatic narratives that come to life, unfolding in time and space as one moves from the entrance door to the altar in the Pauline Chapel (Plate 22).[89] Compositional unity within the borders of the two-dimensional field and from a fixed vantage point have been replaced by a type of cinematic narrative painting pioneered by Titian, absorbed by Michelangelo, and continued by Caravaggio.

Titian undoubtedly was a catalytic factor in reanimating Michelangelo's engagement with painting and pictorial design even if the Florentine artist reentered these arenas on his own terms. The Venetian stimulated an interest that would continue to occupy a surprising amount of Michelangelo's creative energies in the final thirty years of his life. One of the richest, untold parts of our story is how much Titian opened Michelangelo's art and sensibility to color, narrative, and drama. Titian was as important to Michelangelo as the older and more established artist was to him.

* * *

Our story now enters a long hiatus. Due to the disruptive political situation in Italy and the personal and professional preoccupations of both artists, it would be sixteen years before the next chapter of Titian's and Michelangelo's relationship unfolded. They would meet face-to-face once again in Rome, in 1545/46.

PART II
Il Divino vs.
the New Apelles,
1545–1576

In 1545, Michelangelo turned seventy. He was an honorary citizen of Rome and a world-renowned artist. Titian, younger by a decade, was also a celebrity, proclaimed by many as the greatest living painter, the "new Apelles." Both masters had achieved unequalled success in their respective spheres of endeavor. They were the two most famous artists in the world, without question or much competition. Leonardo, Raphael, Giorgione, Giovanni Bellini, and Pordenone were all dead. Given that Giulio Romano had decamped for provincial Mantua, and Sebastiano del Piombo grew lazy enjoying the fruits of a papal sinecure, they were no longer *in gamba*, "in the game." Moreover, both would soon die, Giulio in 1546 and Sebastiano the following year. That left the Florentine Baccio Bandinelli and the Venetian Jacopo Tintoretto, both of whom suffered from a greatly inflated sense of self, which, despite their zealous efforts at self-promotion, never threatened the stratospheric reputations of Titian and Michelangelo.

Thus, when the two artists met for the second time in Rome, there was little question about their position at the pinnacle of their profession, working again for the same important patrons, the current wielder of supreme power, the Farnese family.

When "il Divino" paid a visit to the "new Apelles," they were now on common ground.

Titian's relations with the Farnese family began in Venice in 1542, when he painted the fetching portrait of twelve-year-old Ranuccio Farnese (Plate 23). With his big ears and oblique but attentive glance, the shy yet self-possessed youth—recently invested with the priorship of San Giovanni di Malta in Venice—sports the attire and accoutrements of his new office: belted sword, soft leather gloves, and the silver Maltese cross sewn on his black silk overcoat. It is one of the most sensitive and charming portraits of an adolescent in the entire history of art. Titian sent the completed picture to Ranuccio's older brother Cardinal Alessandro Farnese, whose patronage Titian was actively courting. Michelangelo certainly saw this portrait as he was friendly with its recipient, Alessandro Farnese, as well as with the boy himself since Ranuccio's tutor in Rome was Michelangelo's current closest friend, the prelate Lodovico Beccadelli, whom we will meet shortly.

In 1543, Pope Paul III traveled north to Busseto in Emilia-Romagna to meet the Holy Roman Emperor Charles V. This is when Titian, already the favored painter of Charles, first met and painted a commanding image of the hard-nosed Pope Paul (Plate 24).[1] The canvas barely contains the seated yet imposing figure, whose piercing gaze fixes the viewer. We note the pontiff's dark eyes, stabbing glance, and full white beard against his velvet crimson *mozzetta*. The pope silently queries our intrusion and determinedly awaits our departure, for he will not break the stare. This lifelike portrait achieved instant fame; Pietro Aretino considered it a "miracle." It successfully elicited an invitation for Titian to come to Rome to paint further pictures for the Farnese. As we have seen, one such picture was *Danaë*, painted for Cardinal Alessandro

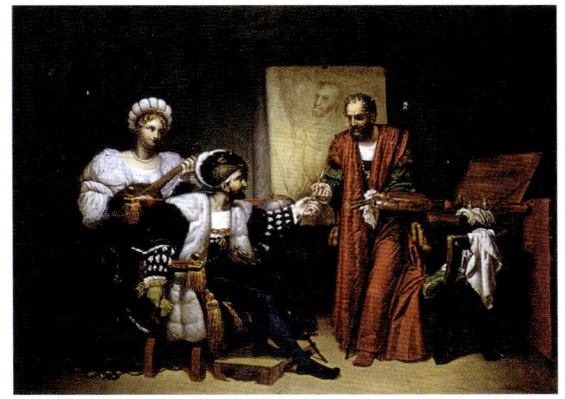

Plate 1. Pierre-Nolasque Bergeret, *Charles V Picking up Titian's Paintbrush*, oil on canvas, 37.75 x 51 in (96 x 129 cm), Musée des Beaux-Arts, Bordeaux, 1808.

Plate 2. Cosimo Gamberucci, *Michelangelo Receives Prince Francesco de' Medici*, oil on canvas, 57 x 55.5 in (145 x 141 cm), Casa Buonarroti, Florence, 1615–17.

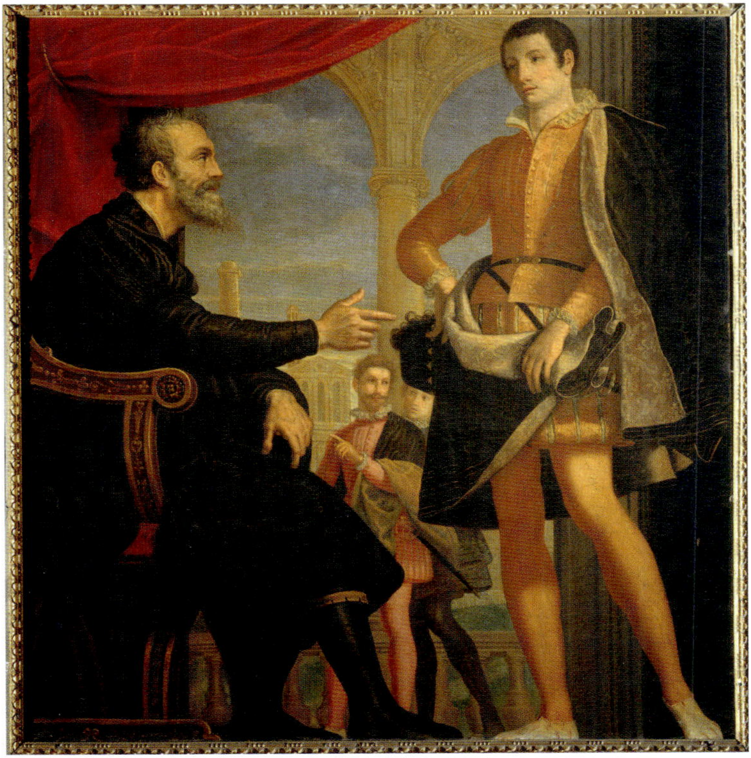

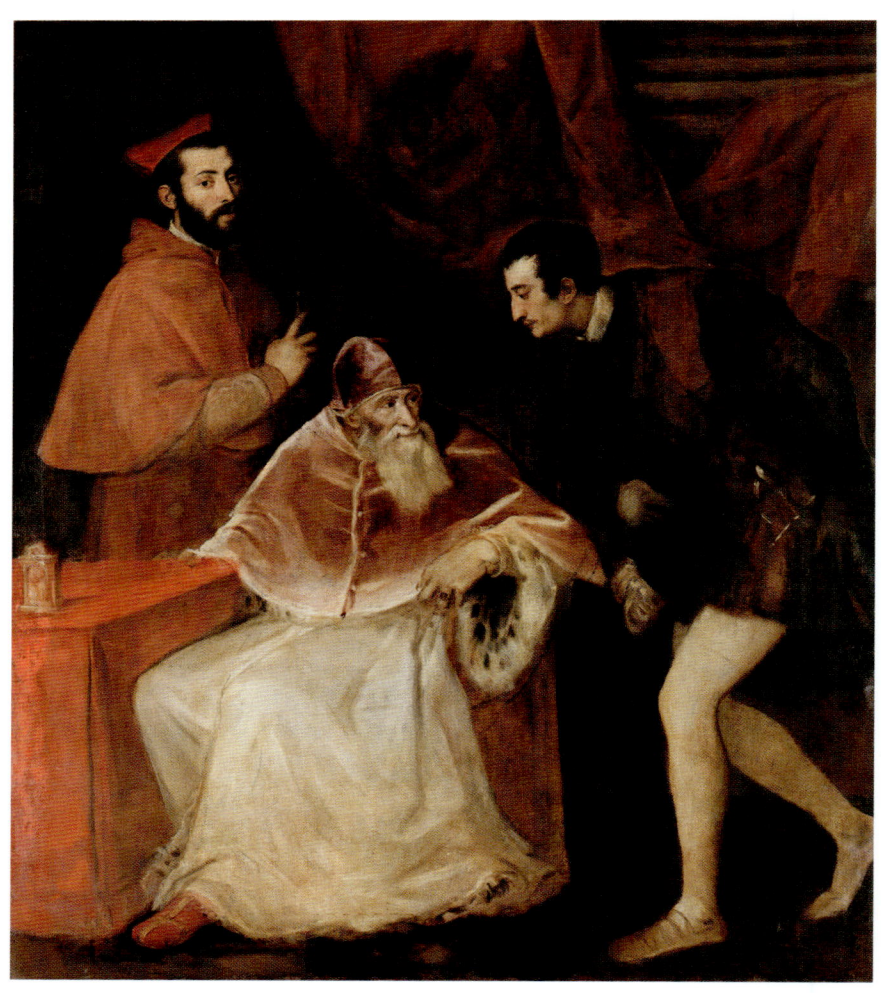

Plate 3. Titian Vecellio, *Pope Paul III and His Grandsons*, oil on canvas, 82.5 x 68.5 in (210 x 174 cm), Gallerie Nazionali di Capodimonte, Naples, 1545–46.

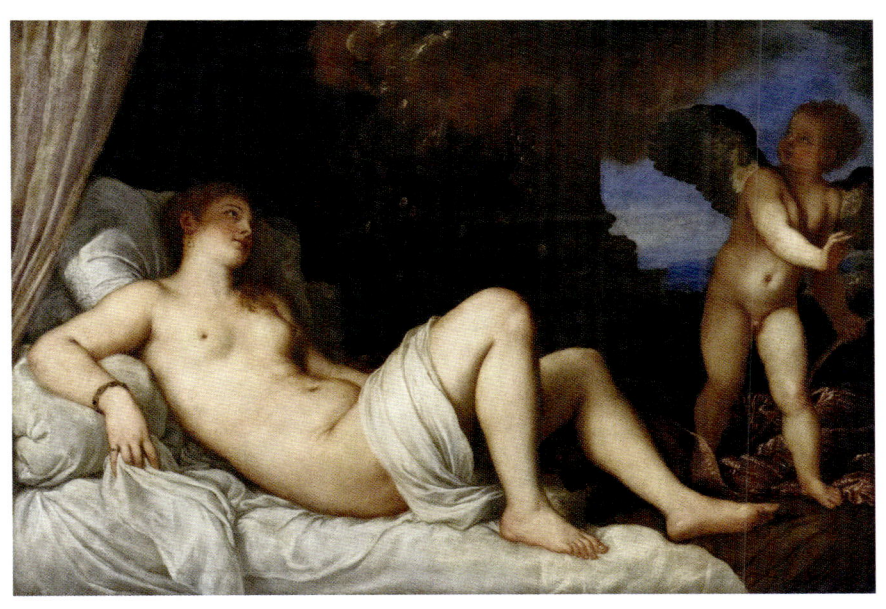

Plate 4. Titian Vecellio, *Danaë*, oil on canvas, 47 x 68 in (120 x 172 cm), Gallerie Nazionali di Capodimonte, Naples, 1544–45.

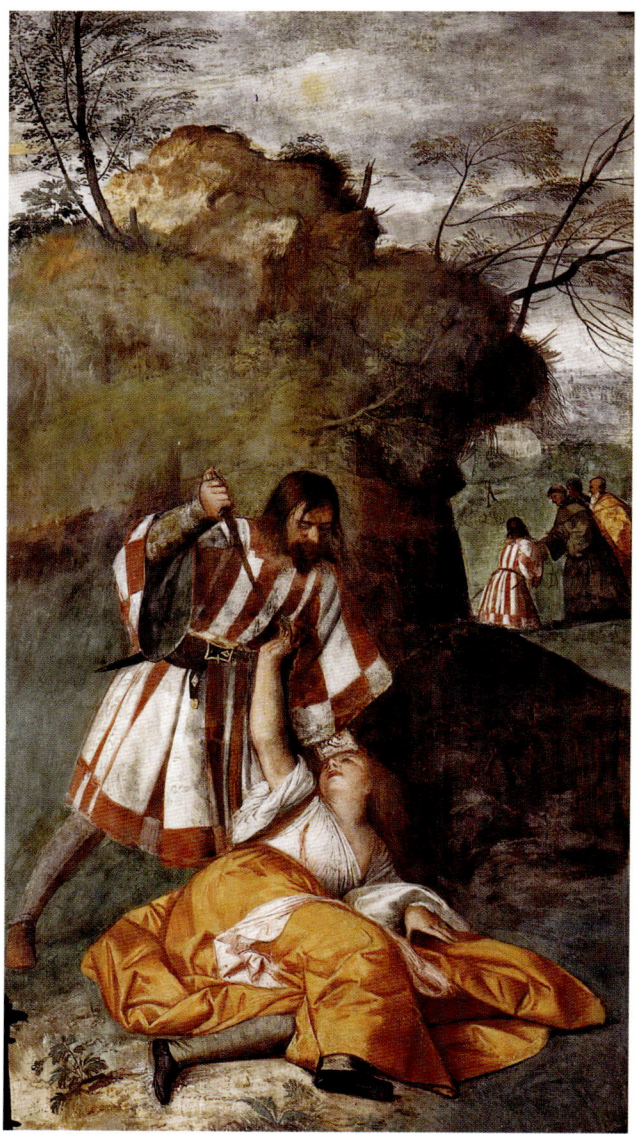

Plate 5. Titian Vecellio, *The Jealous Husband*, fresco, 11 x 6 ft (340 x 185 cm), Scuola del Santo, Padua, 1511.

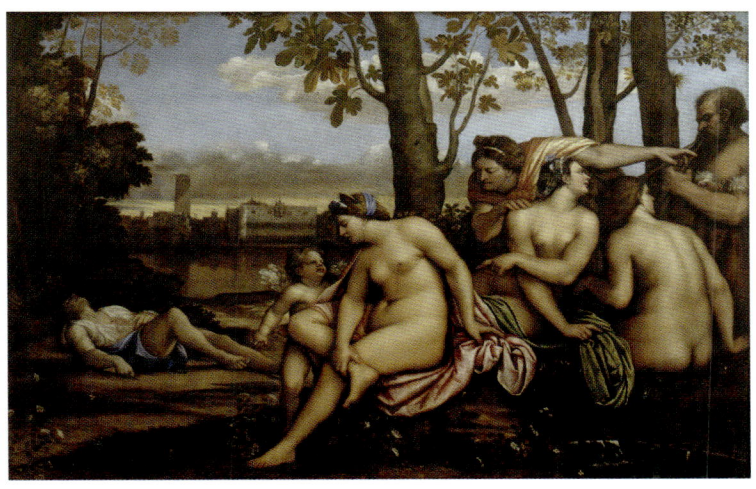

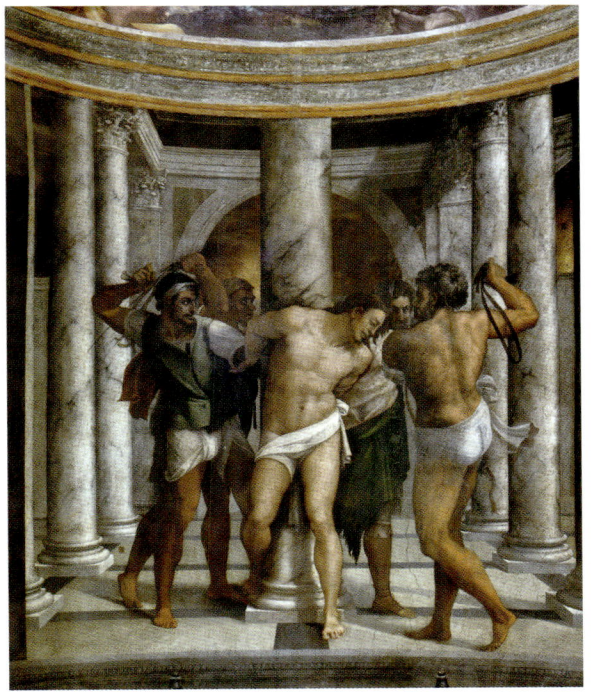

Plate 6. Sebastiano del Piombo, *Death of Adonis*, oil on canvas, 74.5 x 112 in (189 x 285 cm), Galleria degli Uffizi, Florence, c. 1511–12.

Plate 7. Sebastiano del Piombo, *Flagellation of Christ*, mural painting in oil, Borgherini Chapel, S. Pietro in Montorio, Rome, 1516–24.

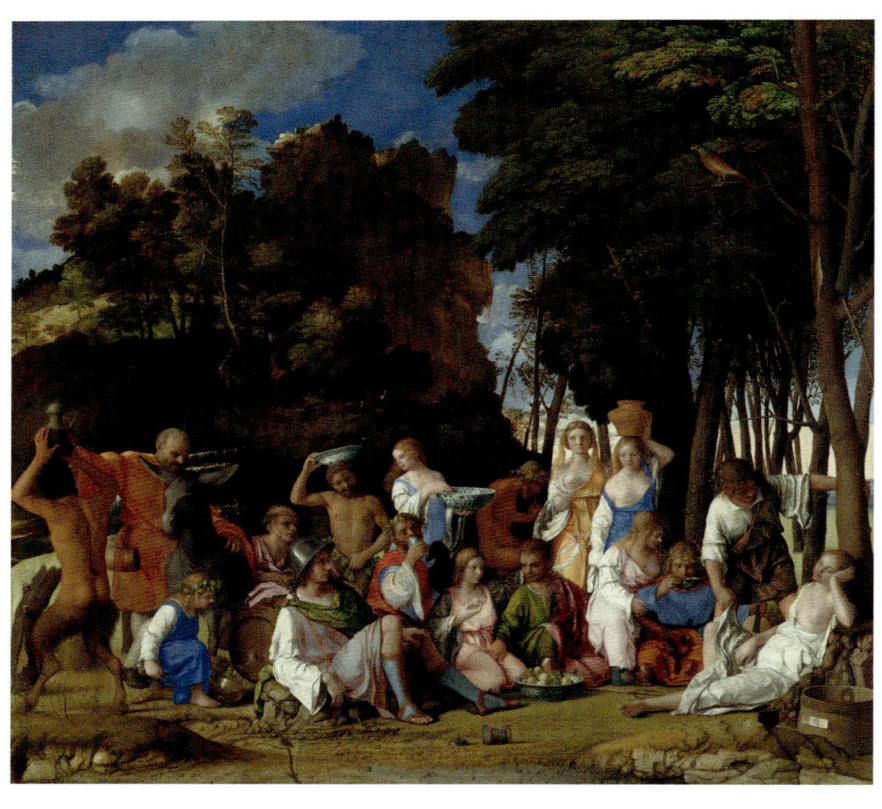

Plate 8. Giovanni Bellini, *The Feast of the Gods*, oil on canvas, 67 x 74 in (170.2 x 188 cm), National Gallery of Art, Washington, DC, 1514.

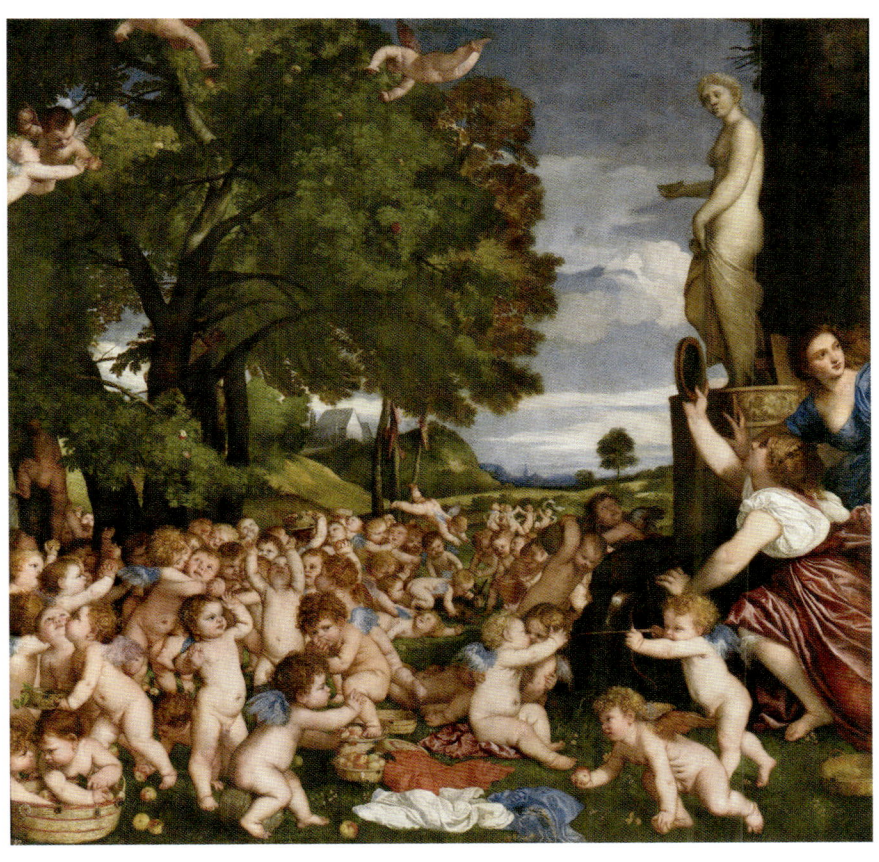

Plate 9. Titian Vecellio, *The Worship of Venus*, oil on canvas, 67.75 x 69 in (172 x 175 cm), Museo Nacional del Prado, Madrid, 1518–19.

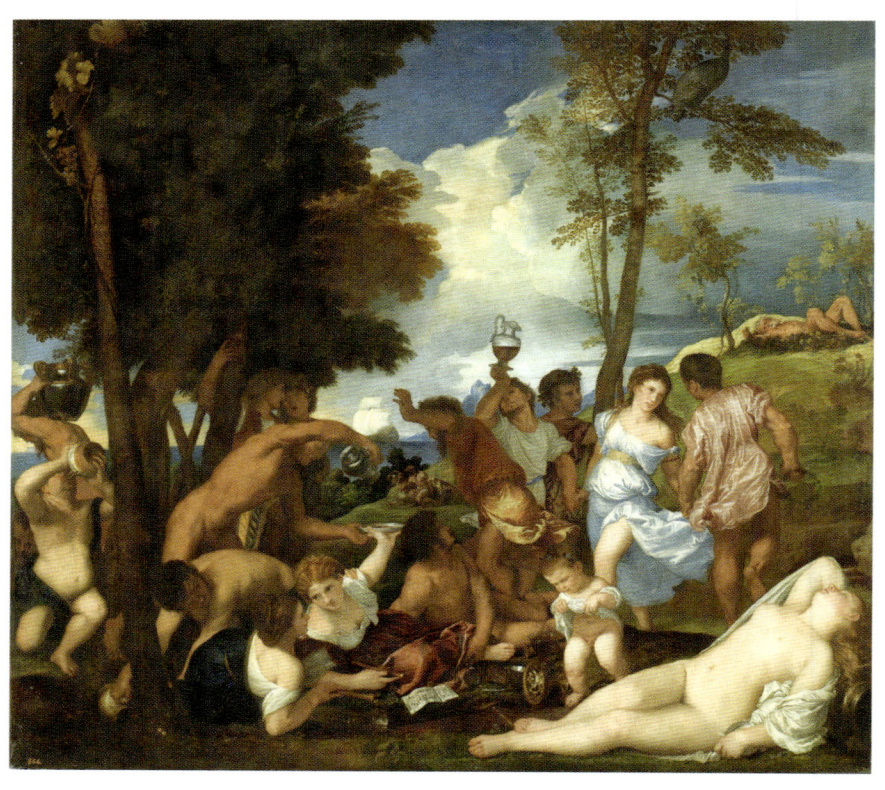

Plate 10. Titian Vecellio, *Bacchanal of the Andrians*, oil on canvas, 69 x 76 in (175 x 193 cm), Museo Nacional del Prado, c. 1519–21.

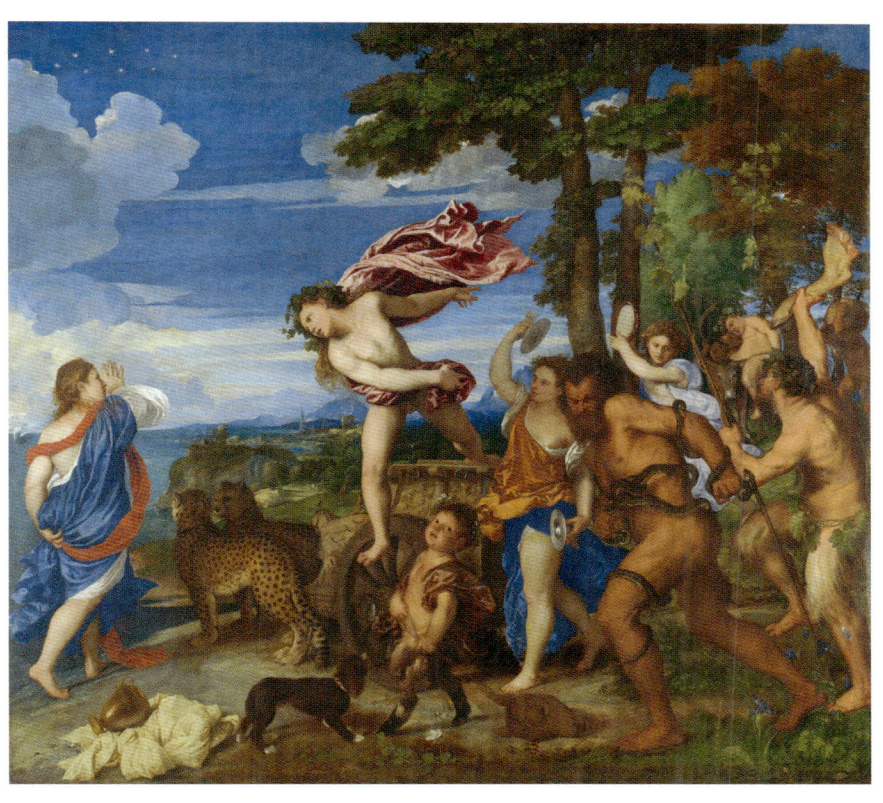

Plate 11. Titian Vecellio, *Bacchus and Ariadne*, oil on canvas, 69.5 x 75 in (176.5 x 191 cm), The National Gallery, London, 1520-23.

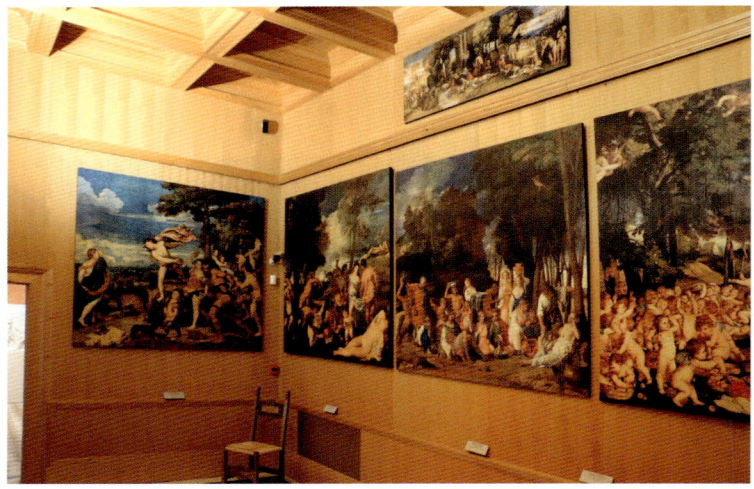

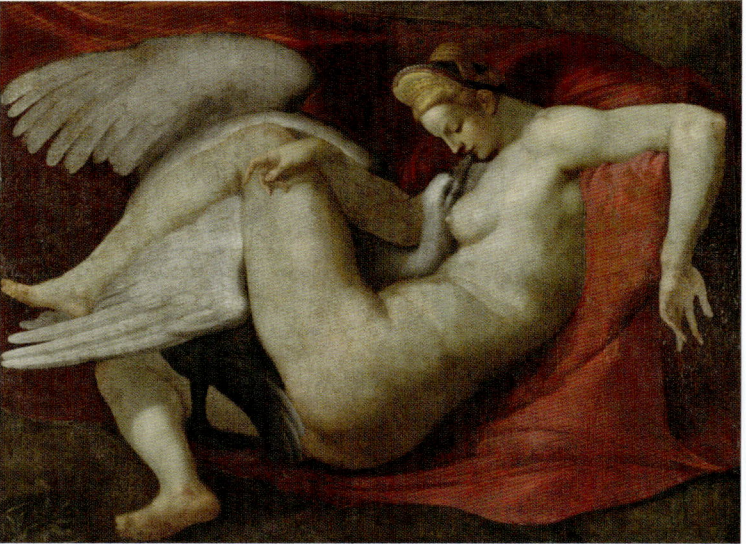

Plate 12. Partial reconstruction of Alfonso d'Este's studiolo.

Plate 13. Rosso Fiorentino after Michelangelo, *Leda*, tempera on canvas, 41.5 x 55.5 in (105.4 x 141 cm), National Gallery of Art, London, 1530/31.

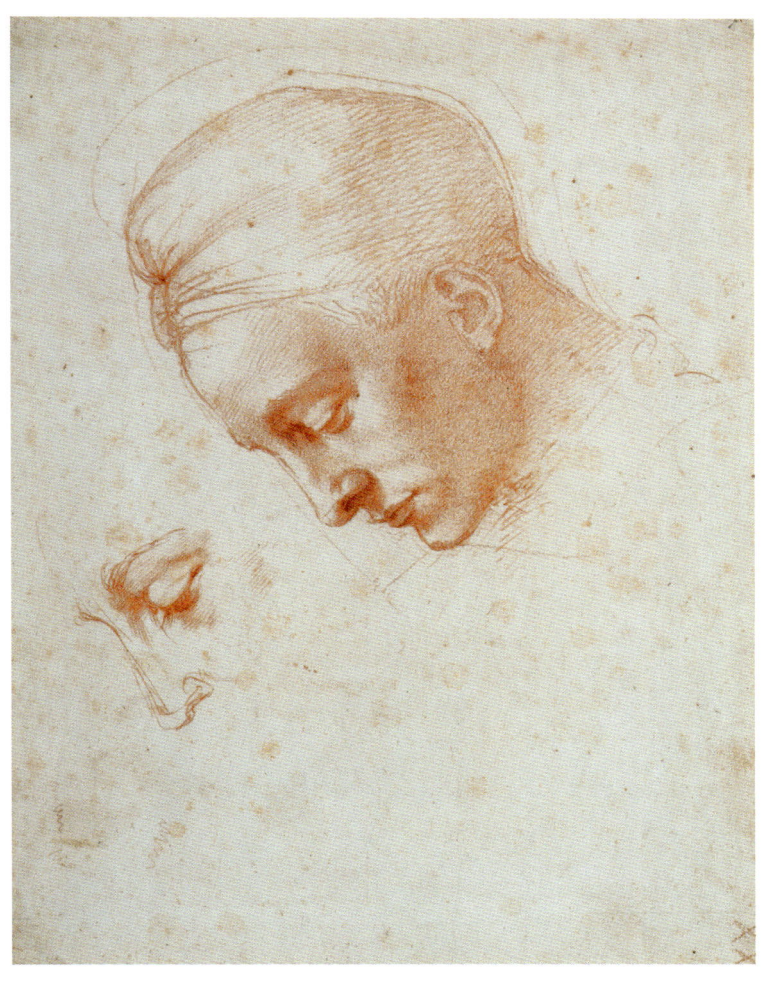

Plate 14. Michelangelo, *Head of Leda*, red chalk on paper, 14 x 10.5 in (355 x 269 mm),
Casa Buonarroti, Florence (no. 7F recto), 1530/31.

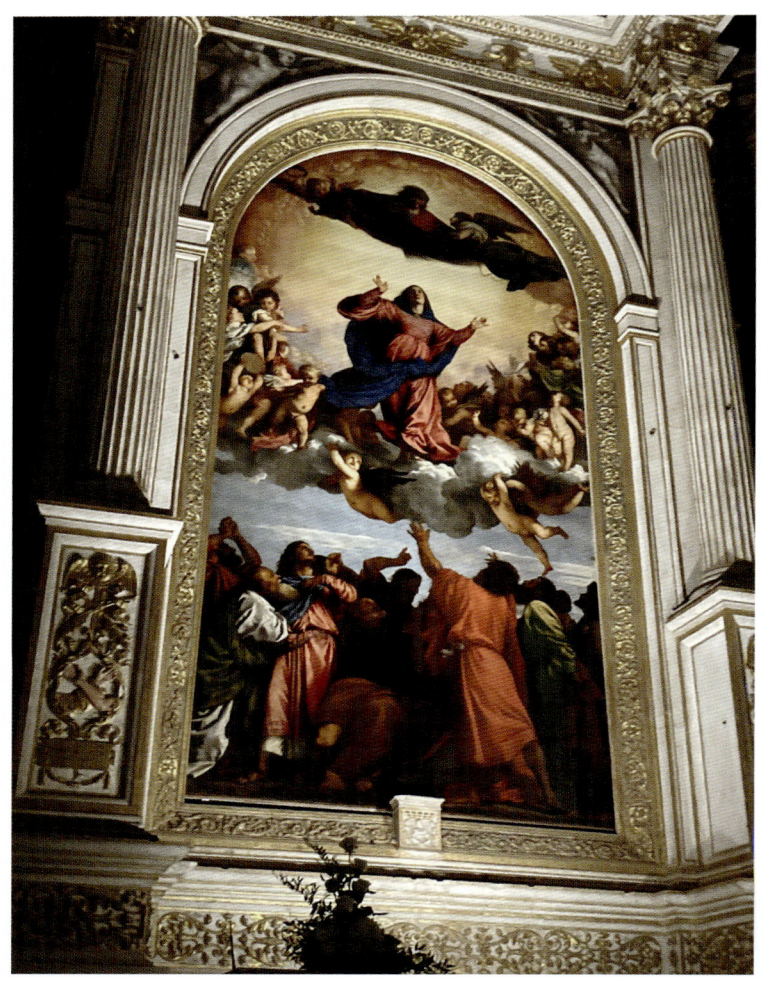

Plate 15. Titian Vecellio, *The Assumption of the Virgin* (*Assunta*), oil on panel, 22.5 x 11.75 ft (690 x 360 cm), Santa Maria Gloriosa dei Frari, Venice, 1515–18.

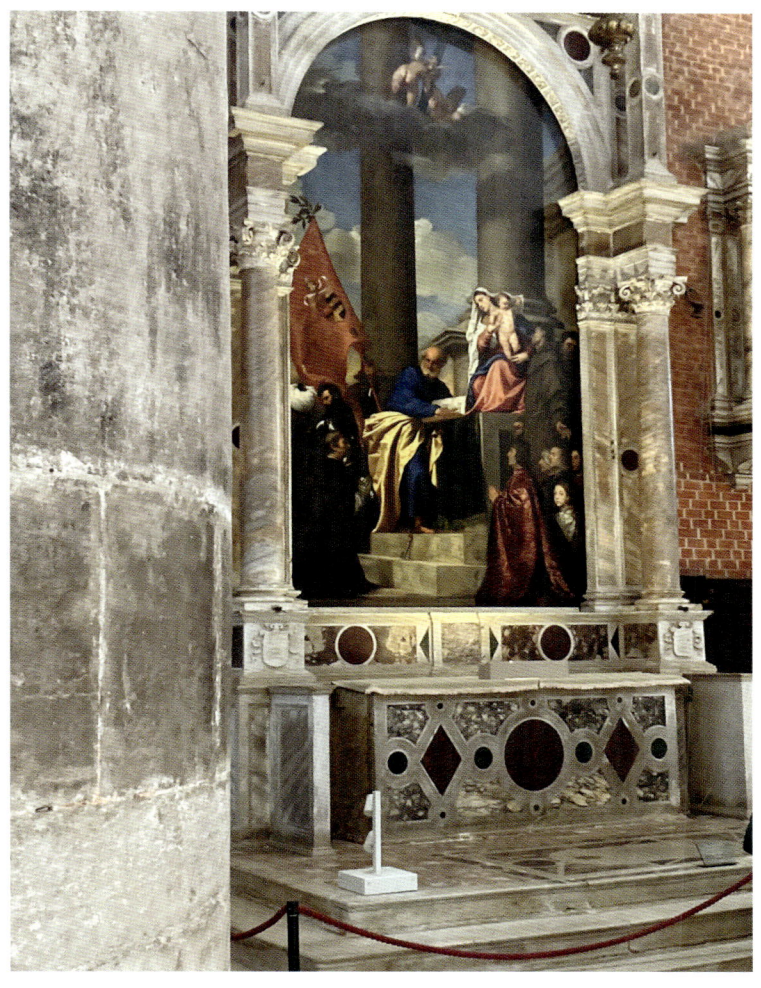

Plate 16. Titian Vecellio, *Pesaro Altarpiece*, oil on canvas, 15.5 x 8.5 ft (478 x 266 cm), Santa Maria Gloriosa dei Frari, Venice, 1519–26.

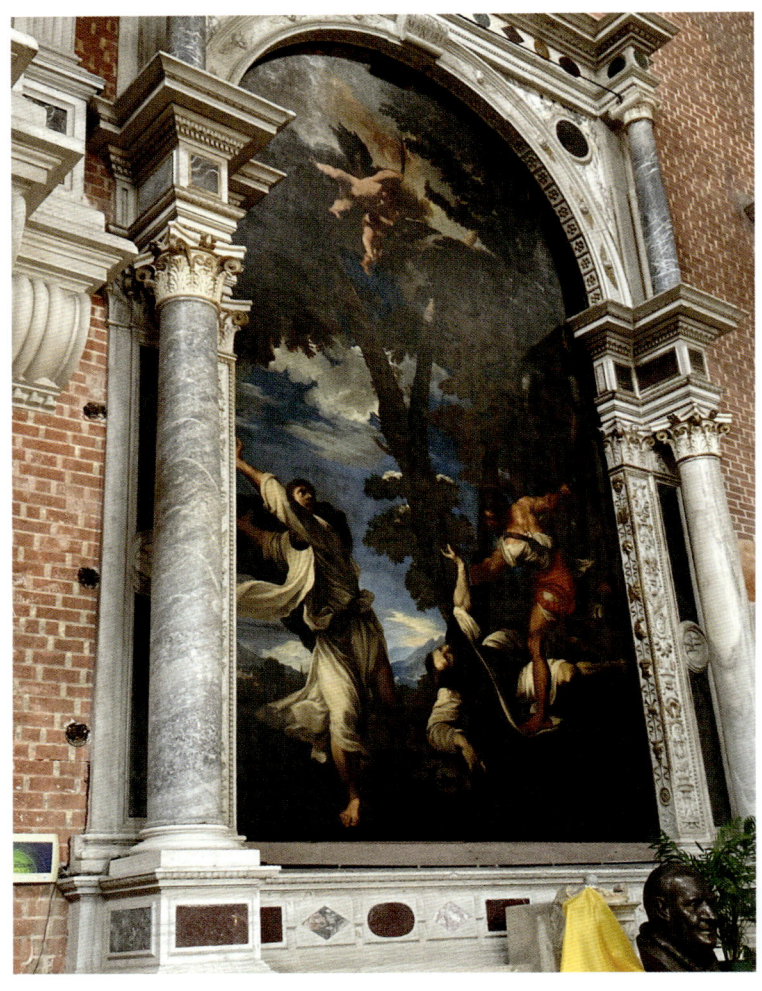

Plate 17. Copy of Titian Vecellio, *The Death of St. Peter Martyr* (Carlo Loth, 1691), oil on canvas, 17 x 10 ft (515 x 308 cm), SS. Giovanni e Paolo, Venice, 1529/30.

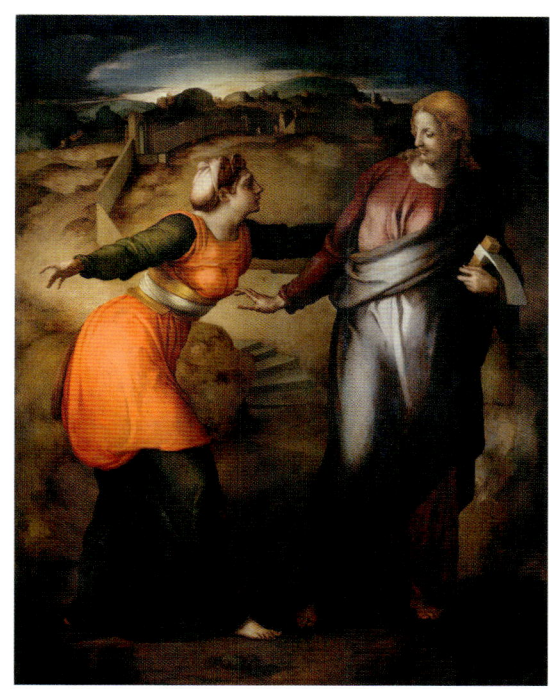

Plate 18. Pontormo after Michelangelo, *Noli me Tangere*, oil on wood panel, 67.75 x 52.75 in (172 x 134 cm), Casa Buonarroti, Florence, c. 1532.

Plate 19. Pontormo after Michelangelo, *Venus and Cupid*, oil on wood panel, 50.33 x 76.33 in (128 x 194 cm), Galleria dell'Accademia, Florence, 1532/33.

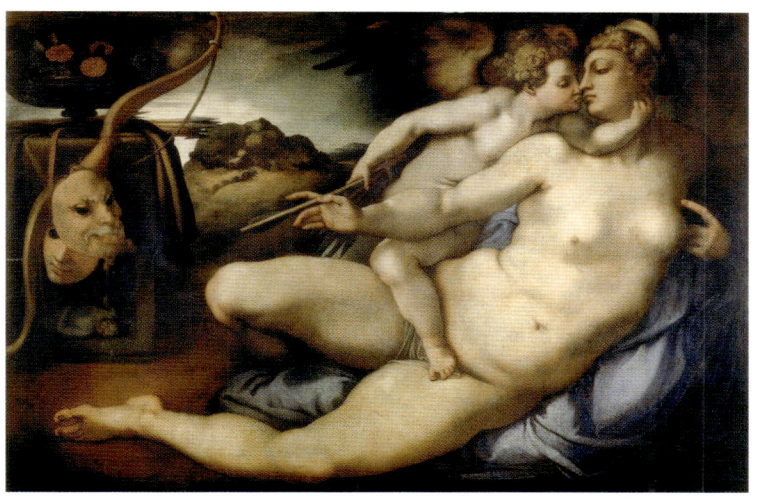

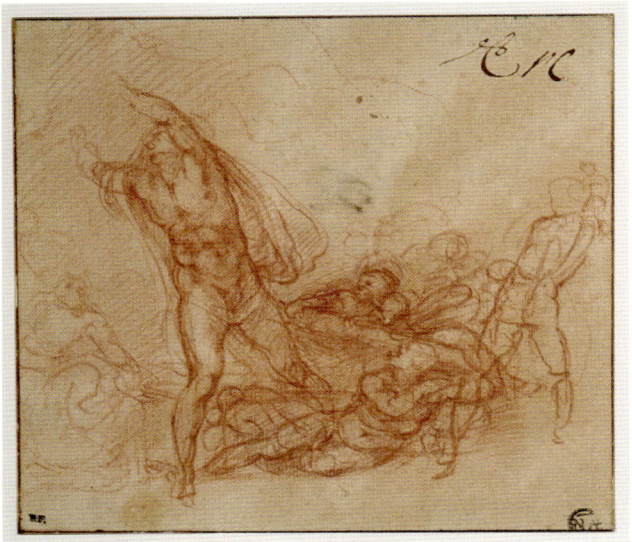

Plate 20. Michelangelo, *Resurrection*, red chalk on paper, 5.75 x 6.5 in (148 x 166 mm), Musée du Louvre, Paris (Inv. N. 691bis recto), c. 1531/32.

Plate 21. Michelangelo, *Resurrection*, black chalk on paper, 9.33 x 13.5 in (238 x 345 mm), Windsor Castle, Royal Library (Inv. N. 12767 recto), c. 1531/32.

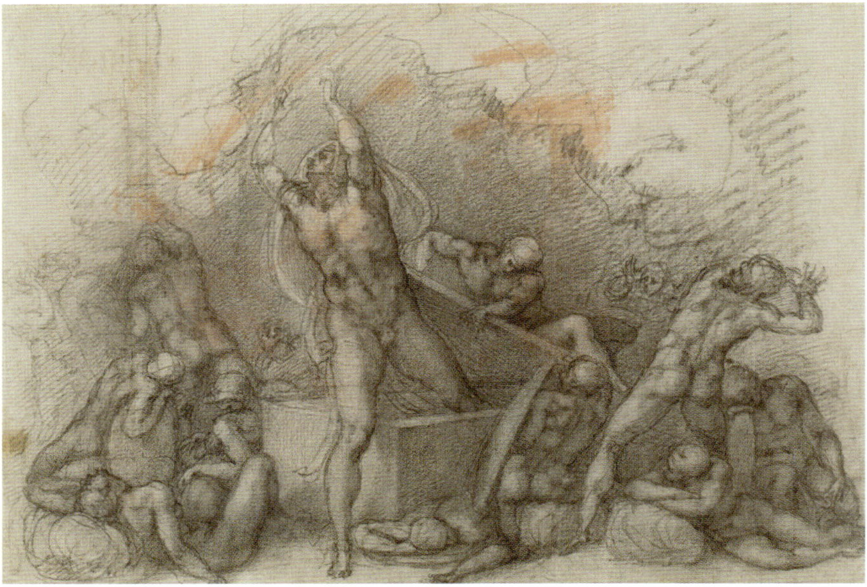

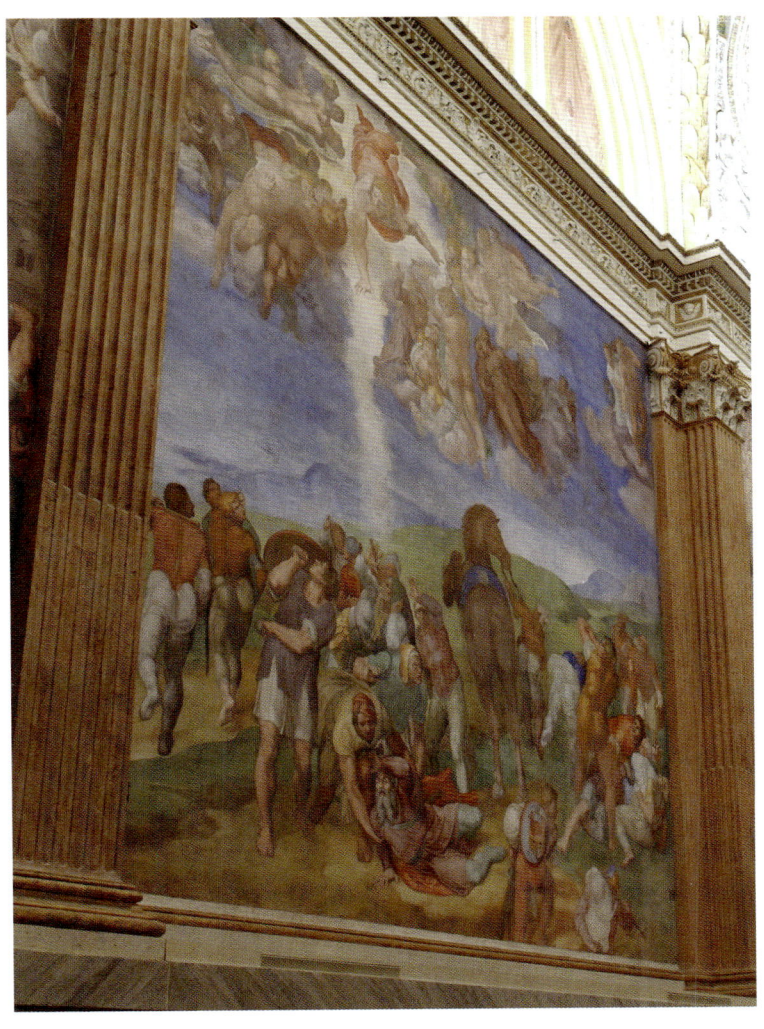

Plate 22. Michelangelo, *Conversion of Saul*, fresco 20.5 x 21.5 ft (625 x 661 cm), Pauline Chapel, Vatican City, 1542–45.

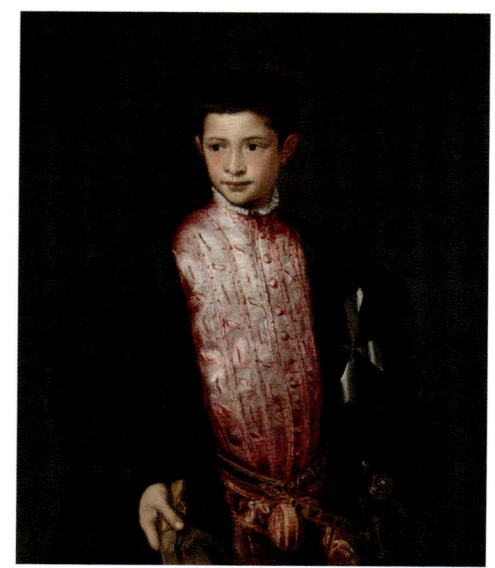

Plate 23. Titian Vecellio, *Ranuccio Farnese*, oil on canvas, 35 x 29 in (89.4 x 73.5 cm), National Gallery of Art, Washington, DC, 1541–42.

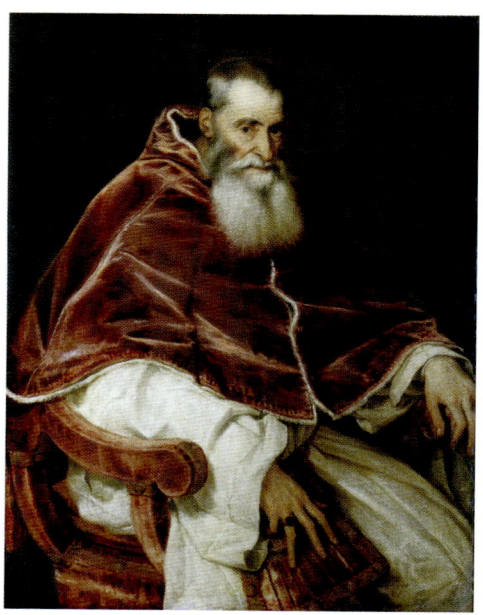

Plate 24. Titian Vecellio, *Pope Paul III*, oil on canvas, 54 x 35 in (137 x 88.8 cm), Gallerie Nazionali di Capodimonte, Naples, 1543.

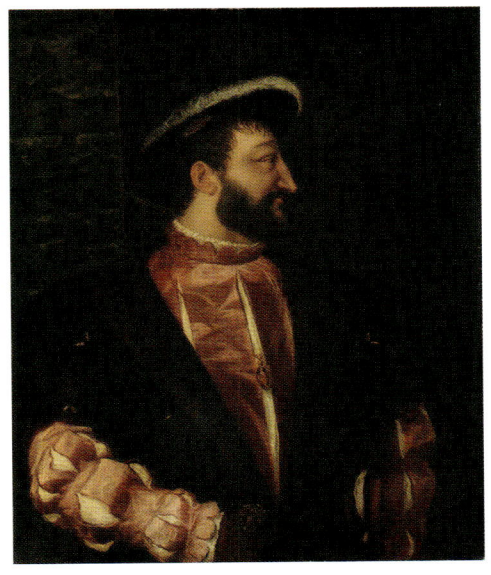

Plate 25. Titian Vecellio, *Francis I, King of France*, oil on canvas, 43 x 35 in (109 x 89 cm), Musée du Louvre, Paris, c. 1538.

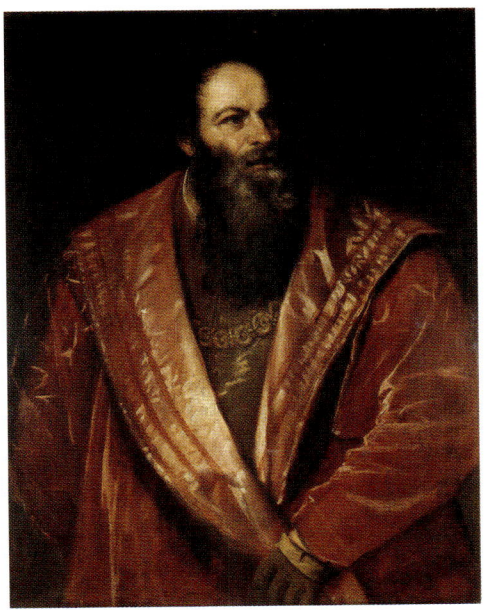

Plate 26. Titian Vecellio, *Pietro Aretino*, oil on canvas, 38 x 30 in (96.7 x 76.6 cm), Galleria Palatina, Palazzo Pitti, Florence, 1545.

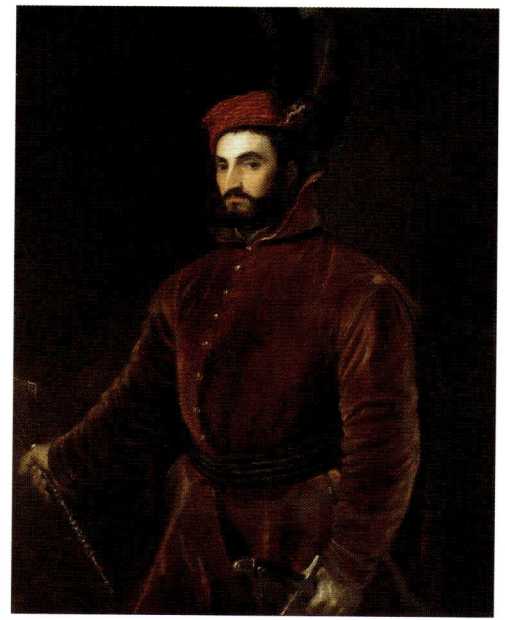

Plate 27. Titian Vecellio, *Ippolito de' Medici*, oil on canvas, 54.75 x 42 in (139 x 107 cm), Galleria Palatina, Palazzo Pitti, Florence, c. 1533.

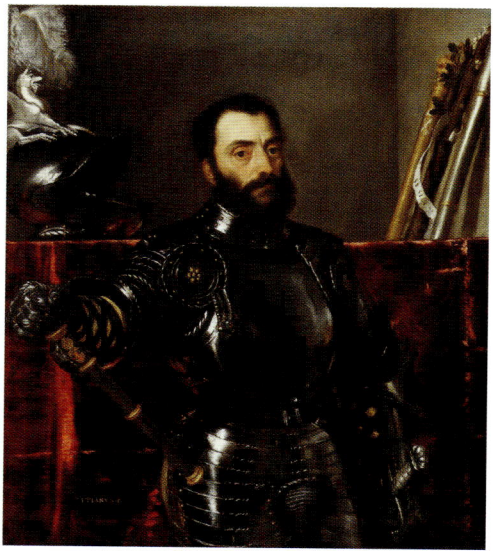

Plate 28. Titian Vecellio, *Francesco Maria della Rovere, Duke of Urbino*, oil on canvas, 45 x 40.5 in (114 x 103 cm), Galleria degli Uffizi, Florence, 1536.

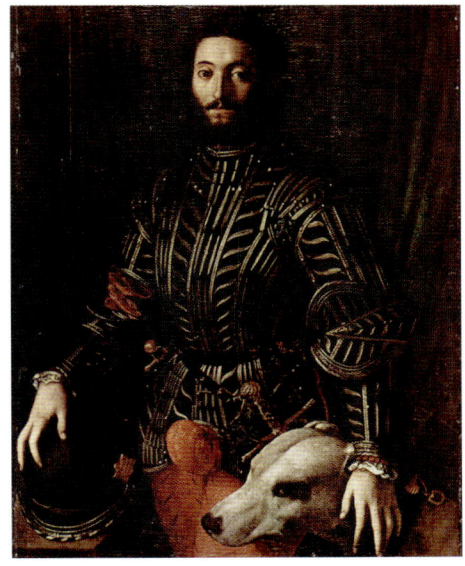

Plate 29. Copy of Titian Vecellio, *Guidobaldo II della Rovere*, oil on canvas, 44.8 x 33.8 in (114 x 86 cm), Galleria Palatina, Palazzo PItti, Florence, c. 1531-32.

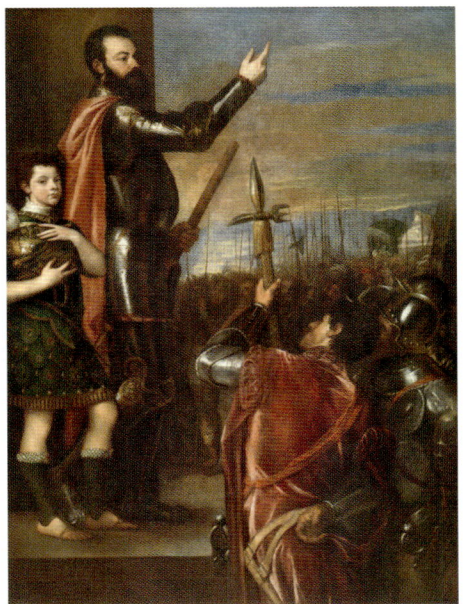

Plate 30. Titian Vecellio, *Allocutio of Alfonso d'Avalos (Allocutio)*, oil on canvas, 87.75 x 65 in (223 x 165 cm), Museo Nacional del Prado, Madrid, 1540-41.

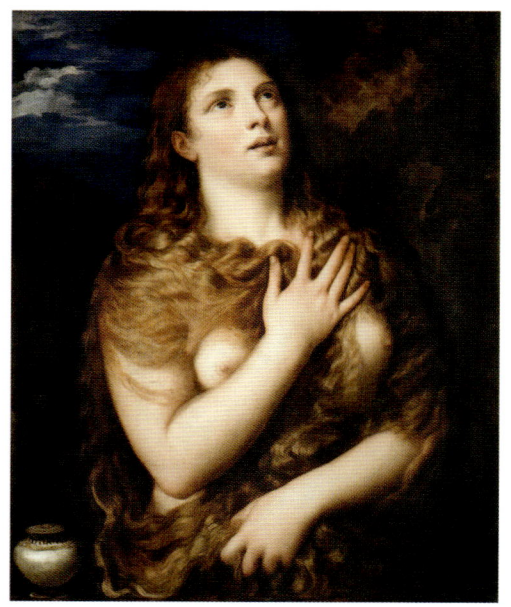

Plate 31. Titian Vecellio, *Saint Mary Magdalene*, oil on panel, 33 x 27 in (84 x 69.2 cm), Galleria Palatina, Palazzo Pitti, Florence, c. 1535.

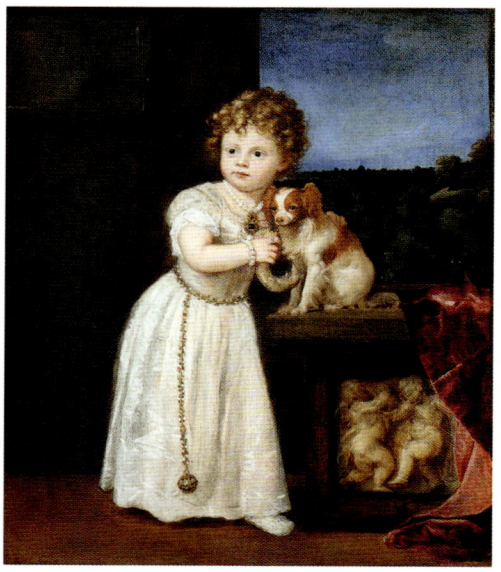

Plate 32. Titian Vecellio, *Clarissa Strozzi*, oil on canvas, 45 x 38.5 in (115 x 98 cm), Staatliche Museen, Berlin, 1542.

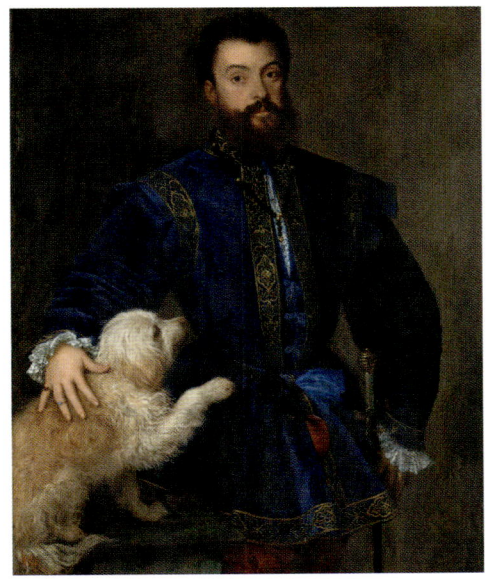

Plate 33. Titian Vecellio, *Federico II Gonzaga*, oil on canvas, 49 x 39 in (125 x 99 cm), Museo Nacional del Prado, Madrid, 1529.

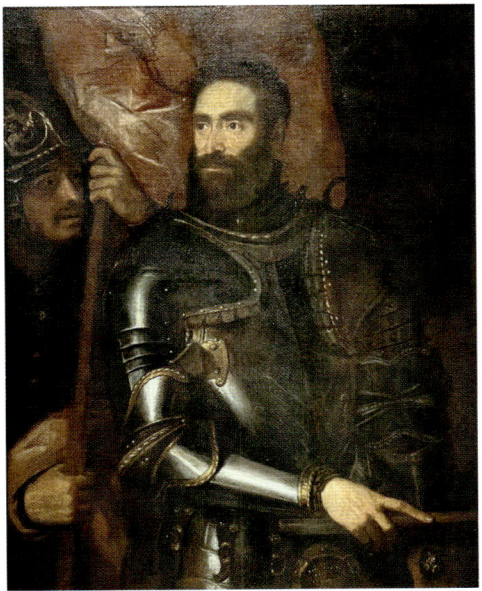

Plate 34. Titian Vecellio, *Pierluigi Farnese*, oil on canvas, 41.75 x 37.5 in (106 x 95 cm), Gallerie Nazionali di Capodimonte, Naples, 1546.

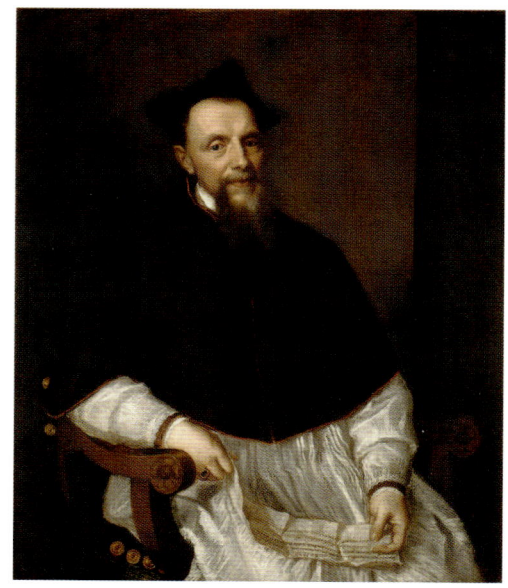

Plate 35. Titian Vecellio, *Lodovico Beccadelli*, oil on canvas, 46 x 38 in (117.5 x 97 cm), Galleria degli Uffizi, Florence, 1552.

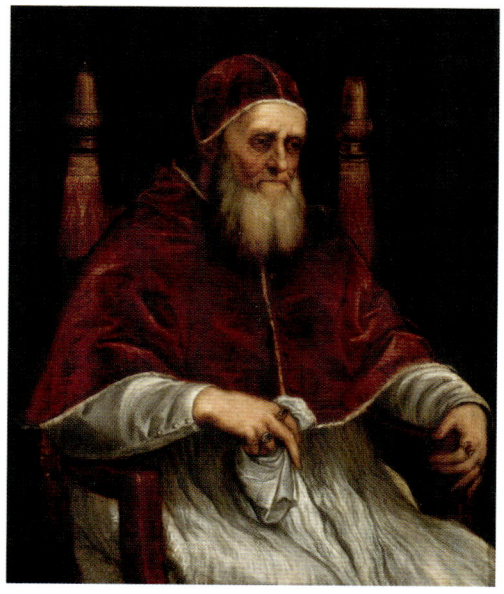

Plate 36. Titian Vecellio (?), *Pope Julius II*, oil on panel, 40 x 32 in (99 x 82 cm), Galleria Palatina, Palazzo Pitti, Florence, 1545–46.

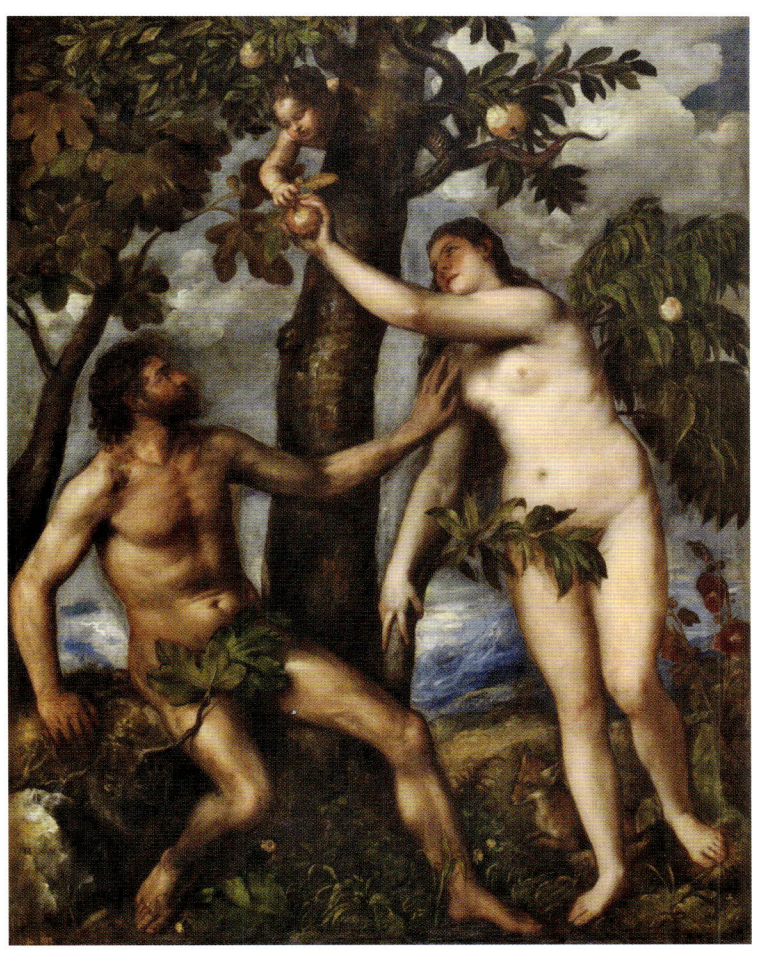

Plate 37. Titian Vecellio, *Adam and Eve*, oil on canvas, 94.5 x 73 in (240 x 186 cm), Museo Nacional del Prado, Madrid, c. 1555–65.

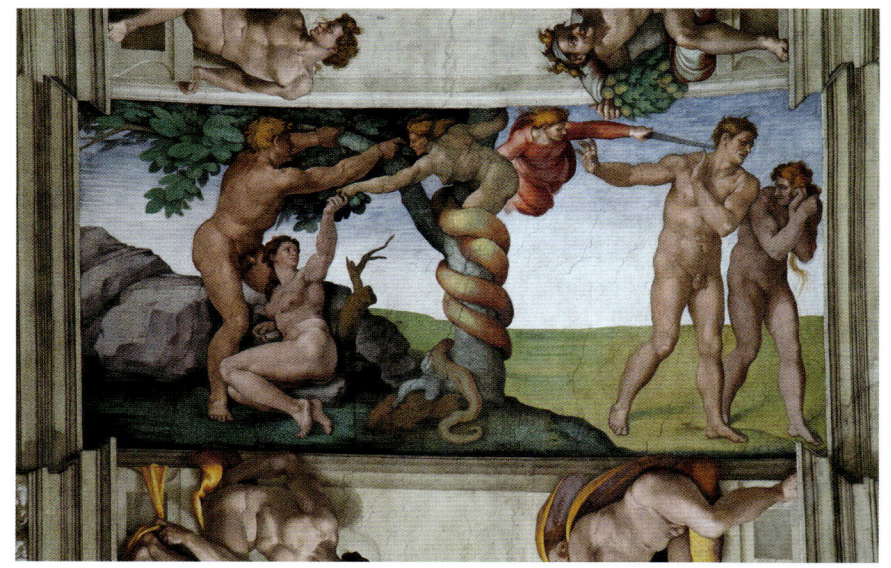

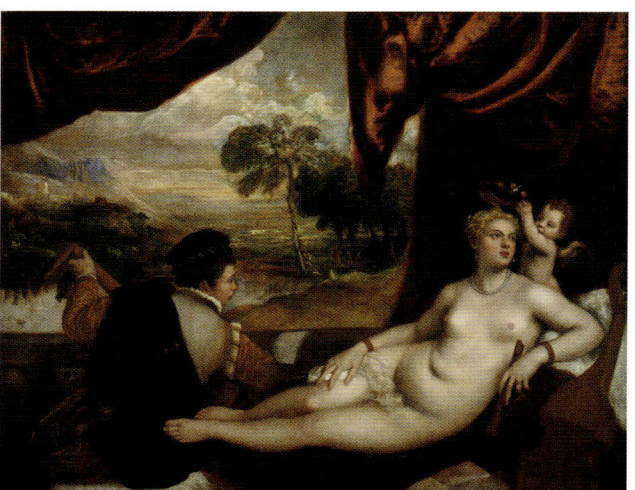

Plate 38. Michelangelo, det. *Fall of Man*, fresco, Sistine Chapel, Vatican, 1508–12.

Plate 39. Titian Vecellio, *Venus and the Lute Player*, oil on canvas, 59 x 77.5 in (150 x 196.8 cm), Metropolitan Museum of Art, New York, c. 1565–70.

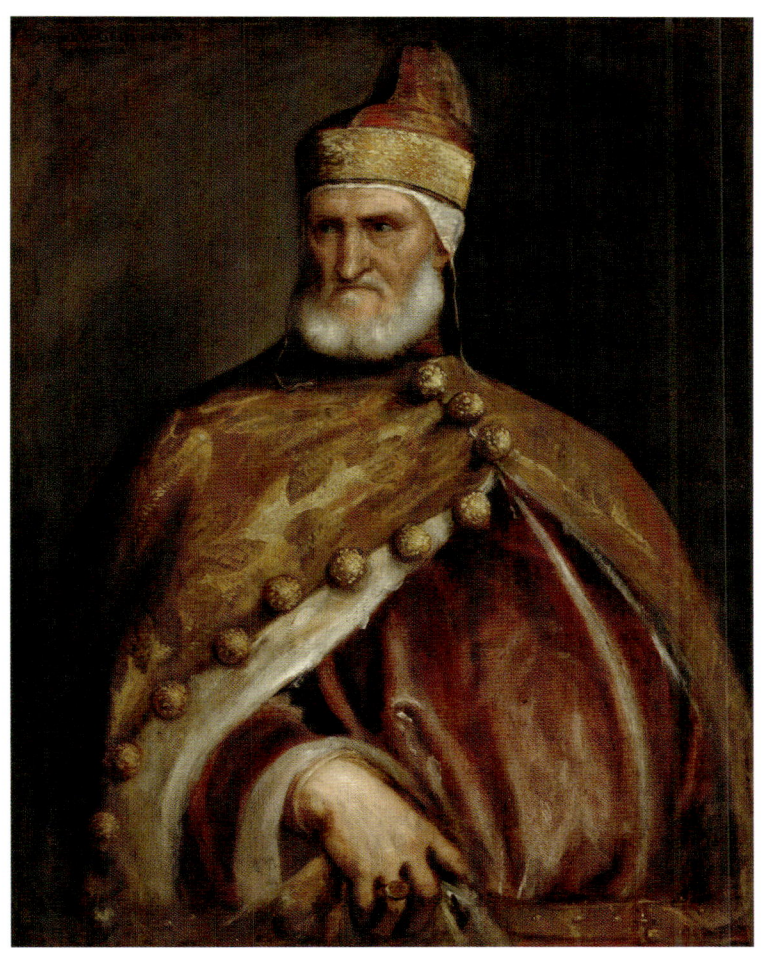

Plate 40. Titian Vecellio, *Doge Andrea Gritti*, oil on canvas, 52.5 x 40.5 in (133.6 x 103.2 cm), National Gallery of Art, Washington, DC, c. 1546–50.

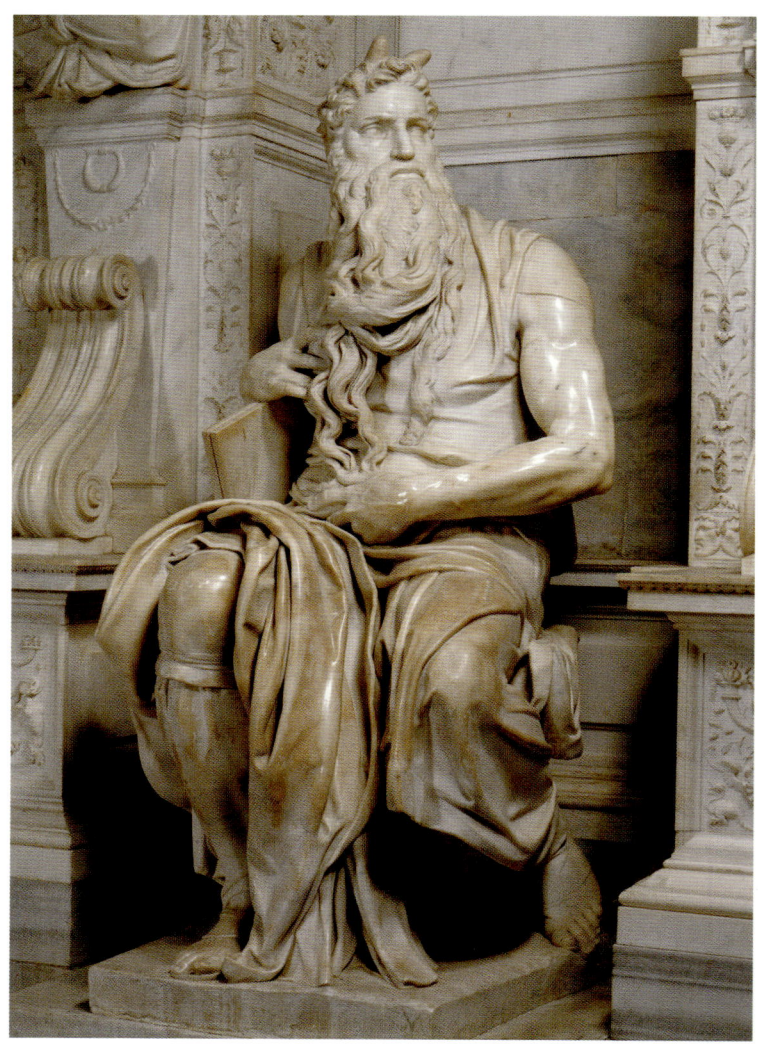

Plate 41. Michelangelo, *Moses*, Tomb of Pope Julius II, marble, h. 7.75 ft (235 cm), S. Pietro in Vincoli, Rome, c. 1506/45.

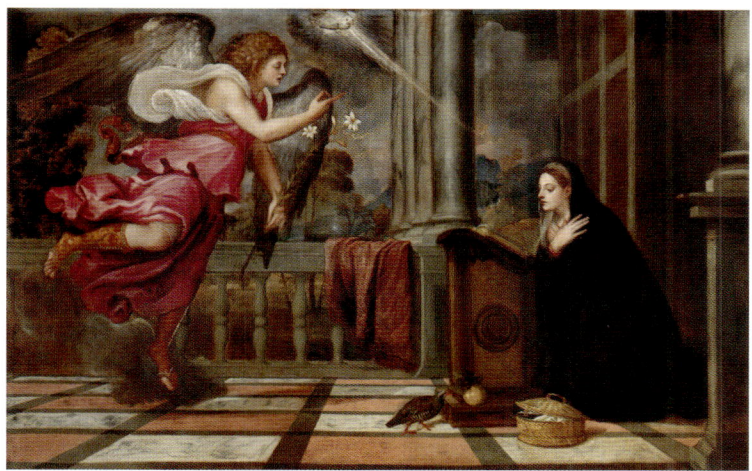

Plate 42. Titian Vecellio, *Annunciation*, oil on canvas, 5.5 x 8.75 ft (166 x 266 cm), Scuola di San Rocco, Venice, c. 1540.

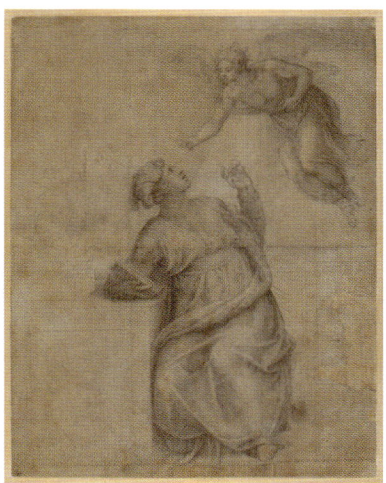

Plate 43. Michelangelo, *Annunciation*, black chalk on paper, 15 x 11.5 in (383 x 296 mm), Pierpont Morgan Library (Inv. N. IV, 7), New York, c. 1543/45.

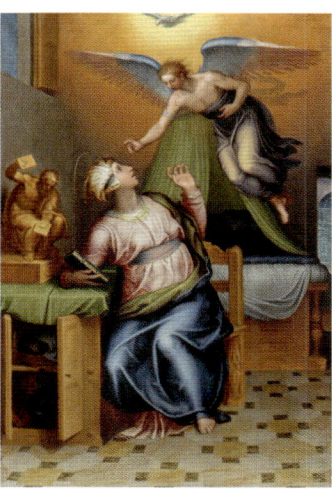

Plate 44. Marcello Venusti small scale copy of lost *Annunciation* altarpiece for Capella Cesi, Santa Maria della Pace, Rome, Gallerie Nazionali Baberini Corsini, Rome, c. 1543/45.

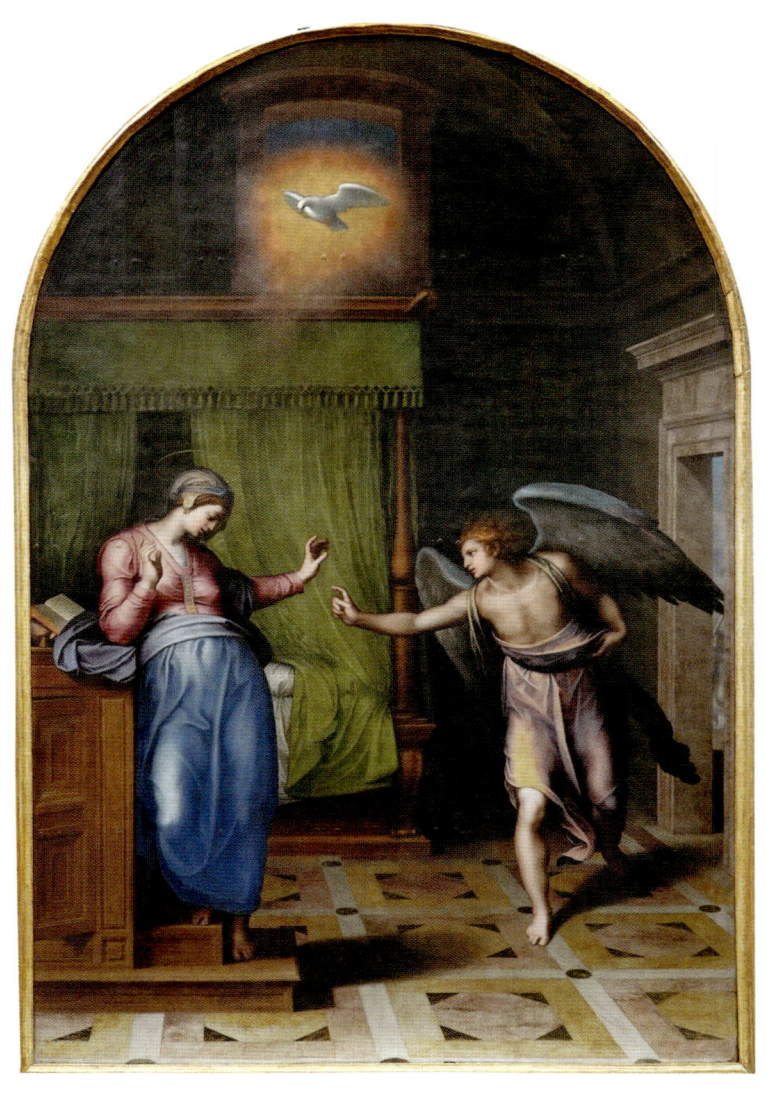

Plate 45. Marcello Venusti, *Annunciation*, oil on panel 10.5 x 7 ft (320 x 210 cm),
San Giovanni in Laterano, Rome, c. 1545/47.

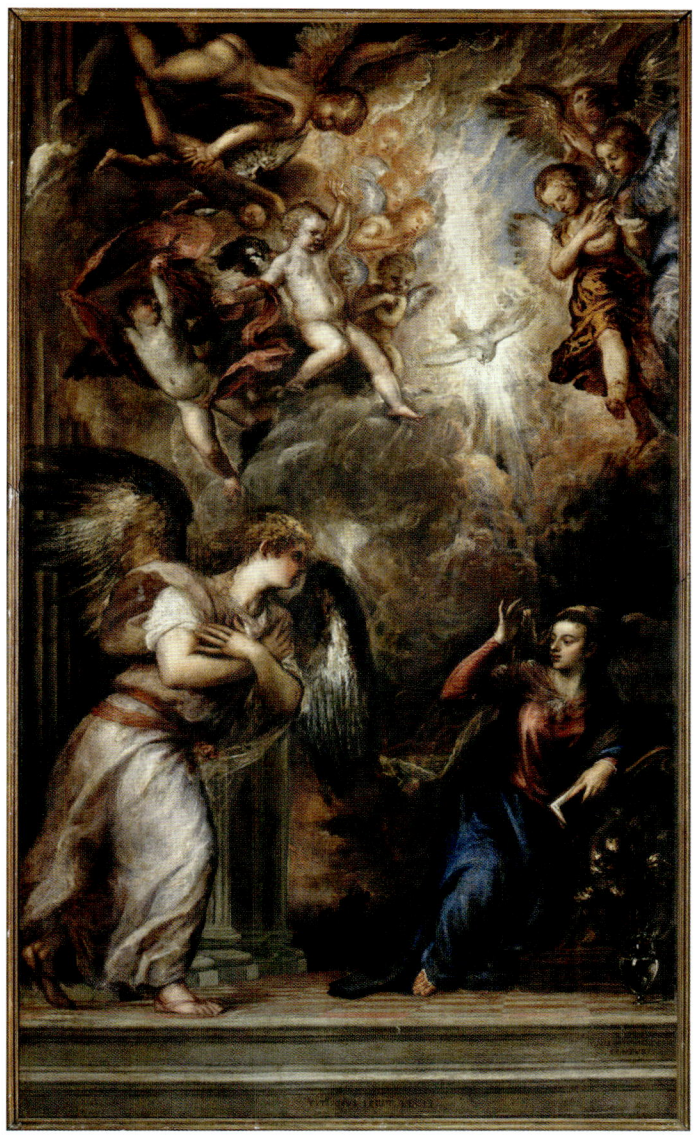

Plate 46. Titian Vecellio, *Annunciation*, oil on canvas, 13 x 7.5 ft (403 x 235 cm),
San Salvador, Venice, c. 1564–66.

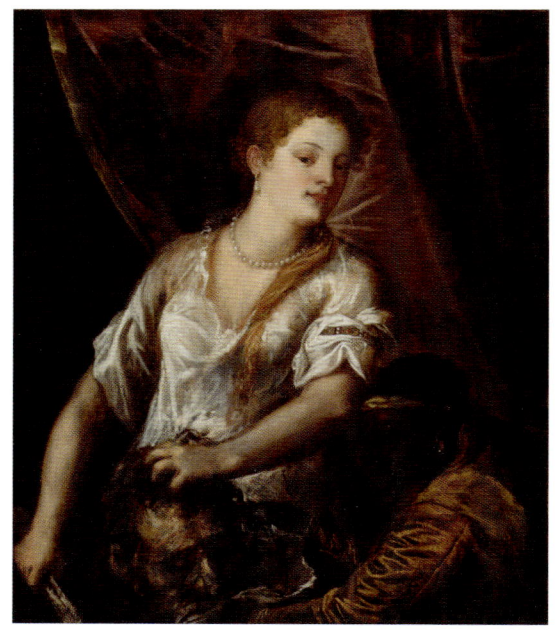

Plate 47. Titian Vecellio, *Judith with the Head of Holofernes*, oil on canvas, 44.5 x 37 in (112.8 x 94.5 cm), The Detroit Institute of Arts, c. 1568/70.

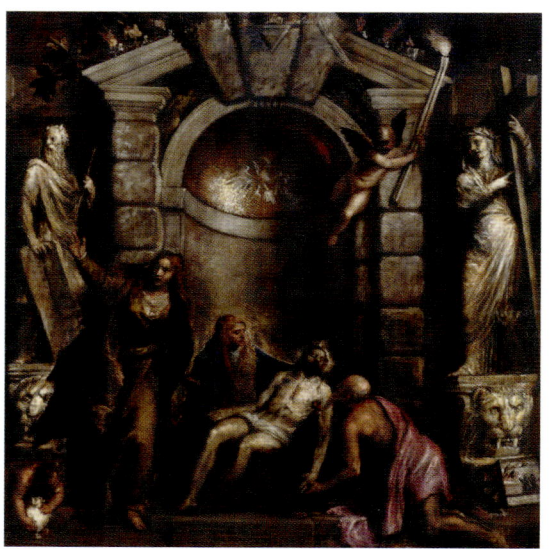

Plate 48. Titian Vecellio, *Pietà*, oil on canvas, 12.5 x 11.33 ft (378 x 347 cm), Gallerie dell'Accademia, Venice, c. 1570–76.

Farnese, the pope's grandson and right-hand counselor. Titian's picture transports us to the bedchamber prison where Danaë welcomes Jove as a shower of gold. This was the painting admired by Michelangelo on his visit to the Belvedere in early 1546 (see Plate 4).[2] It certainly pleased the worldly cardinal and introduced Rome to the best Venetian painter of the day.

Titian to Rome

The desire to deliver the nearly completed *Danaë* to Cardinal Alessandro Farnese finally induced Titian to make his first visit to the Eternal City. Thus, toward the end of 1545, Titian and his younger son Orazio traveled by sea from Venice to Ancona and then by horse to Rome along the well-trodden Via Flaminia. Titian was confident of his art but wary of Rome, a cultural and political world far different from his native Venice. Alessandro Farnese ensured that Titian would be well-received at court. The painter was given rooms in the Vatican Belvedere, which is where Michelangelo and Vasari visited the artist and admired the *Danaë*. The cardinal "recommended Titian to Vasari, who then lovingly kept him company and took him to see the sights of Rome."[3] So began Titian's six-month exploration of the attractions and seductions of the Eternal City: food, flesh, and art.

When not touring, Titian "set his hand to painting the portrait of Pope Paul" with Cardinal Alessandro and Duke Ottaviano.[4] This is the famous triple portrait of *Pope Paul III and His Grandsons* with which we began our story (see Plate 3).[5] Such a large, ambitious picture required the artist to spend time in close quarters with the pope and members of his sometimes uneasy family. The insightful psychology of the picture reveals how far Titian astutely

penetrated the inner sanctum and tense dynamics of the nepotis-
tic Farnese. It is a naked revelation, a precursor to certain equally
revealing portraits by Diego Velazquez and Francisco Goya. Via
his versatile and sometimes trenchant brush, Titian exposed the
Farnese to the world. This court was the same bewilderingly complex political arena that Michelangelo navigated—mostly successfully—on a daily basis, largely due to his close relations with the
very persons portrayed in Titian's painting.

Titian's portraits won him entrance to Farnese favor. Highly
ambitious and ever politic, Titian did his best to parlay artistic
success into personal gain. He launched a multipronged campaign for papal preferment, lobbying incessantly for an ecclesiastic benefice for his eldest son, Pomponio. For more than a
year before his visit to Rome, Titian had zealously marshaled
support, including a bold and completely unexpected petition to
Michelangelo. Having met Michelangelo fifteen years earlier, Titian evidently felt little compunction about approaching him for a
personal favor. Michelangelo must have been surprised, and perhaps alarmed, given that a favor rendered would implicate him
in a web of reciprocal obligations at the highest levels of Vatican
power. Although constantly solicited for small and larger per-
quisites, Michelangelo rarely granted favors except to his closest
friends, preferring to remain outside the tangle of obligations that
such service entailed. He was even reluctant to argue on behalf
of his friend Sebastiano when the latter repeatedly importuned
Michelangelo for a (failed) recommendation to complete the Vatican decorations following the death of Raphael. Sebastiano was
a close friend, Titian barely an acquaintance.

Titian's first approach to Michelangelo elicited no response.
Undaunted, Titian enlisted his friend Pietro Aretino to write a
second letter to Michelangelo. In his most flamboyantly unctuous

manner, Aretino, the "notorious scourge of princes," begged Michelangelo to put in a good word for his friend Titian, "a man of optimum example, of grave and modest life: he, ardent preacher of your superhuman style, has borne witness in writing to you with all due reverence and the hope that the pope will confer a benefice upon his son Pomponio."[6] Such rhetorical bombast again failed to elicit a response, even more so because Aretino sullied the ill-considered request with yet another effort to extort a drawing from Michelangelo. Several times in the past years, Aretino had solicited Michelangelo "with constant devotion" for a gift of a drawing or two. Believing he had Michelangelo's ear, Aretino slathered him with his promiscuous pen: "But if Your Lordship is revered thanks to public acclaim, even by those who are ignorant of the miracles of your divine intellect, why not believe that I too revere you, who am almost able to respond to the excellence of your fatal genius? . . . But why, O Lord, do you not reward my constant devotion, which bows down before your celestial qualities, with a relic of those papers which you care least about? Certainly I would appreciate two chalk marks on a sheet of paper."[7]

Silence. Michelangelo did not respond either to Titian or Aretino. Inundated by requests from all quarters, Michelangelo became increasingly disinclined to act on the myriad appeals made to him. He harbored his energies and worked only for longtime sympathetic clients, reserving rare gifts and favors for his closest friends. It was the age-old custom of gift exchange in which a service rendered would be reciprocated by a service or gift in return, especially expected among members of equal social standing. But Titian was not a social equal, at least not in the estimation of Michelangelo, a Florentine aristocrat who claimed descent from the noble counts of Canossa. The contemporary engraved portrait of Michelangelo by Giulio Bonasone (1546) proclaimed Michelangelo a Florentine patrician in Latin majuscules: MICHEL ANGELVS BONAROTVS PATRITIVS.[8] Titian, a mere craftsman from provincial Pieve di Cadore without any sort of distinguished ancestry, had little social standing in the rigid hierarchy of papal Rome.

Such a favor as Titian was asking required time, effort, and delicate diplomatic maneuvering in the complicated machinations of papal bureaucracy. Michelangelo was grateful to friends who politicked for him, but it was quite another matter to expend effort on behalf of someone who was not a *famigliare*, *amico*, or *vicino*, and not even Florentine. Did Titian not understand the culture of gift and favor that governed advancement in the papal court? Was Venice so different? The advancement of Titian's son Pomponio Vecellio was of no interest to Michelangelo.

Michelangelo must have been perplexed if not bothered by Titian's persistent request, and now, awkwardly, the artist was in Rome working for the same Farnese patrons. In the competitive papal court, there was only so much attention and treasure that any one individual could hope to command. Was Titian here to supplant Michelangelo? As with earlier in his career, Michelangelo could not escape his anxiety that the pope's attention might be distracted by a new artist or project—as when Bramante successfully convinced Pope Julius II to turn his attention (and funds) from Michelangelo's monumental marble tomb to the building of New St. Peter's. The pope—dealing with the international forces tearing Christianity apart—had more pressing priorities than his myriad artistic projects. Having contested with Bramante and Raphael for the attention and finances of a busy pope, a cautious Michelangelo inevitably would be wary of the newly arrived foreigner.

Friendship with a Pope and His Family

Michelangelo had a head start on confidential relations with the Farnese. The pope's cultivated grandson, Alessandro Farnese, known as "il Gran Cardinale," was an admirer and longtime loyal supporter of the artist. He secured lucrative benefices for Michelangelo and assisted him in his fractious negotiations with the heirs of Pope Julius II over the unfinished tomb. The artist was also close to Alessandro's personal secretary, Annibale Caro, who was "much to Michelangelo's taste" and who may have assisted Ascanio Condivi in writing the life of the artist published in 1553.[9] Michelangelo was friendly with a number of others in the large Farnese household, including the pope's chamberlain, Ascanio Sforza, for whom he designed the Sforza Chapel in Santa Maria Maggiore. Most importantly, the artist was on extremely friendly terms with the pontiff himself who, according to Vasari, "felt for Michelangelo such reverence and love that he always went out of his way to please him."[10] Vasari may have been exaggerating, but he heard this from Michelangelo himself and he witnessed their friendship firsthand.

Both the pope and Michelangelo launched their careers in the Florentine Medici court. Although they probably did not meet in the 1490s, Michelangelo and Paul (then Alessandro Farnese) were nurtured in the humanist circle of Lorenzo de' Medici, "il Magnifico." Some fifty years later in Rome, they discovered kindred spirits in one another, founded in no small part on the fact that they were both of venerable age, profoundly Christian, and dedicated to church reform. Confirmation of their intimacy is found in the *motu proprio* issued by Pope Paul appointing Michelangelo supreme architect of St. Peter's: "Our beloved son, Michel Angelo

Buonarroti, a Florentine citizen, a member of our household, and our regular dining companion."[11] A "member of our household," that is, a privileged, intimate member of the pope's innermost circle. And "our regular dining companion."

The amicable relationship—actually, a genuine friendship—is suggested by the unexpected but delicious fact that Michelangelo, as "beloved son," was Paul's dinner companion, albeit more occasional than "regular." The artist brought Tuscan delicacies to the pope's table thanks to his nephew Lionardo who regularly sent foodstuffs to provincial Rome: every June, between three and four dozen flasks of Trebbiano wine and each winter a dozen or more marzolino cheeses (sometimes cacio). Lionardo also sent ravioli, Tuscan sausages, red and white ceci beans, and fruits including apples, plums, and sweet yellow pears. Each time these delicacies arrived, Michelangelo shared them with his close friends, including Pope Paul. Consider the day in mid-June of 1547, when Michelangelo sent Paul a quarter of the forty-four flasks of new Trebbiano wine just arrived from the Buonarroti vineyards. The following spring, Michelangelo shared thirty-three pears with the pope. Fruits—especially since they traveled from distant Tuscany—were a type of aristocratic gift exchanged only among persons of stature and familiarity. The pope "thought they were excellent and was most grateful."[12]

The gift of pears and flagons of excellent Trebbiano wine elicited invitations to dine with the pontiff. Over succulent Buonarroti pears served in a warmed, clove-spiced muscato, Michelangelo and Paul might have spoken of the artist recently arrived from Venice who was painting the pope's portrait. Titian had been invited to Rome, but he was not yet a guest at Paul's table. The pontiff did not extend the same degree of conviviality to his Venetian guest, perhaps because he was not equally at ease with the man's grasping manner and peculiar foreign accent. Would Michelangelo do the pope a favor and call upon Titian? A courtesy visit would be an appropriate gesture, and one that the ever-attentive Giorgio Vasari could readily arrange. Michelangelo, moreover, had good reason to acquiesce to such a request.

Reciprocal Favor

When Titian arrived in Rome in late 1545, Michelangelo had just begun two large frescoes for the pope's eponymous Pauline Chapel. The winter damp, however, prompted him to suspend painting until warmer weather. Moreover, a small fire had recently damaged the roof, and infiltrating water threatened the frescoes. Distraught and irate, the artist threatened to abandon the project altogether. The disconsolate artist remained at home in Via Macel de' Corvi for several weeks. Finally, the pope's request, Giorgio Vasari's offer to accompany him, and Michelangelo's sense of obligation all contributed to his decision to visit Titian in the Belvedere on a cold day in early 1546.

As he and Vasari rode slowly through the wintery city, Michelangelo recalled the time—was it already sixteen years ago?!—when Titian visited him in Venice. As an anxious, disheveled fugitive from war, Michelangelo had been afraid for his life and uncertain of his future. He was forever grateful for the courtesy shown to him by Venice in his hour of desperate need. Although not fleeing for his life, Titian was a colleague who deserved equal consideration. It is even possible that Michelangelo was curious to see for himself the Titian paintings that were the talk of cognoscenti Rome. Hence the visit described at the opening of this book.

In the Belvedere studio, Michelangelo and Vasari saw the ravishing picture of *Danaë*, as well as other superb examples of Titian's painterly ability (see Plate 4). Truly, the Venetian was a swift and assured painter. There were several pictures completed and in progress, including the impressive *Pope Paul III and His Grandsons* (see Plate 3). There was another portrait of the seated pontiff wearing a *camauro* cap, as well as a half-length portrait of the two artists' mutual patron, Cardinal Alessandro.[13] There also was an *Ecce Homo* that Vasari judged somewhat harshly as "not as good as many other Titian paintings, especially the portraits"—a comment that must have annoyed the Venetian when he read it in the second edition of Vasari's *Lives* (1568).[14] It was just one of many reasons for Titian to react negatively to Vasari, as we shall see.

Titian painted the Farnese as unnervingly alive, more so than the comparatively stiff portrait of Alfonso d'Este that Michelangelo "enthusiastically praised" years before (see Fig. 18).[15] It was proper and socially decorous for Michelangelo to admire Titian's paintings, especially since the Venetian was universally acknowledged to be the best portraitist of his time. Of course, the paintings were not the only, nor necessarily the principal topic of conversation. Perhaps they conversed about Pope Paul Farnese or King Francis I. Did they share gossip about their mutual patron, the willful Alfonso d'Este? An importunate Titian may again have brazenly broached the topic of Pomponio's ecclesiastic preferment. Michelangelo would claim old age and perhaps admit to being overwhelmed by requests from insistent lords such as the persistent Alfonso d'Este. It was an awkward moment rescued by the ever-courteous Vasari who turned their attention back to the *Danaë*. This permitted Michelangelo to express his genuine admiration for the picture which "pleased him very much."

"Too Bad Venetians Never Learned to Draw"

By age seventy, Michelangelo had grown comfortably into his aristocratic persona.[16] He knew how to dress properly and negotiate the corridors of power. Although he could be brusque and wielded an acerbic Tuscan wit, Michelangelo had also learned the ways of the court and courtier. He behaved appropriately and properly in praising Titian's painting "as one would with the artist present."[17] His well-known criticism—"It was a shame that Venetians never learned to draw"—was directed to Vasari alone and only after the two had departed Titian's company.[18] Less a criticism of the specific picture, Michelangelo's comment was a general observation regarding Venetian practice, which tended to eschew preliminary drawing for working *alla prima*, that is, directly on canvas, favoring color as a means to define form and composition. Subscribing to the tradition in which he was raised, Michelangelo was devoted to drawing, disegno, as foundational to artistic practice. Therefore, he was perfectly justified in making his observation: the Venetians worked differently from Florentines.

Was there, however, something else, maybe something more personal behind Michelangelo's remark? Was he genuinely commenting on style or practice, or might he have been piqued by Titian's *Danaë* in a manner that he refrained from admitting? Did Michelangelo see the picture for what it partly was—a riposte and a challenge to Michelangelo's recent spate of female nudes? In particular, Titian's *Danaë* is a corrective response to Michelangelo's *Leda* and *Venus and Cupid*, which, in turn, owe much to the Florentine's encounter with Titian's paintings in Ferrara. Titian was not blind to Michelangelo's provocation, nor was Michelangelo blind to Titian's obvious counter-challenge. For some sixteen years, the two artists had been in an unspoken dialogue regarding the painting of sensuous subjects sensuously. For Titian, the *Leda* and *Venus and Cupid* were critical catalysts in this exchange.

Although dispatched to France, the *Leda* was a media sensation of its time and well-known to Titian via word of mouth and widely circulated engravings (see, e.g., Fig. 21).[19] Recall too, that Giorgio Vasari had painted copies of both the *Leda* and the *Venus and Cupid*, which he peddled in Venice in 1540–41.[20] Well-informed of Michelangelo's two paintings, Titian surely would have recognized a competitive threat. Given that the *Leda* was made in purposeful confrontation with Titian's Ferrara pictures, it is not surprising that the Venetian artist would respond in kind. One can almost hear Titian: "*This* is how to paint a sensuous nude." With the *Danaë*, the quietly germinating artistic dialogue between the two artists burst into visible if unspoken confrontation.

Michelangelo was fully cognizant of the challenge. Even as he recognized Titian's originality, Michelangelo must have perceived that *Danaë* was an obvious retort to his *Leda*. Both artists had painted life-size reclining nudes welcoming Jove's divine impregnation: a gentle shower of golden coins versus the disconcerting feathery caress of a lovesick swan. Titian's portrayal of alluring passion challenged discomfiting bestiality, his enticing manner of oil painting contrasted with the hard-edged drawing and flattened palette of tempera. Michelangelo praised Titian's style ("maniera") and coloring, but said nothing about the two artists' quid pro quo. True to his gentlemanly nature, he reserved any negative assessment of Titian's painting until after their meeting. Years later, Vasari used the encounter for his own polemical purposes, but he likely missed (and thus did not write) what more may have lain behind Michelangelo's critical comment. Vasari lacked subtlety when it came to his hero.

Titian and Michelangelo never met again, but this episode resulted in increased mutual attention, regard, and competition. A
creative artistic dialogue continued for the remaining twenty years
of their lives. Beyond professional rivalry, Titian and Michelangelo
had much to offer one another, even if their ongoing exchange was
distant, mostly indirect, and largely unacknowledged. Their devel-
oping liaison would continue to be nourished by countless close
and peripheral figures.

Patrons, Friends, Acquaintances:
Mecenati, Amici, Vicini

Titian and Michelangelo lived in a small but highly interconnected
world. Most importantly, the two artists shared the patronage and
sometimes friendship of many of the most powerful figures of their
time, including prominent members of the Medici, Este, Della Rovere, and Farnese families.

Titian painted or produced works for a half dozen members
of the Farnese family, including the two closest to Michelangelo:
Pope Paul III and his grandson, Cardinal Alessandro Farnese. From
the moment of Titian's arrival in Rome, he and Michelangelo were
aware that they shared and were competing for the attention of "i
grandi." In his portraits, Titian captured the character and fraught
relations among the Farnese, but he never grew close to any of
them. Michelangelo, on the other hand, was an intimate, a "familiare" of the family. Ventriloquizing his hero's sentiments, Condivi
tells us that Michelangelo "loves and honours all the persons of the
Farnese house." He was especially close to Pope Paul, whom he
"recalled with the utmost reverence, and continuously mentioned
him as a good and holy man."[21] It must have been disconcerting for
the world's two greatest artists to find themselves simultaneously

employed by the current pontiff and members of the Farnese *famiglia*, as well as working within close proximity to one another in the Vatican. Yes, they paid close attention to each other.

During Titian's Roman sojourn, another mutual patron added some spice to the artists' escalating competition. As early as 1519, the most Catholic king of France, Francis I (ruled 1515-47), expressed his admiration and love ("amore") for Michelangelo. A voracious collector of Italian art and culture, Francis declared that he fervently wished to own "something of yours" ("cosa del vostro").[22] Michelangelo responded to the flattering request, yet pleaded that he momentarily was preoccupied with the Medici commissions at San Lorenzo. It was not until 1529 that Francis finally obtained a work by the master—the marble *Hercules* once owned by the Strozzi and ultimately installed in the king's garden at Fontainebleau.[23] Francis continued energetically to pursue Michelangelo, especially after the *Leda* arrived in France.

Years after the demise of the Last Republic, Michelangelo and his fellow republicans still looked to France as the best hope of freeing Florence from the tyranny of Medici rule. In 1544, Michelangelo offered to create a bronze equestrian statue if Francis would restore the independent Florentine republic. On behalf of his friend Michelangelo, Luigi del Riccio wrote to Roberto Strozzi, the Florentine ambassador to Francis: "He begs you to remind the king that if his Majesty would restore the liberty of Florence, Michelangelo would make a bronze statue of him on a horse for Piazza della Signoria."[24] Francis was not about to commit to such a dangerous course; however, Michelangelo's overture encouraged the king to request further work from the master.

In February 1546—shortly after Titian's arrival in Rome—Michelangelo received a highly flattering letter from Francis addressed "Au Seigneur Michelangelo." Personally signed "Francoys" in his large looping hand, Francis reiterated his long-standing desire to own "some examples of your work." The king informed Michelangelo that he had charged his current envoy, the Bolognese artist Francesco Primaticcio, to acquire works by Michelangelo, "and I beseech you, if you should have some excellent works already finished when he arrives, to entrust them to him."[25] A knowledgeable and well-informed connoisseur, Francis further requested that Primaticcio be permitted to make plaster molds of Michelangelo's Vatican *Pietà* and the *Risen Christ*.[26] Michelangelo eagerly responded on April 26, 1546: "I know not which is the greater, the favour or the wonder that Your Majesty should deign to write to a man like me, and still further to request of him examples of his work." Michelangelo assured Francis "that for a long time I have desired to serve You, but have been unable to do so."[27] He went on to promise a work in marble, in bronze, *and* in painting. Note that Michelangelo promised more than one work, one of which would be a painting.

Titian, too, courted the patronage of Francis. His friend Pietro Aretino persuaded Titian to paint a portrait of the monarch that could be sent to the king as a gift. (Was Aretino hoping to deflect the monarch's attention from Michelangelo to his Venetian friend?) As a model, Titian used Benvenuto Cellini's medal to create a striking half-length portrait of the monarch (Plate 25).[28] The portrait successfully elicited the gift of a gold chain for Aretino, who proudly wears it in his portraits by Titian (e.g., Plate 26).[29] Michelangelo never saw these paintings, but he certainly was aware that he and Titian shared this royal patron. Yet, as in the case of the Farnese, Michelangelo could claim a much greater degree of familiarity. Francis corresponded directly with Michelangelo but not with Titian. Francis invited Titian to court, but made little effort to obtain further work from the Venetian artist.

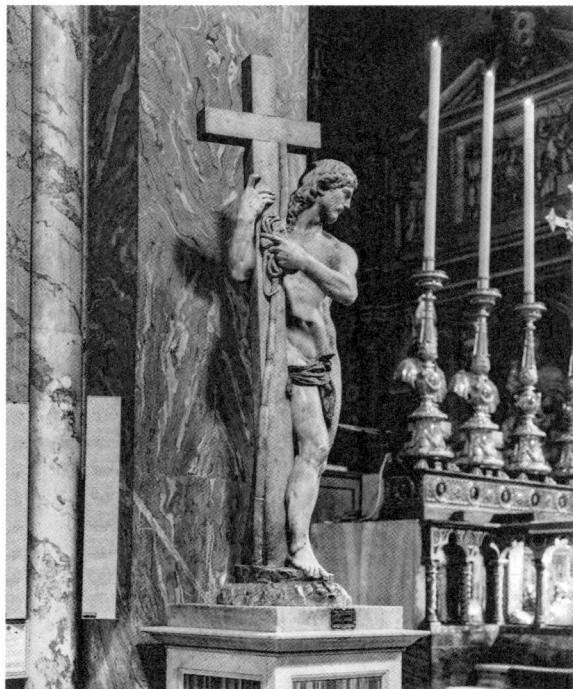

35. Michelangelo, *Risen Christ*, marble, h. 6.75 ft (205 cm), Sta. Maria sopra Minerva, Rome, 1519-20.

Titian's portrait of the king proved to be primarily Pietro Aretino's self-promotional project.

Curiously, toward the end of his visit to Rome, Titian acquired a full-size plaster of Michelangelo's *Risen Christ*, most likely cast from the very mold that Primaticcio made for King Francis I.[30] The *Risen Christ* (Fig. 35) is no longer one of the more admired works of Michelangelo, but such a full-size replica reminds us of a different canon of masterpieces that attracted sixteenth-century viewers and collectors. At the very least, Titian's acquisition confirms that he saw and admired the marble sculpture in Santa Maria sopra Minerva. It would serve as a creative catalyst many years later.

Cardinal Ippolito de' Medici (1511–35) was another grand personage who links our two artists.[31] The natural son of Giuliano, Duke of Nemours, whom Michelangelo immortalized in the Medici Chapel, the young Ippolito was one of the artist's most favored people. Michelangelo was drawn to the Medici cardinal for the refined taste and generosity common to his family, while at the same time he was a committed republican. Ippolito remained a staunch ally of the group of Florentine exiles (*fuorusciti*) who gathered in Rome in the 1530s and '40s, conniving to free Florence of Duke Alessandro de' Medici's tyrannical rule. In the longstanding effort to cultivate Francis I in support of the republican cause, it was Ippolito de' Medici who enlisted Michelangelo for the promised equestrian statue of the king. In thanks, Ippolito presented Michelangelo with the princely gift of a beautiful Arabian horse.[32]

In September of 1533, the cultivated cardinal was among the small group of cognoscenti who descended upon the young Roman nobleman, Tommaso de' Cavalieri, eager to see the exquisite drawings that Michelangelo had presented to his recent infatuation. Cavalieri wrote to inform Michelangelo that Cardinal Ippolito "wanted to have the Tityus and Ganymede made in crystal"—the first translations of these drawings into precious materials.[33] Soon, and in various media, these private inventions became public, spreading far and wide, including to Venice.

Titian painted Ippolito de' Medici in Bologna in 1533, shortly after the cardinal's return from Hungary where the Emperor Charles V was campaigning against the Turks (Plate 27).[34] Dressed in exotic Hungarian costume—a long belted doublet of crushed crimson velvet and feathered cap—the young cardinal-soldier holds a heavy gilded mace in his right hand while firmly gripping his foreign kilij sword in his left. With an aquiline nose and neatly trimmed mustache and beard, Ippolito fixes us with a leveling gaze. It is one of the most handsome portraits of the sixteenth century.

Titian memorably portrayed Ippolito, but Michelangelo knew the young man much better. Listed among Michelangelo's closest friends by Giorgio Vasari, Ippolito was a magnanimous individual, a longtime *familiare* and generous patron of the artist. Unfortunately, Ippolito's controversial politics cut short his life. In 1535, at the tender age of twenty-four, he was poisoned. His death was certainly painful to Michelangelo, although the artist, ever wary of political entanglement, accepted it with characteristic silence.

Michelangelo had no such affectionate feelings for another shared patron: Duke Francesco Maria della Rovere (1490–1538). The nephew of Pope Julius II, Francesco Maria inherited oversight of his uncle's unfinished tomb. In contrast to the executors who preceded him, Francesco Maria exhibited little patience with Michelangelo and became increasingly strident in his demands; indeed, he proved a persistent thorn in the artist's side. For some four years between 1524 and 1528, the duke and several of his loathsome representatives periodically badgered Michelangelo, accusing him of financial dishonesty and embezzlement, words that Michelangelo claimed "penetrated the heart" ("trafisse el core").[35] Michelangelo probably never saw, *nor cared to see*, the martial portrait of the arrogant duke painted by Titian and extravagantly praised by Pietro Aretino (Plate 28).[36]

Michelangelo was finally relieved of the forty-year albatross of the Julius monument when Francesco Maria's son, Guidobaldo della Rovere (1514–74), the great-nephew of Pope Julius II, inherited the responsibility of seeing his ancestor's tomb to completion. Unlike his father, Guidobaldo held Michelangelo in high regard and treated him respectfully. Guidobaldo extended generous terms in a final contract that encouraged the artist to bring the

tomb to a satisfactory conclusion. Guidobaldo was equally generous in his many dealings with Titian. He was the proud owner of
Titian's *Venus of Urbino* as well as an elegant, full-length portrait
of himself, known only from copies (e.g., Plate 29).[37] Guidobaldo
also owned Titian's copy of Raphael's famous portrait of Pope Julius II, which—as we will see—Titian painted while he was in Rome
(see Plate 36). Michelangelo likely saw Titian's copy of Raphael
and probably also his portrait of Guidobaldo.

As a refined connoisseur and collector, Guidobaldo continued to patronize Titian and pursue Michelangelo. In his portrait
of Guidobaldo, Titian captures something of the duke's haughty
character. Although considerate of Michelangelo, the artist experienced Guidobaldo's high-handedness when the duke strong-
armed Michelangelo's former housemate, Cornelia Colonelli (wife
of Michelangelo's assistant Pietro Urbino), into giving up two drawings that Guidobaldo wished to have painted by Michelangelo's
friend and collaborator, Marcello Venusti. Thus, in addition to his
Titians, the duke owned two paintings by the other foremost artist
of the day, even if his "Michelangelos" were painted by proxy.[38]
Moreover, Guidobaldo may have been the intended purchaser of
the painted copies of *Leda* and *Venus and Cupid* that Vasari was
peddling in Venice in 1540–41.

Alfonso d'Avalos (1502–46), the Marchese del Vasto and a lead-
ing general of the imperial armies of Emperor Charles V, also pursued both artists. Titian painted two portraits of Alfonso d'Avalos.
The second, more ostentatious full-length painting, the so-called
"Allocutio," features the successful general addressing his troops
(Plate 30).[39] Following the fall of the Florentine Republic in 1530,
Alfonso pressed Michelangelo for a work by his hand. Given his
tenuous situation in the unsettled political climate, Michelangelo
could not refuse the powerful Marchese. He drew a cartoon for

a *Noli me Tangere* and enlisted Jacopo Pontormo to paint it (see Plate 18). As discussed earlier, this was, along with the *Leda* and *Venus and Cupid*, one of several paintings designed by Michelangelo shortly after his experience of Titian in Ferrara and Venice.

In addition, Alfonso d'Avalos acted as an intermediary for his kinswoman, the Marchese Vittoria Colonna (Fig. 36), who owned Titian's penitent *Mary Magdalene* (Plate 31), and may have been the ultimate recipient of Michelangelo's *Noli me Tangere*.[40] In the 1540s, Vittoria Colonna (1492–1547) became a close companion of Michelangelo and something of a spiritual advisor. In his *Notable Men and Women of Our Time* (1527), Paolo Giovio celebrated Vittoria Colonna's many virtues, including her chastity and grace, noble lineage, and spiritual devotion.[41] Both Michelangelo and Vittoria Colonna were committed to church reform and together confronted the problem of accommodating personal belief within the strictures of institutional orthodoxy.[42] The two friends wrote deeply affecting poetry that sought to reconcile the contradictory obligations of the secular and sacred, the earthly and divine.

Michelangelo and Vittoria Colonna occasionally met to discuss these and other subjects in a lovely little courtyard attached to the church of San Silvestro in Capite on the Quirinale Hill. A young Portuguese painter, Francisco de Hollanda, sometimes joined their distinguished company, and subsequently recalled conversations that transpired over several days. Francisco, a propagandist for elevating the artistic profession in his comparatively backward Iberian world, one day asked Michelangelo if he would "inform me what celebrated paintings there are in Italy."[43] It was a long difficult answer, Michelangelo claimed, yet in his listing of notable works he mentioned: "At Venice there are admirable works by the Cavaliere Tiziano, who excels in painting and in portraits." Michelangelo added that "the whole of that city [Venice] is a good

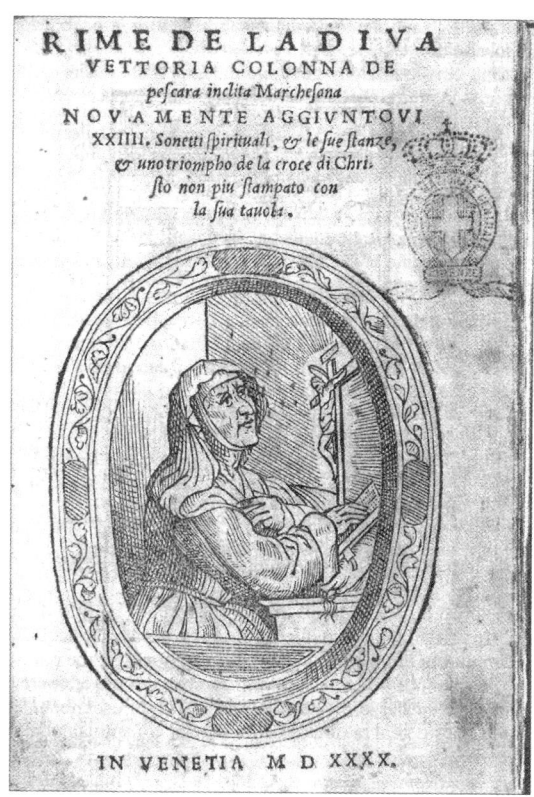

RIME DE LA DIVA
VETTORIA COLONNA DE
pefcara inclita Marchefana
NOVAMENTE AGGIVNTOVI
XXIIII. *Sonetti fpirituali, & le fue ftanze,*
& uno triompho de la croce di Chri-
fto non piu ftampato con
la fua tauola.

IN VENETIA M D XXXX.

36. Anon., Vittoria
Colonna, frontispiece
Rime de la Diva,
woodcut, 5.5 × 3 in
(138 × 77 mm), 1542.

painting." One wishes that Hollanda would have mentioned the friends speaking of Titian's *Magdalene* or Michelangelo's *Noli me Tangere*, although these are paintings that likely would have resided in Vittoria Colonna's private apartments.

Michelangelo and Titian not only crossed paths via mutual patrons and similar subject matter but the two artists both also painted original and erotically charged images of Mary Magdalene. Michelangelo's *Noli me Tangere* and Titian's *Penitent Magdalene* should be considered in dialogue even if they were created independently of one another. They are both paintings of the Magdalene that enlist erotic frisson to engage the spectator in spiritual issues of individual faith, sin, and salvation. In her poetry, Vittoria Colonna displayed a profound interest in and empathy for Mary Magdalene—the central subject of both pictures by Titian and, more unusually, Michelangelo. It is suggestive that the saint—who had not figured in Michelangelo's art previously—plays a prominent role in the *Noli me Tangere* and more unexpectedly in his Florentine *Pietà*, a highly personal work begun shortly after the death of Vittoria Colonna.[44] His friendship with Vittoria Colonna and the challenge of Titian helped prompt Michelangelo's engagement with this hitherto anomalous subject matter.

In 1542, Titian painted an enchanting portrait of the young Clarissa Strozzi (Plate 32), daughter of Michelangelo's longtime family friend and protector Roberto Strozzi (1515–66).[45] In the Strozzi's Roman palace, Michelangelo may well have seen Titian's portrait of the sweet child, bedecked in jewels and holding her pet spaniel. He was certainly aware that once again the two artists shared patronage with yet another prominent person. Michelangelo and his family had maintained ties with the Strozzi for nearly fifty years.[46] Michelangelo grew especially close to Roberto Strozzi during the years when they were both members of the Florentine exile community in Rome. Messer Roberto—as Michelangelo addressed him—spent much of his time in Lyons, France, conducting business with the Florentine merchant community and as a representative to the court of Francis I, which is why Roberto Strozzi was the appropriate intermediary when Michelangelo offered to create an equestrian statue of the French king.

During the pestilent summer of 1544—shortly before Titian arrived in Rome—Michelangelo fell dangerously ill with a debilitating fever. His dear friend, Luigi del Riccio—a business agent of the Strozzi who lived in their Roman palace close to Ponte Sant'Angelo—insisted that the sick artist move into the Strozzi household where he was attended by the family physician during a month-long convalescence. Roberto Strozzi was on business in France, but thanks to regular reports from Rome, he attentively followed Michelangelo's slow return to health.[47] When Michelangelo finally recovered, the artist expressed his heartfelt thanks to Luigi del Riccio by writing a sonnet and, in the accompanying note, swore his "service" to Roberto Strozzi.[48] But he did much more.

Michelangelo presented Roberto Strozzi with the two unfinished marble Captives, the so-called "Rebellious" and "Dying" Slaves, now in the Louvre (see Fig. 10). Technically, the sculptures belonged to the Della Rovere since the marbles originally were destined for the tomb of Pope Julius II. They were an expression of gratitude as well as political alliance, which partly explains Michelangelo's dissimulation; even his contemporary biographers knew little about the sculptures. The unusual gift was a stunning affirmation of Michelangelo's loyalty and intimacy with one of the most important families of his native Florence and contemporary Rome. As with the Farnese, Michelangelo was much closer to the Strozzi than Titian, who merely painted a fetching portrait of their young daughter Clarissa.

*   *   *

Many more connections—increasingly tenuous—conjoin the two artists living in a tightly entwined world of patronage, friendship, and acquaintance (*mecenati, amici, vicini*). For example, Titian painted at least one portrait of the humanist, diplomat, and Este court poet Ludovico Ariosto (1474–1533). Twice Ariosto served as a diplomat to Pope Julius II in Rome, where he saw Michelangelo's completed Sistine ceiling in 1513.[49] He may have met Michelangelo, and certainly did when the artist was in Ferrara in 1529, negotiating with their mutual patron, Alfonso d'Este. In the final version of his epic poem *L'Orlando Furioso* (1532)—read by both Titian and Michelangelo—Ariosto praised Titian but exalted Michelangelo, raising him to the level of divinity: "Michel, più che mortale, Angel divino" (*Orlando Furioso* 33.2). Undoubtedly, a source of irritation for the competitive, thin-skinned Titian.

The rapacious collectors of Mantua, Isabella d'Este (1474–1539) and her son, Federico II Gonzaga (1500–1540), also openly pursued both artists. Twice painted by Titian, Isabella was the proud owner of Michelangelo's *Sleeping Cupid*, and was perpetually hunting for more.[50] Titian also painted a dashing portrait of Isabella's son Federico (Plate 33), who was equally interested in acquiring "either paintings or sculpture . . . and especially something by the hand of Michelangelo."[51] In painting these portraits, was Titian aware that Michelangelo was of equal or greater interest to these collectors? Similarly, when Titian painted a portrait of the Turkish Sultan Suleiman the Magnificent, did he recall that Michelangelo was to build a bridge across the Golden Horn and still had a standing invitation to visit Constantinople?

We gain a bit of intimate access to this tight-knit social world when we read a letter that the Florentine philologist Francesco Priscianese sent to his and Michelangelo's mutual friends, Luigi del Riccio and Ludovico Becci.[52] Writing from Venice, Priscinese described a delightful late summer evening, "ferrare Agosto," spent in the garden of Titiano Vecellio. Priscianese likened Titian's garden to the "most pleasant at Sant'Agata" in Rome which belonged to Niccolò Ridolfi, a patron of Michelangelo, a committed Republican exile (*fuoruscito*), and proud owner of one of Michelangelo's last sculptures, the bust of the tyrannicide *Brutus*.[53]

Joining the illustrious company at Titian's garden soiree were "some of the most rare intellects that are found today in this city," including the other members of the Venetian triumvirate, Pietro Aretino and Jacopo Sansovino. The letter's recipient, Luigi del Riccio, undoubtedly shared the gossipy news of the enchanting evening with his dear friend Michelangelo. Thus, a small but closely related group of friends and acquaintances—known to both Titian and Michelangelo—are linked together in this single letter. This is a documented example of the oral culture of information, gossip, and hearsay that circulates "a bocca," but rarely finds its way into the written record. One further example helps illuminate this world, bringing the two artists into ever greater proximity.

On his return to Venice from Rome in 1546, Titian painted another portrait of a member of the Farnese family, Pier Luigi Farnese (1503–47), Duke of Parma and Piacenza (Plate 34).[54] In the 1540s, Pier Luigi was the guarantor of Michelangelo's lucrative source of income from the Passo del Po ferry.[55] Pier Luigi was also the father of another of Michelangelo's principal benefactors, Cardinal Alessandro Farnese, whom Titian painted in Rome in 1545/46, and of Alessandro's younger brother, Ranuccio Farnese.[56] Ranuccio was the favored grandson of Pope Paul III who raised him to the cardinalate at the tender age of fifteen. The pope ensured that the young Ranuccio received an excellent education while also conferring a number of lucrative benefices on the boy. Despite his rapid advancement, Ranuccio was well-liked for his endearing personality and good character, beautifully captured in Titian's first-ever Farnese portrait (see Plate 23). Wishing to provide the best education for the precocious boy, Pope Paul appointed the eminently appropriate Lodovico Beccadelli to be Ranuccio's personal tutor.

Lodovico Beccadelli

Lodovico Beccadelli (1501–72) was a refined, well-educated prelate and poet from a prominent Bolognese family and an ideal mentor for Ranuccio, who reciprocated tender feelings for his teacher. He was also one of Michelangelo's closest and dearest friends.[57] Younger by almost forty-five years, Beccadelli was one of the beautifully mannered, urbane younger men to whom Michelangelo was repeatedly drawn, especially in his later years. Additionally, Beccadelli was a friend of Vittoria Colonna and others of the same literary and spiritual circle: Cardinal Reginald Pole, Pietro Bembo, and Giovanni della Casa.

When Michelangelo took over the construction of St. Peter's in 1546, Beccadelli proved a loyal supporter and an invaluable ally since he sat on the fractious board of the *Fabbrica di San Pietro*, the deputies charged with overseeing the building fabric. The two friends shared a tender and deeply mutual regard. They grew extremely close and began exchanging intimate letters and poetry. Beccadelli was one of those rare friends with whom Michelangelo shared his conflicting feelings of carnal desire and spiritual yearning, simultaneously pining for relief from earthly concerns while fully accepting his obligations as a servant of God. Once, the artist wrote longingly: "We'll meet in heaven; but before our final breath, I would still like us to enjoy each other here on earth . . . you are always in my thoughts."[58] Beccadelli frequently was assigned duties that took him far from Rome, causing Michelangelo to greatly miss his friend. Only in separation did the two friends have reason to correspond; therefore, their time together in Rome is a mostly unwritten history that transpired not via letters, but "a bocca."

In 1550, Beccadelli was appointed papal legate to Venice, where he was painted by Titian, who successfully captured the intelligent, thoughtful, and sensitive man's warm, unpretentious character (Plate 35).[59] Having previously painted Beccadelli's precocious pupil Ranuccio Farnese, and having spent six months in Rome with the teacher and his pupil, Titian was at the pinnacle of his abilities in portraying the warmhearted tranquility of the man's genial character. Titian must also have been aware of the deep and sympathetic attachment between Ranuccio and Beccadelli and between Beccadelli and Michelangelo. Unfortunately, Michelangelo probably never saw Titian's affecting portrait.

*   *   *

By 1545, a dense skein of threads entwined the two artists. Titian knew his sitters via his commissions and brilliant brush; Michelangelo knew many intimately as longtime friends. They belonged to the same tight-knit, geographically compact world of sixteenth-century Florence, Venice, and Rome. The two artists were pursued by many of the same and sometimes would-be patrons: Francis I, Andrea Gritti, Alfonso d'Avalos, Federico Gonzaga, Alfonso and Isabella d'Este, Francesco and Guidobaldo della Rovere, Ippolito and Cosimo de' Medici, Vittoria Colonna, Lodovico Beccadelli, and most recently, the Farnese family—Pope Paul III, and his progeny, Alessandro, Pier Luigi, and Ranuccio Farnese. They shared a few friends: Sebastiano del Piombo, Jacopo Sansovino, Annibale Caro, and with reservations on the part of one or the other, Pietro Aretino and Giorgio Vasari. Then there is the legion of mutual acquaintances including the humanists Pietro Bembo and Giovanni della Casa, artists Giulio Clovio and Giovanni Bernardi in the Farnese household, and the Florentine pedant Benedetto Varchi who championed Michelangelo's poetry and was painted by Titian.[60] Constantly inserting himself in this intersecting web of overlapping relations was the longtime third wheel in the Titian / Michelangelo story: Pietro Aretino, friend of one and nemesis of the other.

Pietro Aretino (1492–1556) (see Plate 26), Titian's closest friend and Michelangelo's longtime bête noire, was the most frequent and vocal intermediary between the two artists.[61] He is first mentioned in Michelangelo's correspondence in a letter from Sebastiano del Piombo of April 1525. Sebastiano reported that Aretino had seen a recent Michelangelo missive and had the effrontery to declare that "he [Aretino] alone was unique" ("che tocca a lui esser l'unico"). Although a friend and godfather to Aretino's child, Sebastiano was clearly affronted by Aretino's brash self-promotion. Sebastiano affirmed to Michelangelo that *he, not* Aretino, was "the only one, above all the others. And, that is all [*Et basta*]."[62]

Some years later, Aretino initiated a back-and-forth correspondence when he wrote directly to "divino Michelagnolo."[63] Thus began an epistolary exchange—which rapidly deteriorated into an epistolary assault—on a mostly unresponsive Michelangelo. Aretino alternately larded Michelangelo with flattery (e.g., "intelletto Divino") and then annoyance when the artist ignored his pointed criticisms of the *Last Judgment*. Frustrated, Aretino went on the attack, making snide allusions to the artist's untoward affections for younger men.[64] While intervening on behalf of Titian, Aretino was simultaneously soliciting Michelangelo for one or more drawings ("una reliquia di quelle carte").

When his overtures were met by silence, Aretino tried a new approach, writing directly to Titian in Rome. Impatiently, Aretino awaited Titian's return to Venice, but in the meantime he wished to hear his friend's opinion of Michelangelo who "does not come close to Raphael in painting."[65] Michelangelo was never going to win that contest, but it is significant that Aretino wished to judge him, not as a sculptor or architect, but as a painter. One wonders how Titian responded, certainly not by letter as Titian was a hampered writer, but more likely "a bocca" when the two friends were once again reunited in Venice. Aretino, the social media champion of his time, was a frequent and unwelcome intermediary in Michelangelo's relations with Titian.

Titian, Tourist in Rome

Winter turned to spring in the early months of 1546, and Titian had ample time to explore Rome. He remained in the city for more than six months—longer than a college semester abroad. One can see a lot in this time. Let us consider Titian's experience "abroad," and follow him around Rome, first in the company of his assigned cicerone (guide), Giorgio Vasari, and sometimes with his Venetian compatriot Sebastiano del Piombo. There is no record of a further meeting between Titian and Michelangelo, although Lodovico Dolce suggests that Michelangelo saw the *Danaë* "more than once" and "with amazement."[66] Both artists were working in close proximity at the Vatican and for the same Farnese patrons. Since Titian was frequently in the company of two artists who claimed intimacy with Michelangelo, Vasari and Sebastiano, it is possible there were further encounters. Certainly, there was plenty of gossip.

When not occupied with the myriad problems at St. Peter's, Michelangelo labored over two large frescoes in the Pauline Chapel. Did Titian see these grand works in progress? Did he, like Michelangelo in Venice, pay a courtesy visit to the artist's final and most innovative paintings? Titian would have encountered and heard about Michelangelo everywhere in Rome, such that he may have felt a bit like the American Mark Twain who protested in *Innocents Abroad*: "Enough, enough, enough! I do not want

Michael Angelo for breakfast—for luncheon—for dinner—for tea—
for supper—for between meals."[67]

While Michelangelo had some six weeks to see works in Venice,
Titian had more than six months to see what Rome had to offer.
What might Titian have seen? As an admirer of Raphael, Titian
most wanted to see his frescoes in the Vatican Palace. Sebastiano
accompanied Titian on the visit, which was not without some awkward moments, particularly when the two stepped into the Sala di
Costantino. Following Raphael's death in 1520, Sebastiano solicited Michelangelo's help in securing the commission to complete
the unfinished decorations. Despite Michelangelo's recommendation, Pope Leo X awarded the lucrative undertaking to Giulio
Romano and his minions. We do not know how Titian responded
to the frescoes or to Sebastiano's evident disappointment.

Sebastiano would have been happier accompanying Titian to
San Pietro in Montorio on the Janiculum Hill. There, Sebastiano
waxed eloquent about his masterpiece, *The Flagellation of Christ* in
the Borgherini Chapel (Fig. 37). Sebastiano bragged of his collaboration with Michelangelo and may have shown Titian some of the
sketches the master had furnished for the project. As Sebastiano
blathered on about his various experiments in fresco, oil, and on
slate, Titian's attention was drawn elsewhere.

Raphael's final and most celebrated painting, the *Transfiguration*, graced the high altar of San Pietro in Montorio (see Fig. 25).
At more than thirteen feet tall (405 cm), the brilliantly colored
painting dominated the church and Titian's interest. In scale and
magnificence, the painting rivaled Titian's own masterpiece, the
Assunta in the Frari in Venice (see Plate 15). It is delightful to imagine the garrulous Sebastiano chattering away while Titian wanders
off fixated on Raphael. History rarely records such moments, but
we are familiar enough with the personalities to envisage a friendly

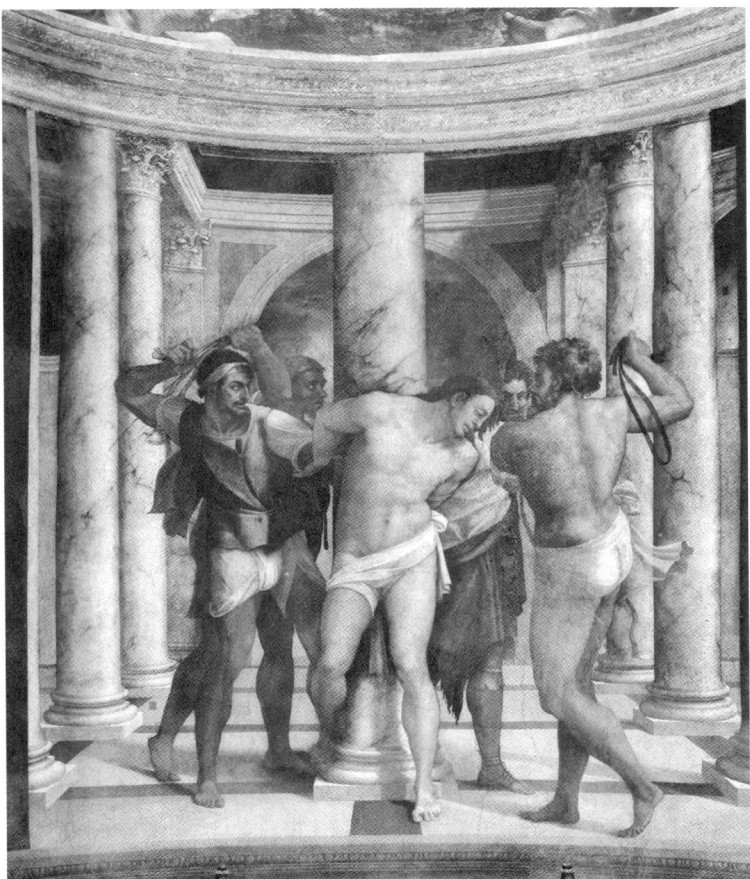

37. Sebastiano del Piombo, *Flagellation of Christ*, mural painting in oil, Borgherini Chapel, San Pietro in Montorio, Rome, 1516–24.

conversation peppered with banter, gossip, and festering jealousy. Lodovico Dolce recounts one such instance when the two were looking at some figures restored by Sebastiano. Suddenly, Titian wondered aloud, "Who is the presumptuous and ignorant fellow who put daubs on these faces?"[68] Sebastiano, of course, was the guilty dauber as Titian probably knew. Like Michelangelo, Titian could wield a wicked tongue.

Down the steep Janiculum hill was the luxury villa of Agostino Chigi, which we know Titian visited with Giorgio Vasari. Vasari recollected that Titian—like many visitors—was enthralled by the room painted in perspective by Baldassare Peruzzi: "And I remember that when I took the Chevalier Tiziano, a most excellent and honoured painter, to see the work, he would by no means believe that it was painted."[69] Whether or not Sebastiano was part of this particular visit, his fresco of the giant Polyphemus must have interested Titian less than Raphael's alluring *Galatea* immediately adjacent. Titian's admiration for Raphael is well documented by contemporaries and was manifested in concrete terms when he saw the seated portrait of Pope Julius II in Santa Maria del Popolo. Desirous of copying the painting (Plate 36), Titian obtained permission to have the picture brought to the Belvedere where he could study it closely and under good lighting conditions.[70] Titian painted his copy of Julius II at the very moment that Michelangelo was installing the tomb of the same deceased pope in San Pietro in Vincoli.

As with most first-time visitors to Rome, Titian immediately went to see "tante belle cose antiche" ("many beautiful antique things").[71] Thanks to his residence in the Belvedere palace, Titian would have seen the most famous antiquities in the papal collection on a daily basis, including the Apollo Belvedere and the astonishing Laocoön, the fame of which long ago had reached Venice.[72] Just one thousand muddy roman feet across Bramante's still incomplete Belvedere court brought Titian to the Sistine Chapel, which he—along with the rest of Rome—surely visited. The recently completed *Last Judgment* was a lightning rod of criticism and sometimes salacious gossip. One of the first critics of the fresco, Pietro Aretino, propagated some outrageous slander that may have prejudiced Titian even if it did not prevent him from admiring Michelangelo's achievement.

No amount of prior knowledge can adequately prepare a visitor to the Sistine Chapel for the experience of the work in person. The chapel and its frescoes never fail to astonish, and there is no reason to think that Titian reacted differently. He surely admired the vast undertaking, absorbed things of interest, and was stimulated to respond creatively, even if not immediately. For contemporaries, the Sistine proved to be a font of inspiration. As a fully mature artist, Titian scarcely required inspiration; on the other hand, he certainly could be inspired and challenged by his highly regarded contemporary.

Years later Titian would paint his version of *Adam and Eve*, albeit in his own preferred medium of oil (Plate 37).[73] In a verdant landscape, Adam and Eve are approached by a cherubic-faced temptress. Titian exposes their weak resistance, leaving open the question—as did Michelangelo—of who is principally at fault for transgressing God's commandment. Adam raises a hesitant and ineffectual hand to forestall Eve, yet he lacks the will and certitude to act more decisively. While Eve, a gloriously luminous ingenue, fearlessly accepts the forbidden fruit, swarthy Adam is rooted to the earth, trembling with indecision.

Although very different, Titian's unique portrayal of the scene reveals an acute understanding of Michelangelo's representation of the same subject (compare Plates 37 and 38). Titian imagines a similarly fraught moment in which Adam is equally at fault for failing to obey God's commandment. Adam impotently watches, reacting with a half-hearted gesture that fails to prevent Eve from accepting the apple. The thumb of his raised hand brushes the roseate nipple of her pert breast, thus exciting an erotic charge where previously there was only innocent nudity. So did Michelangelo electrify the moment by entwining his two figures in a sexually suggestive pose. Has Titian once again upped the ante? He increased the sensuality of the subject by translating Michelangelo's hard-edged drawing and masculinized nudes into the soft, coloristic medium of oil paint. Both artists effectively employed landscape to heighten the psychological drama: the empty plain of Michelangelo's *Expulsion* suggests the bleak life beyond the garden; similarly, Titian's turbulent sky and mountainous landscape anticipate the couple's traumatic exile far from idyllic Eden. Titian's *Adam and Eve* might fruitfully be considered an original invention informed by his experience of Michelangelo: two highly original but not wholly independent visions of sin and transgression.

We see a further example of Titian's intelligent appreciation of Michelangelo's Sistine inventions in his assimilation of the *Libyan Sibyl* (Fig. 38). Along with many contemporaries, Titian was drawn to the muscular yet serene beauty of the north-African Sibyl (a land hazily known to Titian as a result of Venetian commerce and slave trafficking). Michelangelo portrayed the Sibyl in a highly inventive, unnaturally contorted pose. More than a decade later, Titian adapted the figure for the relaxed posterior pose of the lute player in his *Venus and Cupid with a Lutenist* (Plate 39).[74] Titian's is a different genre of picture-making in a radically different context, such that one might be forgiven for doubting any connection between the two. But consider the extreme contrapposto, for which Michelangelo was famous, and the exploitation of the back view to lure the viewer into the picture. Titian has transformed Michelangelo's imposing, uncomfortably twisted Sibyl into a languid lute player engaged in a plushy bedside seduction. One might imagine Titian painting this michelangelesque figure looking longingly at luscious Venus, a supreme example of the artist's own forte: the soft and sensuous nude. Titian has so transformed the figure that it seems

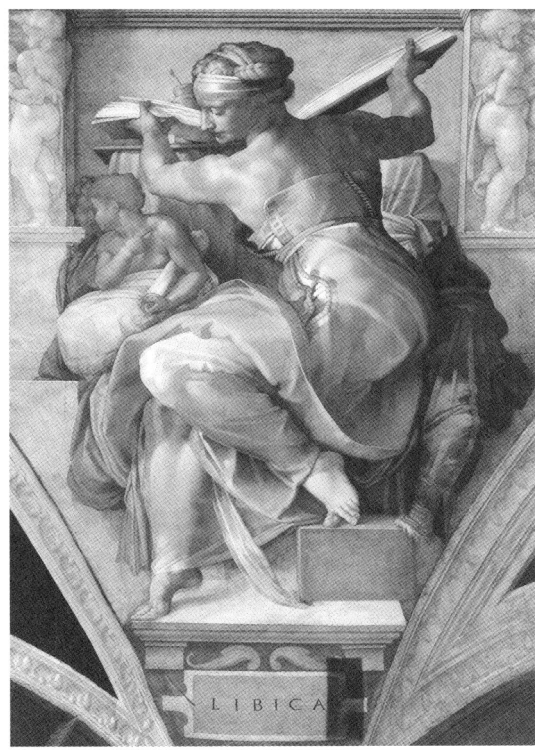

38. Michelangelo,
Libyan Sibyl, fresco,
Sistine Chapel, Vatican
City, 1508–12.

gratuitous to cite Michelangelo as a "source"; however, to overlook Titian's metamorphosis is a failure to acknowledge that he was equally capable of turning artistic ideas into original inventions.

Let us continue to follow Titian around Rome. Even if such peregrinations were limited and brief, and documentation lacking, we can be reasonably certain that Vasari, papal courtiers, or Titian's own curiosity led him to visit another major monument. After a forty-year struggle, and just months prior to Titian's arrival in Rome, Michelangelo finally completed and installed the tomb of Pope Julius II in San Pietro in Vincoli (Fig. 39). In relating the

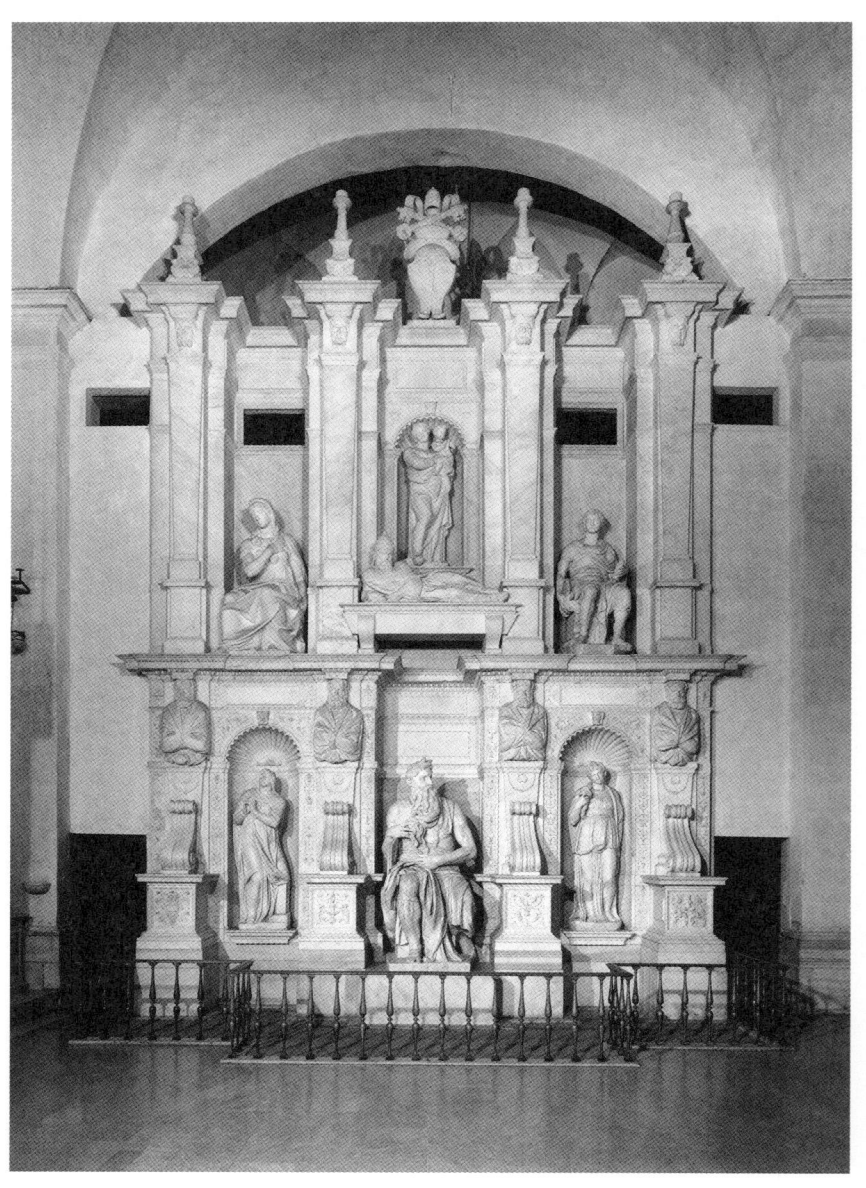

39. Michelangelo, *Tomb of Pope Julius II*, marble, San Pietro in Vincoli, Rome, 1505-45.

long, tortuous history of the project, Ascanio Condivi resorted to calling it a "tragedy." Surely he was characterizing Michelangelo's feeling that "I lost the whole of my youth, chained to this Tomb."[75] Yet, in the end, Michelangelo created one of the grandest and most notable funerary ensembles of the Renaissance, which Condivi concluded "is yet the most impressive to be found in Rome and perhaps anywhere else."[76] It is difficult to imagine that Titian, who must have heard about the project "a bocca" at times during its forty-year gestation, would *not* visit Michelangelo's grandest work of sculpture. It was, moreover, their mutual patron, Guidobaldo della Rovere, who was largely responsible for encouraging Michelangelo to bring the project to completion. In visiting San Pietro in Vincoli, Titian may have been reciprocating the courtesy visit that Michelangelo recently paid him in the Belvedere. Moreover, in having eagerly copied Raphael's masterful portrait of Julius II, the Venetian might reasonably have wished to see how his rival portrayed the "terrible" pope in the artist's preferred medium of marble. While Titian—like many modern visitors—may have paid scant attention to the reclining figure of the pope on the second level of the tomb, he was certainly—as is *every* visitor—struck by the majestic figure of *Moses*.

It was not until many years after his sojourn in Rome that Titian painted a portrait of the Doge Andrea Gritti (Plate 40).[77] Not only would Titian recollect his encounter with the titanic figure of Michelangelo's *Moses*, but he would certainly remember that it was Gritti who first brought the two artists together in Venice in 1529.

Painted shortly after his Roman sojourn and well after Gritti's death in 1538, Titian's commanding image of the doge depends less on life than on Michelangelo, and his recollection of *Moses* (Plate 41). The two imposing figures share similarly assertive poses, fierce gazes, and emphatic hand gestures. Moses glares right, Gritti glares left; both figures, although seated, are composed in a slow-turning contrapposto. A long, sinuous line extends from Moses's horns through his copious beard, spreading into a broad delta of drapery folds. Gritti's lineaments begin with his doge's *corno*—a horned hat—and continue around his bushy beard and down the s-shaped curve of padded buttons adorning his brocaded cloak. In both conceptions, mighty arms and gripping hands forcefully assert themselves, grabbing the viewer's attention. The similarly strong grasping hands alone have convinced many scholars that Titian held Michelangelo's awe-inspiring figure in mind when he painted Gritti.

These are titanic figures—in art and reality. They fill and command space, demanding attention and inspiring awe, one in marble ready to erupt, the other painted on the verge of speaking. Fully aware that they shared Andrea Gritti as an erstwhile patron, it seems particularly appropriate that Titian immortalized the doge by drawing inspiration from Michelangelo's image of awesome grandeur and transcendent majesty.

*   *   *

After six months, it was time for Titian to return to his beloved Serenissima. Like any tourist, Titian brought back to Venice a treasure chest of trinkets, drawn and painted recollections, and probably a selection of prints. Sending these things home, Titian secured a license for a muleteer to travel outside papal territory with a consignment of plaster casts ("pronti di gesso"), clothes ("vestimenti"), and "other stuff" ("alter sue robbe").[78] It is likely that among the three hundred pounds of "pronti di gesso" was his newly acquired plaster cast of Michelangelo's *Risen Christ*, which will make an appearance, much transformed, in Titian's late *Pietà*.

Michelangelo the Painter

One little-considered aspect of Michelangelo's relationship with Titian is his ever-increasing involvement with the art of painting. His claim that "painting is not my art" ("non è mia arte") was more an effort to avoid unwanted tasks than a description of his interests or abilities. Although claiming not to be a painter, Michelangelo repeatedly was drawn to the medium, even if, over the years, he more frequently furnished drawings and designs for others to execute. Initially, friendship with Sebastiano and the challenge of Raphael spurred Michelangelo to enter the lists, that is, compete even if mostly by proxy. In subsequent years, Michelangelo worked with other brilliant colorists: Jacopo Pontormo, Marcello Venusti, and Daniele da Volterra. Each of these collaborations proved to be stimuli to Michelangelo's creativity and a means to imaginatively extend himself in new and widely influential directions. Michelangelo's early reputation was founded on the creation of unique, inimitable works—*Pietà*, *David*, Sistine ceiling; however, he eventually came to recognize the power of multiple production through collaboration and reproduction. How much of this activity—unexpected given his many other obligations—can be credited to his encounters with Titian?

Much in the same manner that he collaborated with Sebastiano and Pontormo previously, Michelangelo furnished drawings to fellow artist Daniele da Volterra (1509–66). A spectacular example of their collaboration is the tour de force, double-sided painting the two artists made for Michelangelo's close friend, the humanist writer Giovanni della Casa, who also happened to be a patron of Titian (Fig. 40).[79] Together, Michelangelo and Daniele designed a painting of *David and Goliath*, showing the same violent decapitation from opposite viewpoints on the front and back of a two-sided slate

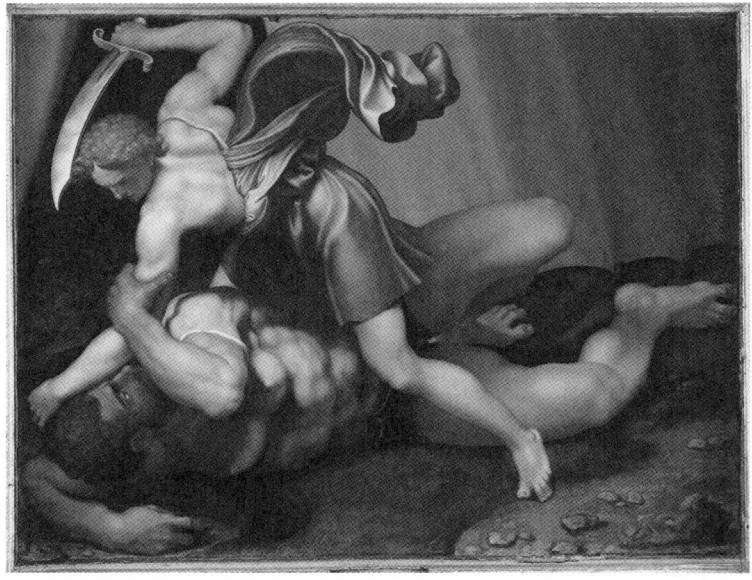

40. Daniele da Volterra, *David and Goliath*, oil on slate, 52.3 × 67.7 in (1.3 × 1.7 m), Musée du Louvre, Paris, 1550s.

panel. Encouraging the viewer to walk around, the scene unfolds in three dimensions, as if it were a sculptural group. In terms of the contemporary *paragone* debate regarding the superiority of painting versus sculpture, this single brilliant panel demonstrates both.

A fierce and determined young David straddles a wounded Goliath who looks in terror at the gleaming scimitar that is about to deliver the decapitating blow. Even twenty years later, Michelangelo recalled the murderous scene from Titian's most famous painting, the *St. Peter Martyr* (Fig. 41). But Michelangelo and Daniele have not only invented a similarly violent murder, they have shown it from opposite vantage points. In a bit of one-upmanship, Michelangelo demonstrated his inventive superiority by turning the murderous scene into a spectator-engaging three-dimensional

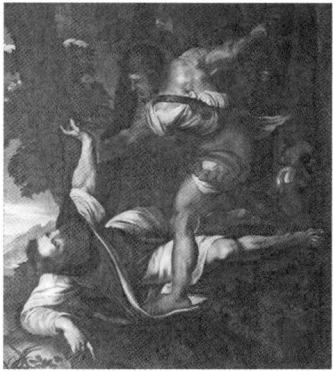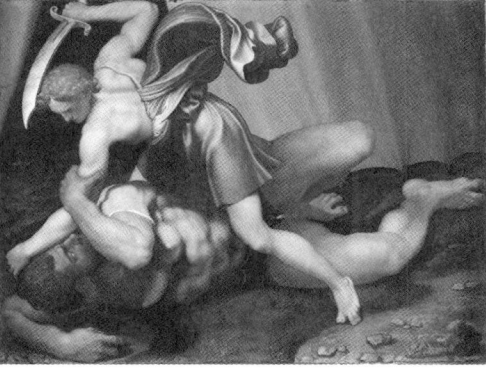

41. Comparison, det. Titian, *Peter Martyr*, and det. Daniele da Volterra, *David and Goliath*.

experience. And he accomplished this in Titian's preferred medium of paint. Recognizing Daniele's ability, Michelangelo continued to furnish drawings to the younger artist, who created paintings after them, including a drawing for an equestrian statue originally destined for the French court.

Marcello Venusti

Shortly after Michelangelo began furnishing sketches to Daniele da Volterra, he embarked on a long and fruitful collaboration with the unassuming but talented painter Marcello Venusti (1512–79).[80] After his disappointment with an increasingly lazy and sometimes irritating Sebastiano (who offered unwanted advice and help in painting the *Last Judgment*), Michelangelo discovered an ideal partner in Venusti. We should take special note here. In the busiest years of his life, and at the height of his creative powers and international fame, Michelangelo *elected* to collaborate with a painter, *this* painter. Michelangelo's extended relationship with Marcello

Venusti is especially surprising given that the septuagenarian was busier than ever, overseeing a half dozen architectural projects in Rome including directing the gigantic enterprise (*cantiere*) of New St. Peter's.

Well before his extended collaboration with Michelangelo, Marcello Venusti enjoyed a successful independent career as a painter of altarpieces and decorative schemes for many important Roman churches. Undoubtedly, he came to Michelangelo's attention when his current patron and supporter, Cardinal Alessandro Farnese, commissioned Venusti to paint a large-scale copy of the *Last Judgment*, now in the Capodimonte museum in Naples. Venusti can be numbered among the many younger men— some forty years younger—to whom Michelangelo was repeatedly drawn in his sunset years. These include Tommaso de' Cavalieri, who was chief among them, as well as Lodovico Beccadelli, the lesser-known Florentine noble Andrea Quaratesi, and the artist's biographer Ascanio Condivi. Each contributed in various ways to enriching Michelangelo's life and stimulating his creativity. The importance of Michelangelo's partnership with Venusti is suggested by the fact that contemporaries referred to Veunsti as "Vostro Marcello," and Michelangelo stood as godfather to Venusti's first child, named Michelangelo.[81]

Michelangelo recognized Venusti's obvious abilities as a painter and chose to work with him on a number of novel creations that enjoyed widespread fame. In this collaborative enterprise, Venusti must be considered much more than a factotum, pupil, or mere imitator of Michelangelo. Michelangelo was drawn to Venusti's highly finished, enamel-like painting, a style much admired, imitated, and copied in the sixteenth century. It was a style diametrically opposite to Titian's increasingly rapid, almost unfinished, "stained" manner (*pittura all macchia*), yet there is good reason to add the Venusti-Michelangelo collaborations to the ongoing dialogue between the Venetian and the Florentine.

Marcello Venusti became a creative partner whose paintings were recognized as Michelangelo inventions, and universally attributed to him, "by his hand" ("di sua mano"). By harnessing Venusti's color to his own precisely made drawings, Michelangelo perfected a union of drawing (disegno) and color (colorito) that he occasionally achieved in his collaborations with Sebastiano and Pontormo but found wanting in Titian's work, as evidenced by his criticism of the *Danaë*. As Michelangelo told Vasari, he admired Titian's color but the painting lacked the discipline of good drawing. With Venusti, Michelangelo struck his ideal balance: precise drawing married to luminous color, a style described by contemporaries as "devoto" and "diligente" (devout and diligent).[82] Moreover, Venusti proved to be a more accommodating partner than Sebastiano who, in any case, was soon to be deceased (d. June 1547).

Together, Michelangelo and Venusti created altarpieces for two important Roman churches: Santa Maria della Pace and San Giovanni in Laterano. Titian saw the Pace altarpiece in person and was aware of the other via a widely circulating engraving. Titian would eventually respond to these original creations, especially given that they were both Annunciations, a subject altogether new to Michelangelo but one that Titian—along with sensuous nudes—could claim as *his* métier.

Prior to his Roman sojourn, Titian had painted the Annunciation at least three times: for Treviso cathedral, for the Scuola di San Rocco in Venice (Plate 42), and for the nuns of Santa Maria degli Angeli on the island of Murano. When the latter painting was completed, the penurious nuns balked at the high price demanded by the artist. Pietro Aretino, who extravagantly praised the picture, suggested sending it instead as a gift to Emperor Charles V. Titian

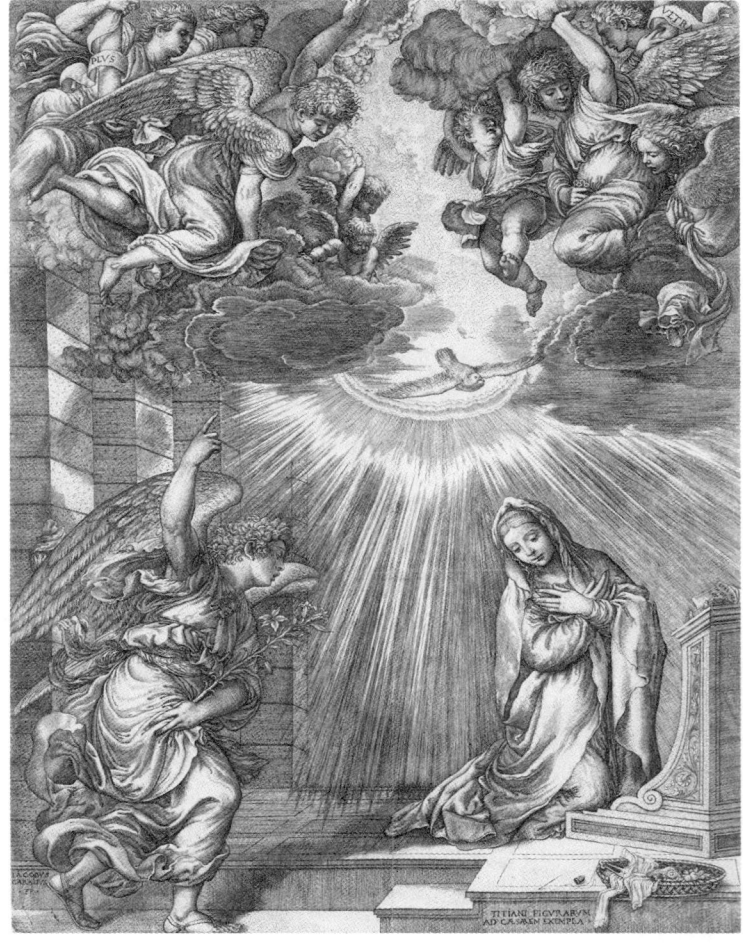

42. Jacapo Caraglio, *Annunciation* after Titian, engraving, 17.87 × 13.62 in (45.5 × 34.4 mm), Metropolitan Museum of Art, New York, 1537.

did so and was handsomely rewarded. Having escaped the provincial nuns of Murano, the painting gained international fame and attention, especially when it was engraved by Jacopo Caraglio in 1536 (Fig. 42).[83] The painting is now lost, but Caraglio's print circulated widely and surely was known to Michelangelo. Thus, well before he and Venusti painted the two major Annunciation altar-pieces in the 1540s, Michelangelo was well aware of this stunning example of the subject. The Annunciation had never before figured as a subject of interest to Michelangelo. Why now, in the 1540s? Is this another case of Michelangelo consciously or unconsciously absorbing the inventions of his contemporary rival?

Michelangelo and Venusti first collaborated on an altarpiece for the Cesi Chapel in Santa Maria della Pace. Michelangelo made a highly finished drawing of an Annunciation that Venusti translated into vivid, metallic colors (Plates 43 and 44). The suffusing light of the Holy Spirit fills the Virgin's Spartan but well-appointed bed-chamber. The claustrophobically close approach of an unusually large, hovering angel causes Mary to turn in startled torsion. She reacts to Gabriel's address with questioning eyes, open mouth, and raised hand—at once a protective and receptive gesture. Compared with hundreds of more conservative precedents, this is a strik-ingly original composition painted with a resplendent color pal-ette. Vasari considered the picture a "novel thing"—a rather tame means of describing something radically new in Michelangelo's art.[84] Vasari was not alone in admiring this highly original painting for it was immediately copied, which was not yet a common prac-tice, especially for altarpieces. Michelangelo's collaborations with Marcello Venusti helped initiate an era of reproductive activity.

Immediately adjacent to the Cesi Chapel is the lavishly deco-rated Chigi Chapel adorned with a frescoed lunette of sibyls by Raphael. The grand yet lyrically expressive figures, painted im-mediately after completion of the Sistine ceiling, were Raphael's response to Michelangelo. We can be certain that Titian visited Santa Maria della Pace, either with Vasari, who was an enthusias-tic admirer of Raphael's sibyls, or with Sebastiano, who was com-missioned to paint the altarpiece "under the figures of Raphael," for which Michelangelo provided the spectacular drawing of the

Resurrected Christ, previously discussed (see Fig. 14).[85] At the same time, Titian inevitably would have seen the newly installed "Michelangelo"—for that is how contemporaries referred to the altarpiece—in the adjacent Cesi Chapel (see Plate 44). Would Titian have perceived another artistic challenge on the part of the self-proclaimed sculptor? Titian had his own ideas about how to paint the subject.

San Giovanni Annunciation

Following the Cesi commission, Michelangelo and Venusti entered into an even more important collaboration—an altarpiece of the *Annunciation* for the Cathedral of Rome, San Giovanni in Laterano. Michelangelo made another highly finished drawing (Fig. 43), translated into radiant color by Venusti, who added the stately domestic setting (Plate 45).[86] The matronly Madonna is interrupted at her reading desk by the sudden appearance of a charging celestial messenger who has just alighted on the marble pavement of her lofty bedchamber. A startled Mary throws open her arms while lowering her gaze to her miraculously full, impregnated womb. Rescued from years of undeserved neglect, the conserved painting is astonishing today for its imposing scale, lustrous color, and three-quarter-life-size figures.

The San Giovanni altarpiece was almost certainly completed after Titian departed Rome; however, as with the Cesi altarpiece, the San Giovanni *Annunciation* was repeatedly copied, and, quite exceptionally, soon appeared as an engraving (Fig. 44). The burgeoning Roman print industry favored prominent monuments and buildings, famous antiquities, and notable ruins. A survey of some three hundred religious prints published by Antonio Lafreri and his heirs reveals that only a handful reproduce altarpieces, usually

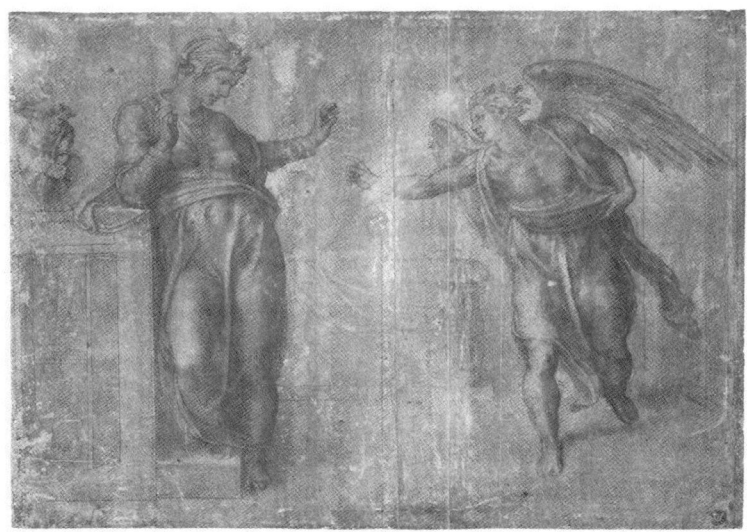

43. Michelangelo, *Annunciation*, black chalk on paper, 16 × 21.5 in (405 × 545 mm), Uffizi G.D.S. (Inv. 229F recto), Florence, 1545/46.

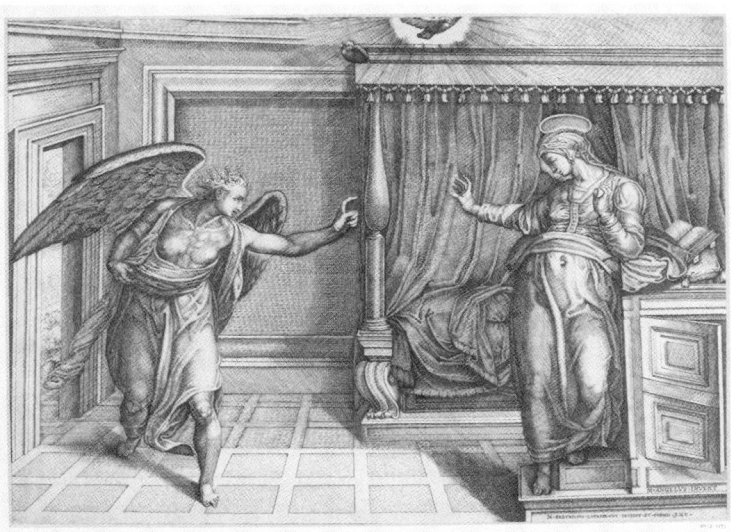

44. Nicholas Beatrizet, *Annunciation* after Michelangelo, engraving, 12 × 16.5 in (304 × 423 mm), Victoria and Albert Museum, London, after 1558.

because the work was part of an important pilgrimage site.[87] It is notable that Michelangelo's altarpiece was engraved almost the moment it was installed in San Giovanni. This is how Titian, having heard about the work in progress, "saw" the San Giovanni *Annunciation* once he returned to Venice in 1546.

The print reverses Michelangelo's composition and reproduces only the lower half of the San Giovanni altarpiece, thereby privileging the two large figures filling a claustrophobically miniaturized space. A broad-winged, bare-chested Gabriel rushes at us even as the angelic apparition turns to gesture emphatically toward an alarmed Mary. The dove of the Holy Spirit descends in a radiating burst of light. The engraving may have attracted Titian's attention precisely because it approximated some of the Venetian's own innovations in representing the Annunciation.

Comparing the engraved images of the two artists' respective Annunciations (see Figs. 42, 44) reveals several similar novel elements, including the aggressive advance and arresting gesture of the large-winged, earth-bound Gabriel, as well as the supernatural illumination that accompanies the descent of the Holy Spirit. Of course, there are many significant differences. In Michelangelo's invention, a standing Mary turns from her tall reading desk and raises her arms in a startled, protective response while Titian's virginal Mary is the model of modesty and *humilitas*. She humbly receives Gabriel while a burst of light and a rhapsodic heavenly host descends upon her interrupted meditations. Although set in a palatial interior, Titian's operatic staging looks nothing like the quietly domestic, high-ceilinged bedchamber that Venusti invented for Michelangelo. Most obviously, Michelangelo eschewed Titian's operatic, proto-Baroque heavenly host for a concentration upon the two protagonists and their significant, multivalent gestures.

Interested in Titian's famous picture but avoiding the Venetian's theatrical extravaganza for a more sober aesthetic, Michelangelo and Venusti created two altarpieces of comparatively restrained invention and easily understood content and spirituality, consonant with the norms of sixteenth-century Counter-Reformatory Rome.[88] Titian, in the more permissive environment of Venice, felt no such constraints. He insisted on having the last word on how to paint an Annunciation.

Return to Venice

As the heat of the Roman summer approached, Titian longed for the lagoon and cooler climes of seaborne Venice. He had painted several masterpieces in Rome, and had experienced the best the city had to offer. But he was glad to return to the pungent smells, mellifluous sounds, and less pervasive religious life of Venice. He would not forget Rome, nor the persons and art he had seen there, but he never would return. He would grow old and ever more distant from his difficult son Pomponio, teach painting to his younger children Orazio and Lavinia, and ultimately find rest in his beloved city. But he still had things to contribute in his ongoing dialogue with a now-distant, ever-overshadowing Michelangelo.

On his way north in June of 1546, Titian stopped in Florence, prompted as much by his avaricious desire to cultivate the Medici ruler as to see the Florentine works of Michelangelo.[89] He met Cosimo de' Medici but no commission was forthcoming, probably because Cosimo already had a favored court portraitist in Agnolo Bronzino, and the Florentine duke failed to appreciate the Venetian's painterly style or bumptious manner. Titian certainly saw Michelangelo's *David* and may have visited the disordered construction site of the still incomplete Medici Chapel. However, his Florentine visit was brief, and he soon resumed his journey home.

Having experienced infertile ground in Florence, Titian renewed his assault upon Farnese favor. Soon after his return to Venice and still hoping to obtain a benefice for his eldest son, Titian wrote to Alessandro Farnese affirming his willingness to continue in the cardinal's service.[90] Ultimately, Titian ceded the Farnese to Michelangelo, turning his primary attention to Emperor Charles V and his son Philip II, the most important patrons and collectors of Titian paintings.

Some considered Michelangelo the greatest contemporary artist, but he, Tiziano Vecellio, was secure in his position as the superior painter—the "Prince of Painters" the "new Apelles." Carrying with him the baggage of his Roman sojourn, Titian was not only at the apex of painting but was more than ready to make his own final statements in the medium of which he reigned supreme. Since Titian would never again visit Rome, his competition with Michelangelo necessarily evolved into a distant, mostly personal affair. As they entered their twilight years, both Michelangelo and Titian became ever more dedicated to their legacies and the social advancement of their families. Contemporaries may have described Michelangelo as "Divine," but he, Titian, certainly could paint a more impressive, dramatic, and sublime Annunciation.

San Salvador Annunciation

Some fifteen years after his return to Venice, Titian had the opportunity to paint another *Annunciation*, for the church of San Salvador close to the Rialto bridge (Plate 46).[91] At the apogee of his inventive and painterly maturity, Titian created a stunning work that openly declares his genius in reimagining this familiar, much beloved, traditional subject. In a shallow but grandiose space flanked by lofty fluted columns, Mary and Gabriel enact a theatrical salutation while a multitudinous angelic host descends in a cloudburst of supernatural light. The large-winged and larger-than-life Gabriel alights on the checkered marble pavement, abruptly interrupting Mary's devotions. Her arm rests on her prie-dieu, and her long, elegant fingers lightly clasp a book. Light suffuses the picture and illumines her face as she half turns in startled surprise, instinctively raising hand and arm in a defensive gesture that, with the open-handed lifting of her veil may simultaneously be read as a receptive greeting. Thus, a picture of dramatic action eloquently expresses a range of successive emotions, from disquiet to eventual submission, from initial alarm to humble acceptance. Once again, the master painter has transformed a church altarpiece and a staid religious subject into a melodramatic narrative.

Is there some recollection of Michelangelo in the aggressive advent of the angel Gabriel, the precipitate torsion of the Madonna, and her startled, multivalent gestures (compare Fig. 44 and Plate 46)? Was Titian piqued by Michelangelo's foray into his domain of expertise—as presumptuous as if Titian had the temerity to carve marble or create a *Pietà* (which, in fact, he would do shortly)? We might see Titian's San Salvador *Annunciation* as a delayed response to Michelangelo—a declaration of his inventive and painterly superiority, of Venetian colorito over the dry and antiquarian manner of Florentine and Roman disegno.

Among the many novel aspects of Titian's picture is the unusually physical and sensual Virgin with full, accentuated bosom.[92] Although clothed, Titian's figure exudes a physicality far more seductive than Michelangelo's amply bosomed, manly Madonnas. In the engraving of the San Giovanni altarpiece (see Fig. 44), Gabriel's exposed breasts and nipples are not remotely sensuous or appealing. Titian was the artist who knew how to heighten sexual intensity, even in a religious picture. Michelangelo's attempts at erotically charged religious picture making—from the *Noli me Tangere* to the Annunciations painted in collaboration with Venusti—leave us mostly perplexed and coolly indifferent.

Titian's generous handling of paint and heavy *impasto* are diametrically opposite—and perhaps a critique of—Michelangelo's tightly drawn figures and Venusti's highly finished, enamel-like manner. Painted in his late, bravura style, Titian's picture is a theatrical extravaganza that explodes with light and color, sound and spectacle. He transforms the supposedly humble abode of the Virgin into an airy, colonnaded marble palace, more reminiscent of the architecture of Rome than anything in Venice. Determined to demonstrate that *he* was the master of sensuality, dramatic narrative, and captivating color, Titian was not going to allow his intermittent tit-for-tat rivalry with Michelangelo to end on a dry Tuscan note. With the San Salvador *Annunciation*, Titian created a Venetian Baroque opera compared to Michelangelo's arid Roman oratory.

In Titian's Thoughts

On a cold February day in 1564, Titian learned of Michelangelo's death in Rome. Titian's success in outliving his greatest rival was tinged with melancholic thoughts of his own advanced age and imminent demise. Now Titian could decisively claim to be the greatest *living* artist. There was some local competition from an aggressively ambitious Jacopo Tintoretto and a rapidly rising Paolo Veronese, but Titian was indisputably the reigning genius of Venetian painting.

Giorgio Vasari concluded his first edition of his *Lives of the Artists* (1550) with a hagiographic paean to his Tuscan hero,

Michelangelo, the *only* living artist warranting inclusion. Titian was barely mentioned, and did not merit a life of his own. Clearly irritated by the short shrift given to Venetians, Lodovico Dolce, who deemed Titian "another Michelangelo," wrote his dialogue *L'Aretino* (1557), in which he asserted the superiority of both Raphael and Titian to Michelangelo.[93] Just a decade later, responding to suggestions and criticisms, Vasari published his much-expanded *Lives of the Artists* (1568). And this, for Titian, was the last straw.

Vasari traveled to Venice in 1565/66 specifically to gather material for the new edition of his *Lives*. He visited Titian's studio, but showed little sympathy for the painter's late style because "his natural powers started to decline."[94] Titian had every reason to be highly irritated with the myopic Vasari. In his second edition of the *Lives*, Vasari included a life of Titian; however, it was a paltry account, one-fifth the length of the bloated life Vasari devoted to Michelangelo.[95] Vasari never once referred to Titian as "divine," a sobriquet he used nearly forty times in reference to Michelangelo and his work. The Venetian was a "pittore eccellente" who painted many "bellissimi" pictures for which he was well paid, but in Vasari's view Titian was not Michelangelo's equal, nor did he ever rise to the level of "divine."

How might Titian have reacted to such an ungenerous amputation of his life and reputation? Of course, complaints about bias and inadequacies in Vasari are legion. For example, a generation later Annibale Carracci was infuriated at Vasari's deficient treatment of Titian, writing blistering comments in his copy of the bestselling book.[96] Surely, Titian was equally annoyed, if not outraged. As Michelangelo was prompted to respond to Vasari with a counternarrative written by his friend and pupil, Ascanio Condivi, so Titian had good reason to offer a riposte, expressed in his preferred medium of paint.

In the Detroit Institute of Arts hangs a late painting of *Judith with the Head of Holofernes*, Titian's only known depiction of this subject (Plate 47).[97] We do not know why or for whom Titian painted this picture, and why now, shortly after the appearance of the new edition of Giorgio Vasari's *Lives of the Artists* (1568). Judith, an attractive, nubile woman in a low-cut, translucent chemise glances slyly at us with disconcerting self-assurance. Gripping a sword in her right hand, she thrusts an ugly decapitated head at the viewer. She is the biblical heroine, Judith, adorned with pearl earrings and necklace, who seduced and murdered the Assyrian general, Holofernes—the ruthless oppressor of her people. Clutching the disheveled hair, Judith is about to drop the heavy head into the sack held open by her Black servant. Likely an adolescent North African slave, Judith's accomplice wears a worn velvet doublet, cloth headband, and pearl earring. After first noting Judith impassively looking at us, we are drawn to the young page staring intently at the grotesque head. We note the broad forehead, receding hairline, sunken eyes, large misshapen nose, and a glimpse of facial hair. Is this horrible thing a recognizable likeness? It is well known that Titian, like Giorgione before him and Caravaggio afterward, sometimes imposed his own image when depicting evil and despicable figures. But this horrific apparition is *not* Titian.

Judith's triumph seems less heroic than vindictive. Fastening us with a supercilious expression, she forcefully thrusts the head at us, almost demanding that we look upon the dreadful visage. Could this be Michelangelo who, Titian would recall, painted the same subject in a Sistine ceiling spandrel? The head bears a striking resemblance to the woodcut portrait of Michelangelo included in the 1568 edition of Vasari's *Lives of the Artists* (Fig. 45). Or, is Titian directing his ire at Giorgio Vasari, given that the head also bears some semblance to Vasari's self-portrait included in the same second edition of his *Lives* (Fig. 46)?[98] Using his daughter Lavinia as

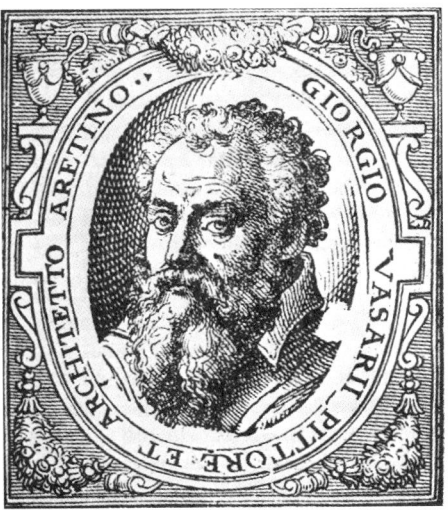

45. *Portrait of Michelangelo* from Giorgio Vasari, *Lives of the Artists*, woodcut, 1568.

46. *Portrait of Giorgio Vasari* from Giorgio Vasari, *Lives of the Artists*, woodcut, 1568.

a model for Judith, Titian successfully decapitates both his rival artist and the niggardly writer. Or, might Titian's daughter Lavinia, also a painter, have painted this vindication of her slighted father? The painting might also be read as a larger statement of the superiority of Venice over Florence. Judith, a masculinized popular heroine of Venice, has decapitated the sculptor of David, the homoerotic hero of Florence.

Having outlived his greatest rival, and thoroughly annoyed by Vasari, the Detroit painting is a declaration of Titian as ultimate victor, triumphant over all, *the* greatest living artist.

*   *   *

Michelangelo was dead, yet his passing could have afforded Titian small comfort. Yes, Titian was alive and still painting, but like most elderly septuagenarians, he was preoccupied with thoughts of death and his legacy. Was he aware that Michelangelo had been similarly obsessed with his legacy and the future of the Buonarroti family? Michelangelo's fame was enshrined in the written biographies that he helped shape. Titian, at the uncontested pinnacle of *his* fame, turned to paint in order to create a fitting and lasting memorial.

Titian heard about the lavish funeral rites accorded Michelangelo, and may even have seen the sumptuous volume published in commemoration of the extravagant event.[99] He certainly heard about the peculiar sanctification of Michelangelo whose "incorruptible" body was still sweet-smelling more than three weeks after his death. "Il Divino" was interred in an impressive monument in the Florentine pantheon of Santa Croce where he joined the most illustrious Florentines of previous centuries, Machiavelli and Leonardo Bruni among them. Shortly after Michelangelo's internment, Titian sent a letter praising Michelangelo's funerary arrangements, inquiring whether he might also be inscribed as member of the Florentine Academia del Disegno, knowing full well that Michelangelo had been appointed honorary head of the newly established institution.[100] Even in death, Titian continued the rivalry with his Florentine counterpart . . . to little avail.

The Two Pietàs

In his eighties, Titian began one of the largest and most ambitious paintings of his career, the *Pietà* now in the Accademia gallery in Venice (Plate 48).[101] It was the picture that Titian intended as his personal grave memorial, something of a last will and testament. Like Michelangelo, who had similar intentions in carving the Florentine *Pietà*, Titian never finished the painting. Perhaps he could

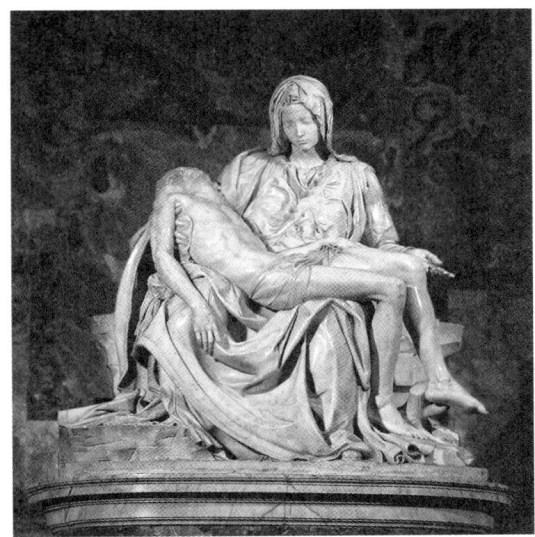

47. Michelangelo, *Pietà*, marble, 5.75 × 6.25 ft (174 × 195 cm), St. Peter's Basilica, Vatican City, 1497–99.

not finish his *Pietà* for the same reason that stymied Michelangelo: to complete the work was to acknowledge the end of life and resign oneself to death. Both artists—in their respective media of marble and paint—included themselves in these final unfinished testaments, as humble supplicants in physical contact with Christ their savior.

Titian's *Pietà* is a large canvas, nearly thirteen by eleven feet, painted in his late, bravura *alla macchia* manner (literally "stained," roughly finished).[102] A distraught Mary Magdalene rushes at us in disheveled distress, gesturing wildly, drapery flying, a plangent cry issuing from her open mouth. Seated in an ample Roman niche under a glittering mosaic, Mary tenderly presents us with the ravaged body of her son. The rusticated architecture suggests Rome; the central figure group recalls Michelangelo's Rome *Pietà* (Fig. 47). Thirty years after seeing Michelangelo's early sculpture, Titian adapted the sublime invention of his rival and the architecture of the Eternal City to express his own harrowing image of death.

Titian portrays himself as the kneeling, beseeching penitent; gently grasping Christ's dangling arm and hand. As Michelangelo cast himself as Nicodemus helping to lower the body of Christ in his Florentine *Pietà*, so Titian partakes in the last rites, yearning to touch his Lord and assist in his burial. In the lower left corner, a putto bends over a white vase in a pose similar to many that Titian may have seen in Michelangelo's *Last Judgment* or the Pauline Chapel. Likewise, the cross-body gesture of the Hellespontic Sibyl embracing the cross—including her explicitly pointing index finger—recalls Michelangelo's *Risen Christ*, a plaster cast of which Titian acquired during his Roman sojourn. As *Moses* sat in Michelangelo's studio for forty years—a perpetual reminder of unfinished work—so might the cast of Michelangelo's *Risen Christ*, which Titian brought back from Rome, have perpetually reminded him of his Florentine rival. Knowing that Michelangelo was celebrated as the master of the three arts of painting, sculpture, and architecture, so Titian displays his artistic virtuosity by including all three in this single painting. But, in the final analysis and at this late moment in Titian's career, such instances of artistic reference were inspired less by rivalry than reverent emulation, subservient to Titian's similar desire for salvation and the forgiveness of his sins.

Titian's *Pietà* is a highly personal statement that pays subtle and sensitive tribute to the only contemporary who challenged his position as the world's greatest artist. With Michelangelo dead for more than a decade, the question of jealous rivalry had subsided. In painting his epitaph, Titian confronted their shared concerns about death and salvation, legacy and immortality.

Conclusion

Titian's San Salvador *Annunciation* and his *Pietà* were the final instances of his extended artistic dialogue with Michelangelo. But at the end of this forty-year exchange, we are left with Titian's pressing desire for the last word. The San Salvador *Annunciation*, the Detroit *Judith*, and the *Pietà*, in different ways, were all declarations of Titian's preeminence. Michelangelo had his sycophantic biographers, Titian his supremely articulate brush. Ultimately, however, print proved more powerful than paint. In writing of Titian, Giorgio Vasari echoed Michelangelo's criticism of Venetian art when he wrote of Titian's late paintings: "But these works, though they have some good aspects . . . in fact fall short of the perfection of his other pictures."[1] In clinging to disegno, proper drawing, and the principles of central Italian picture making, Vasari was unable to appreciate the genius of Titian's late bravura painting.

Titian had his own literary paladins in Pietro Aretino and Lodovico Dolce, both of whom were relentless in promoting their friend. Yet, no one could match Vasari's success in the contemporary literary arena. It was Vasari—not the Venetian authors Pietro Aretino, Lodovico Dolce, Paolo Pino, Francesco Sansovino, or Carlo Ridolfi—who wrote a best-selling book. More than anyone,

Vasari shaped and codified our notion of Renaissance art, the superiority of Tuscan disegno, and the supremacy of Michelangelo in all fields of artistic endeavor. Still today, undergraduates want to learn first about the heroes of Florentine art: Giotto, Botticelli, Leonardo and, above all, Michelangelo, well before they embrace the great Venetian artists.

In the centuries following their deaths, Titian's artistic production continued to have a profound and widespread impact, while Michelangelo's fame and importance faded, to be revived in the nineteenth century, spurred by the fourth centenary celebrations of his birth in 1875.[2] Titian's paintings are found in museums and collections throughout the world, but this widespread dispersal makes it more difficult to measure his legacy and popularity. Today, Michelangelo's Rome *Pietà*, *David*, and the Sistine Chapel are among the most popular tourist destinations in the world. Titian does not enjoy comparable crowds of admirers, nor does his art elicit similar Stendhal-syndrome-like reactions from his viewers.

Scholars have traditionally linked the two artists mainly by comparing figural poses with Titian being the primary beneficiary of these formal comparisons and presumed borrowings. However, as we have seen, the two artists' early careers developed largely independent of one another. Each artist had only vague and indirect knowledge of the other and no direct experience of their respective art. This all changed with Michelangelo's diplomatic visit to Ferrara in 1529 when, in encountering Titian's paintings for the first time, scales fell from his eyes. Michelangelo, in fact, was the first to see a work by the other, and the first to react to the challenge posed by what he perceived to be a formidable contemporary rival.

The unspoken competition between the two most famous artists of their time was fueled by two brief encounters and a long, albeit distant rivalry characterized by sincere interest and mutual competitive regard. Michelangelo and Titian were *already* famous by the time they first met in 1529, and they were extravagantly famous by the time they met again in Rome in 1546. They did not *need* to compete, but they did . . . in their own way, unbeknownst to many, for it was mostly a private dialogue carried on intermittently by the artists themselves.

Over the course of their exceptionally long lives and careers, the two artists dealt with an astonishing number of the same persons and patrons, including a king and a pope, a doge and a sultan, five dukes, four Marchesi, and at least two cardinals and a bishop. They shared a handful of friends and dozens of acquaintances. They were known to and gossiped about by everyone. For forty years, they were attentive, admiring, and sometimes emulating, intermittently competing, yet never imitating one another. They were polite but not friends, mostly distant but constantly aware of the other. Ultimately, the two artists faced the same imperatives of money, fame, family, frustration, war, plague, legacy, old age, and finally death. Four hundred years later, Matisse and Picasso would engage in a similar longtime rivalry that spurred both artists to ever greater creativity and invention.

* * *

The entire artistic and literary community of Florence gathered to memorialize Michelangelo's death in 1564. Duke Cosimo de' Medici underwrote the extravagant exequies and Lionardo Buonarroti, Michelangelo's nephew and heir, paid for the expensive funerary monument erected in Santa Croce. Whether or not we admire Michelangelo's tomb, it is a sumptuous memorial created to pay respectful homage to Florence's greatest artist and reclaimed native son (Fig. 48). At Titian's death in August 1576, the

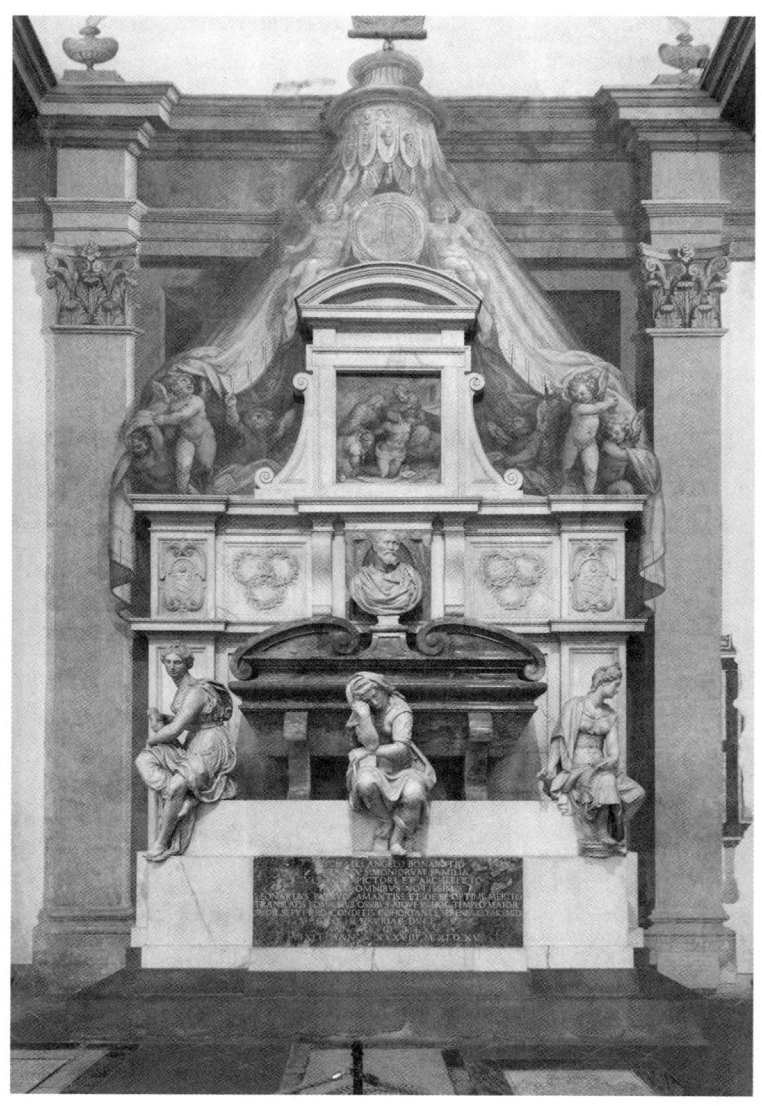

48. *Tomb of Michelangelo*, marble, h. c. 20 ft (c. 600 cm), Sta. Croce, Florence, 1570.

artistic community of Venice made elaborate plans to pay equal respect to *their* most famous artist, modeled on those honoring Michelangelo. But unfortunately, Titian died during a virulent outbreak of plague and nothing came of these efforts.[3] Titian was buried not in Venice's Pantheon of San Giovanni e Paolo but hurriedly in the lesser basilica of Santa Maria Glorioso dei Frari, where his grave was marked by a simple floor tile.

Only in the nineteenth century—nearly three-hundred years after Titian's death—did Luigi Zandomeneghi erect the pompous neoclassical wall monument that we see in the church today (Fig. 49).[4] While thousands of tourists pay daily homage to Michelangelo's tomb, few persons pay equal or any attention to the bombastic pile honoring Titian. The respective funerary monuments of the two greatest artists of the Renaissance tell a tale of their posthumous reputations, but not the interesting story of their long-term mutual regard and reciprocal creativity—a tale of genius and rivalry, a tale of titans.

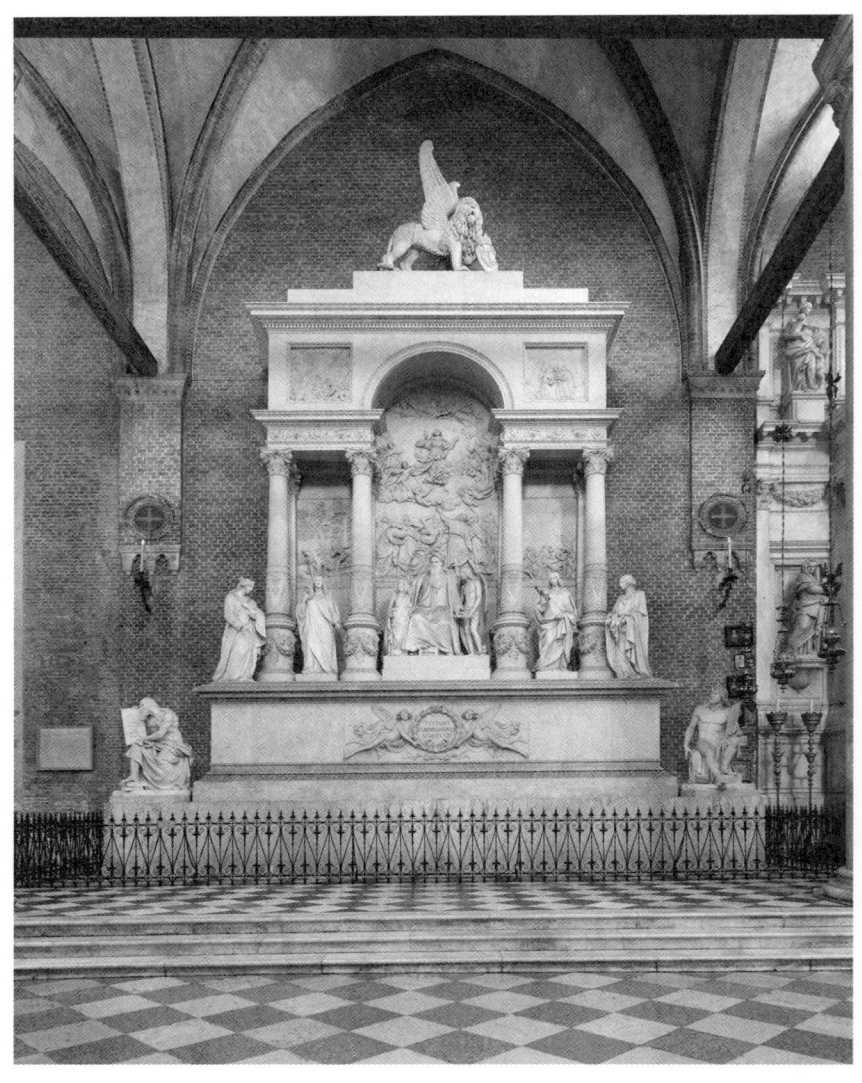

49. Luigi Zandomeneghi, *Tomb of Titian*, marble, Santa Maria Gloriosa dei Frari, Venice, 1838–52.

Acknowledgments

This book is the fruit of a forty-five-year career studying and writing on Michelangelo. Indeed, the seeds of this story were sown in my PhD dissertation written with the late Howard Hibbard and David Rosand (Columbia University, 1983). Generous and considerate mentors, Hibbard and Rosand excited my interest in Tuscan/Roman *disegno* and Venetian *colorito*. In subsequent years, I incurred many debts—far too many to list here. Rather, I wish to acknowledge those persons who specifically helped me in completing this book.

First and foremost, my sincerest and deepest thanks are extended to Paul Barolsky, Deborah Parker, and Maria Ruvoldt, each of whom read the entire manuscript, offering invaluable suggestions and necessary corrections. Errors, however, remain mine.

In multiple ways, the following persons have helped and advised me in this project; the impersonal alphabetical list, however, does not reflect the true importance of these *cari amici*: Bernadine Barnes, C. D. Dickerson, Andrea Donati, Martha Dunkelman, Esther Gabel, Charles Hope, Paul Joannides, Ralph Lieberman, Livio Pestilli, and James Saslow.

I thank Patrick Hathaway for the beautifully crafted maps of Rome and Venice. I am happy to acknowledge the insightful ideas of my current PhD students: Julie James, Caitlin Petty, and Emily Thompson. I am deeply indebted to Betha Whitlow, Hannah Weir, and Mary Sulavik for handling—with competence and good cheer—the tangled world of images and rights.

Michelle Komie has been a friend, editor extraordinaire, and enthusiastic champion of this idea from the beginning. Thank you.

And finally, I am deeply grateful for Beth Fagan, my partner, tireless editor, and companion in all things Italian, a half century after meeting in Bologna in 1974.

Notes

Preface

1. The anecdote is related by Carlo Ridolfi, *Le maraviglie dell'arte: Ovvero, Le vite degli illustri pittori veneti e dello stato* (Venice, 1648); see Carlo Ridolfi, *The Life of Titian*, ed. and trans. Julia and Peter Bondanella (University Park, PA, 1996), 95.

2. Pliny, *Nat. Hist.* XXXV:85.

3. William E. Wallace and Eric Denker, "Michelangelo and Seats of Power," *Artibus et Historiae* 72 (2015): 199–210.

4. Francesco Sansovino, *Sansovino's Venice*, trans. Vaughan Hart and Peter Hicks (New Haven, 2017), 266n173.

Prologue

1. Enzo Noè Girardi, *Rime: Michelangiolo Buonarroti* (Bari, 1960), no. 267.

2. Ruth Wedgwood Kennedy, "Apelles Redivius," in *Essays in Memory of Karl Lehman: Marsyas Supplement 1* (New York, 1964), 160–70. See also Paul Hills, *Venetian Colour* (New Haven, 1999), 201; Norman E. Land, "Poetry and Anecdote in Carlo Ridolfi's *Life of Titian*," in *The Cambridge Companion to Titian*, ed. Patricia Meilman (Cambridge, 2004), 216–20, and Tamara Smithers, *The Cults of Raphael and Michelangelo: Artistic Sainthood and Memorials as a Second Life* (New York, 2023), 36–41 and passim. Michelangelo was first described as "divine"—"Michel, più che mortale, Angel divino"—by

Lodovico Ariosto in the second edition of *Orlando Furioso* (1532), the same edition in which Titian is first mentioned; see Paul Barolsky, *Michelangelo's Nose: A Myth and Its Maker* (University Park, PA, 1990), and Patricia A. Emison, *Creating the "Divine" Artist: From Dante to Michelangelo* (Leiden, 2004), 134–54 and passim.

3. Giorgio Vasari, *Le vite de' più eccellenti pittori, scultori e architettori nelle redazioni del 1550 e 1568*, ed. Rosanna Bettarini, 6 vols. (Florence, 1966–87), 6:164 (hereafter cited as Vasari-Bettarini); English translation from Giorgio Vasari, *Lives of the Artists*, trans. George Bull (London, 1965), 455 (hereafter cited as Vasari-Bull). Lodovico Dolce confirms that Michelangelo saw the *Danaë* "with amazement more than once"; see Mark Roskill, ed., *Dolce's "Aretino" and Venetian Art Theory of the Cinquecento* (New York, 1968), 110–11.

4. "Una femina ignuda, figurata per una Danae, che aveva in grembo Giove trasformato in pioggia d'oro" (Vasari-Bettarini, 6:164; trans. Vasari-Bull, 455). The painting of *Danaë* is currently in the Capodimonte Museum in Naples; see Harold E. Wethey, *The Paintings of Titian*, vol. 3, *The Mythological and Historical Paintings* (London, 1975), cat. no. 5 (hereafter, Wethey, *Titian: Mythological and Historical Paintings*); Peter Humfrey, *Titian: The Complete Paintings* (Ghent, 2007), cat. no. 144 (hereafter Humfrey).

5. "Dopo, partiti che furono da lui, ragionandosi del fare di Tiziano, il Buonarruoto lo comendò assai, dicendo che molto gli piaceva il colorito suo e la maniera, ma che era un peccato che a Vinezia non s'imparasse da principio a disegnare bene" (Vasari-Bettarini, 6:164; trans. Vasari-Bull, 455).

6. See Leatrice Mendelsohn, *Paragoni: Benedetto Varchi's Due Lezioni and Cinquecento Art Theory* (Ann Arbor, MI, 1982).

7. Paola Barocchi and Renzo Ristori, eds., *Il Carteggio di Michelangelo*, 5 vols. (Florence, 1965–83) 4:265–66 (hereafter cited as *Carteggio*); trans. E. H. Ramsden, *The Letters of Michelangelo*, 2 vols. (London, 1963), 2:75 (hereafter cited as Ramsden).

8. Rona Goffen, *Renaissance Rivals: Michelangelo, Leonardo, Raphael, Titian* (New Haven, 2002), chap. 7; Paul Joannides, "Titian and Michelangelo / Michelangelo and Titian," in *The Cambridge Companion to Titian*, ed. Patricia Meilman (Cambridge, 2004), 121–45.

9. *Carteggio*, 1:8.

Part I: 1500–1545

1. See William E. Wallace, "Michelangelo's *Leda*: The Diplomatic Context," *Renaissance Studies* 15 (2001): 487.

2. *Carteggio*, 4:3.

3. On diplomats and diplomacy, see, Garrett Mattingly, *Renaissance Diplomacy* (New York, 1970); Donald E. Queller, *The Office of the Ambassador in the Middle Ages* (Princeton, 1976); Melissa M. Bullard, "The Language of Diplomacy," in *Lorenzo il Magnifico: Image and Anxiety, Politics and Finance*, ed. Melissa M. Bullard (Florence, 1994), 81–109; Paulo Preto, *I servizi segreti di Venezia* (Milan, 1994); Isabella Lazzarini, "Renaissance Diplomacy," in *The Italian Renaissance State*, ed. Andrea Gamberini and Isabella Lazzarini (Cambridge, 2012), 425–43; Catherine Fletcher, *Diplomacy in Renaissance Rome: The Rise of the Resident Ambassador* (Cambridge, 2015), and Stefano Andretta, Lucien Bély, Alexander Koller and Géraud Poumarède, eds., *Esperienza e diplomazia: Saperi, pratiche culturali e azione diplomatica nell'Èta moderna (sec. XV–XVIII)* (Rome, 2020). Eric Dursteler has noted "the elusive character of quotidian dialogue . . . speech acts are fleeting and words are slippery witnesses—they are uttered and immediately evaporate, rarely leaving even a faint archival residue" (Eric Dursteler, "Language and Gender in the Early Modern Mediterranean," *Renaissance Quarterly* 75, no. 1 [2022]: 3). On the Florentine penchant for *ricordanze*, diaries, histories, and chronicles, see Ann E. Moyer, *The Intellectual World of Sixteenth-Century Florence* (Cambridge, 2020), esp. chap. 3, "Florentine Histories," 71–122.

4. William E. Wallace, "Michelangelo's O," *Source: Notes in the History of Art* 40, no. 4 (2021): 234–40, with references.

5. William E. Wallace, "Michelangelo in and out of Florence Between 1500 and 1508," in *Leonardo, Michelangelo, and Raphael in Renaissance Florence from 1500 to 1508*, ed. Sarah Hager (Washington, DC, 1992), 55–88; William E. Wallace, "How Did Michelangelo Become a Sculptor?," in *The Genius of the Sculptor in Michelangelo's Work* (Montreal, 1992), 151–67; and William E. Wallace, *Michelangelo: The Artist, the Man and His Times* (New York, 2010), chap. 3.

6. Ascanio Condivi, *Michelangelo: Life, Letters, and Poetry*, trans. George Bull (Oxford, 1987), 61 (hereafter cited as Condivi-Bull). On the episode, see Caroline Elam, "'Che ultima mano?': Tiberio Calcagni's *postille* to Condivi's

Life of Michelangelo," in Ascanio Condivi, *Vita di Michelagnolo Buonarroti*, ed. Giovanni Nencioni (Florence, 1998), xlii–xliv (herafter Condivi-Nencioni). A fictional but credible account of Michelangelo's sojourn to Constantinople is related by Mathias Énard, *Tell Them of Battles, Kings & Elephants* (New York, 2010).

7. On ekphrasis, see Ruth Webb, *Ekphrasis, Imagination and Persuasion in Ancient Rhetorical Theory and Practice* (Burlington, VT, 2009); Michael Baxandall, *Giotto and the Orators* (Oxford, 1971), esp. 85–96, and, as it relates to Michelangelo, see Jaś Elsner, "Art History as Ekphrasis," *Art History* 33 (2010): 10–27 (I thank Nate Jones for this latter reference).

8. Condivi-Bull, 24–25. The marginal notation in Condivi reads: "Questa era, disse, una pazzia venutami per detta. Ma s'io fusse sicuro di vivere 4 volte quanto son vissuto, sare'vi io entrato" (Condivi-Nencioni, xlii).

9. Harold E. Wethey, *The Paintings of Titian*, vol. 1, *The Religious Paintings* (London, 1969), cat. no. 95 (hereafter Wethey, *Titian: Religious Paintings*); Humfrey, cat. no. 15c.

10. Johannes Wilde, *Venetian Art from Bellini to Titian*, ed. Giles Robertson (Oxford, 1974), 123. As is generally recognized, the observation was first made by Theodor Hetzer in the *Allgemeines Lexikon der bildenden Künstler*, ed. Ulrich Thieme and Hans Becker, vol. 34 (Leipzig, 1940), 161. Among the many scholars who have repeated and expanded upon the Hetzer / Wilde observation are Charles Hope, *Titian* (London, 1980), 27–28; Creighton E. Gilbert, "Some Findings on Early Works of Titian," *Art Bulletin* 62 (1980): 36–75; Paul Joannides, *Titian to 1518. The Assumption of Genius* (New Haven, 2001), 115–16; Paul Joannides, "Titian and Michelangelo," 125–26, and Goffen, *Renaissance Rivals*, 267–68.

11. Gilbert, "Some Findings," 36, 38, and Creighton E. Gilbert, "Titian and the Reversed Cartoons of Michelangelo," in *Michelangelo on and off the Sistine Ceiling* (New York, 1994), 151–55. The comparison depends on the group being reversed, as in an engraving. However, in 1511 when Titian was painting in the Santo, there were no such reproductive engravings, which mainly began appearing in the 1540s; see Bernadine Barnes, *Michelangelo in Print: Reproductions as Response in the Sixteenth Century* (Surrey, UK, 2010), 3, and Alida Moltedo, ed., *La Sistina Riprodotta* (Rome, 1991). Early engravings focused mainly on individual figures of the prophets and sibyls, as well as the series of the *ignudi* engraved by Adamo Scultori. There are no early engravings or

drawings of the narratives, especially not from a moment when even the papal curia had limited access to the still incomplete chapel.

12. Discussing various hypotheses regarding Lorenzino de' Medici, the assassin of his relative Duke Alessandro de' Medici, Stefano Dall'Aglio notes multiple instances where "a legitimate hypothesis is transformed into an uncontested historical fact"; see Stefano Dall'Aglio, *The Duke's Assassin* (New Haven, 2015), 127.

13. Wethey, *Titian: Religious Paintings*, cat. no. 93; Humfrey, cat. no. 8A.

14. Wethey, *Titian: Religious Paintings*, cat. nos. 80 and 16, respectively; Humfrey, cat. nos. 34 and 35.

15. Wethey, *Titian: Religious Paintings*, cat. nos. 119 and cat. no. 63, respectively; Humfrey, cat. nos. 18 and 78.

16. Wethey, *Titian: Religious Paintings*, cat. no. 92; Humfrey, cat. no 63.

17. Harold E. Wethey, *Titian and His Drawings* (Princeton, 1987), cat. 22: "unquestionably one of Titian's major drawings." See also Paul E. A. Joannides, "On Some Borrowings and Non-Borrowings from Central Italian and Antique Art in the Work of Titian, c. 1510–c. 1550," *Paragone*, no. 487 (1990): 31–32, and Gilbert, "Some Findings," 39. In general, see Wethey's discussion, "Titian and Central Italian Art," in Wethey, *Titian: Religious Paintings*, 17–21.

18. See Maria Ruvoldt, "Michelangelo's *Slaves* and the Gift of Liberty," *Renaissance Quarterly* 65, no. 4 (2012): 1029–59.

19. Ridolfi, *The Life of Titian*, 84.

20. Craig Hugh Smyth first proposed the hypothesis in "Venice and the Emergence of the High Renaissance in Florence: Observations and Questions," in *Florence and Venice: Comparisons and Relations*, ed. Sergio Bertelli, Nicolai Rubinstein, and Craig Hugh Smyth (Florence, 1979), 1:209–52, and Craig Hugh Smyth, "Michelangelo and Giorgione," in *Giorgione: Atti del convegno internazionale di studi, Castelfranco 1978* (Venezia, 1979), 213–20. The latter was reprinted with light editing in Lynn Catterson and Mark Zucker, eds., *Watching Art: Writings in Honor of James Beck/ Studi di storia dell'arte in onore di James Beck* (Todi, 2006), 241–45. While Smyth's suggestion has been frequently repeated—as probable (e.g., Joannides, "Titian and Michelangelo," 128), or as bald fact (e.g., Goffen, *Renaissance Rivals*, 93 and 102)—it is important to insist that Michelangelo's trip to Venice in 1494/95 is an undocumented hypothesis.

21. Debra Pincus, "Lo scorrere del tempo: Antonio Rizzo, Pietro e Tullio Lombardo e Michelangelo," in *Tullio Lombardo: Sculture e arhitetto nella*

Venezia del Rinascimento; Atti del Convegno di studi Venezia, Fondazione Giorgio Cini, 4–6 April, 2006, ed. Matteo Ceriana, (Venice, 2007), 283–88.

22. *Carteggio*, 1:51 and *Carteggio*, 1:19. For the Bologna sojourn, see Wallace, "Michelangelo in Bologna 1506–08," in *Michelangelo*, 80–88.

23. Craig Hugh Smyth is again the principal scholar who hypothesized a trip to Venice sometime during Michelangelo's long second sojourn in Bologna—a hypothesis that has been repeated so often that it has been uncritically accepted by many—e.g., Andrea Donati, "The Sistine Ceiling with Regard to Jews and Turks, and Michelangelo's Two Journeys to Venice," *Studi Veneziani* 74 (2017): 257–91.

24. See Smyth, "Venice and the Emergence of the High Renaissance," 210–15, and Pincus, "Lo scorrere del tempo," 283–88.

25. Vasari-Bull, 275.

26. Smyth, "Michelangelo and Giorgione," 213–20, and Smyth in *Watching Art*, 241–45. Sydney Freedberg suggested that Giorgione may have been influenced by Michelangelo's Battle of Cascina cartoon; see Smyth in *Watching Art*, 241.

27. See Joannides, "Titian and Michelangelo," 129, and Matthias Wivel, "'A Meeting of Minds': The Extraordinary Artistic Partnership of Michelangelo and Sebastiano," in Matthias Wivel, *Michelangelo and Sebastiano* (London, 2017), 15–39. Generally, for Sebastiano's career and art, see Michael Hirst, *Sebastiano del Piombo* (Oxford, 1981).

28. *Carteggio*, 3:305, 306.

29. *Carteggio*, 2:206.

30. *Carteggio*, 3:426.

31. "Et si per desgratia advenise, che Dio nol voglia, che vui mancasti, l'opera non se finiria né a una via né a l'altra, perché non piovano i Mechelagnioli" (*Carteggio*, 3:317). I have modified the quotation slightly in order to capture the sense of Sebastiano's quip.

32. *Carteggio*, 3:342.

33. On Michelangelo's humor, see Paul Barolsky, *Infinite Jest: Wit and Humor in Italian Renaissance Art* (Columbia, MO, 1978), esp. chap. 3, and William E. Wallace, "Michelangelo Ha Ha," in *Reading Vasari*, ed. Anne Barriault, Andrew Ladis, Norman E. Land, and Jeryldene M. Wood (London, 2005), 235–43.

34. British Museum, London, Inv. 1895-9-15-501. Charles de Tolnay, *Corpus dei disegni di Michelangelo*, 4 vols. (Novara, 1975–1980), no. 263. Such sketch /

doodling was common Michelangelo practice, even on sheets with radically divergent content; see William E. Wallace, "Instruction and Originality in Michelangelo's Drawings," in *The Craft of Art: Originality and Industry in the Italian Renaissance and Baroque Workshop*, ed. Andrew Ladis and Carolyn Wood (Athens, GA, 1995), 113–33.

35. *Carteggio*, 3:156. See Costanza Barbieri, "Sebastiano as Portraitist and a Case Study: The *Portrait of Michelangelo Pointing to His Drawings*," in *Sebastiano del Piombo and Michelangelo: The Compass and the Mirrror*, ed. Matthias Wivel (Turnhout, 2021), 197–218.

36. *Carteggio*, 3:250.

37. On Michelangelo as designer of fortifications, see Renzo Manetti, *Michelangiolo: Le fortificazioni per l'assedio di Firenze* (Florence, 1980); Pietro C. Marani, ed., *Disegni di fortificazioni da Leonardo a Michelangelo* (Florence, 1984), and William E. Wallace, "'Dal disegno allo spazio': Michelangelo's Drawings for the Fortifications of Florence," *Journal of the Society of Architectural Historians* 46 (1987): 119–34.

38. Condivi-Bull, 47. Condivi's account is substantiated by the Florentine ambassador, Galeotto Giugni; see Wallace, "Michelangelo's *Leda*," 478.

39. Condivi-Bull, 47–48; Vasari-Bull, 370–71.

40. See Bette Talvacchia, *Taking Positions: On the Erotic in Renaissance Culture* (Princeton, 1999).

41. Ludovico Ariosto, *La Lena*, ed. Guido Davico Bonino (Torino, 1976). The play was first presented in Ferrara during Carnival, 1528, and again a year later, shortly before Michelangelo's visit to Ferrara.

42. On Alfonso's studiolo, see Charles Hope, "The Camerini d'Alabastro of Alfonso d'Este," *Burlington Magazine* 113 (1971): 712–21; Philipp Fehl, "The Worship of Bacchus and Venus in Bellini's and Titian's Bacchanals for Alfonso d'Este," in *Studies in the History of Art* (Washington, DC, 1975), 37–87; Dana Goodgal, "The Camerino of Alfonso d'Este," *Art History* 1, no. 2 (1978): 162–90; and Anthony Colantuono, "*Dies Alkyoniae*: The Invention of Bellini's *Feast of the Gods*," *Art Bulletin* 73 (1991): 237–56.

43. Vasari-Bull, 371, 448. Vasari tells of Alfonso showing Michelangelo his portrait in both the lives of Michelangelo and Titian. Published in Michelangelo's lifetime and likely read by him, Lodovico Dolce also noted the Florentine's praise for Titian's portrait: "Michelangelo saw this same portrait and admired and praised it beyond bounds, saying that he would not have believed that art

could achieve so much, and that Titian alone deserved the title of painter" ("Il quale veduto poi da Michel'Agnolo, ei lo ammirò e lodò infinitamente, dicendo, ch'egli non haveva creduto, che l'arte potesse far tanto: e che solo Titiano era degno del nome di Pittore") (Roskill, ed., *Dolce's "Aretino"*, 108-9).

44. Condivi-Bull, 48.

45. See Wallace, "Michelangelo's *Leda*," 479.

46. Wallace, "Michelangelo's *Leda*," 485.

47. Francesco Guicciardini, *The History of Italy*, ed. and trans. Sidney Alexander (New York, 1969), 415.

48. Barnes, *Michelangelo in Print*, 169; see also *Fortuna di Michelangelo nell'incisione: Catalogo della mostra*, ed. Mario Rotili (Benevento, 1964), cat. no. 33.

49. Along with Michelangelo, Rinaldo Corsini was declared a rebel of Florence on September 30, 1529 (Archivio di Stato di Firenze [ASF], Otto di Guardia 206, fol. 28r-v). Another Corsini, Bertoldo Corsini, worked with Michelangelo as a supervisor (*procuratore*) on the bastions.

50. *Carteggio*, 3:280-81; trans. Ramsden, 1:175-76.

51. Lucilla Bardeschi Ciulich and Paola Barocchi, eds, *I ricordi di Michelangelo* (Florence, 1970), 262-63.

52. ASF, Otto di Guardia 206, fol. 28r-v. The text of the *bando* is reprinted in Giorgio Vasari, *La vita di Michelangelo nelle redazioni del 1550 e del 1568*, ed. Paola Barocchi, 5 vols. (Milan, 1962), 3:1067-68. A proclaimed rebel according to Florentine law could be killed with impunity; see Lauro Martines, *Fire in the City: Savonarola and the Struggle for Renaissance Florence* (Oxford, 2006), 202. More generally on exile, see Christine Shaw, *The Politics of Exile in Renaissance Italy* (Cambridge, 2000).

53. *Carteggio*, 3:282. On Battista della Palla, see Caroline Elam, "Art in the Service of Liberty: Battista della Palla, Art Agent for Francis I," *I Tatti Studies* 5 (1993): 33-109.

54. Paola Barocchi, Kathleen Bramanti, and Renzo Ristori, eds., *Il Carteggio indiretto di Michelangelo*, 2 vols. (Florence, 1988 / 1995), 1:52 (hereafter *Carteggio indiretto*). On Michelangelo's aristocratic persona and his concern regarding proper dress and comportment, see William E. Wallace, "Miscellanae Curiositae Michelangelae: A Steep Tariff, a Half-Dozen Horses, and Yards of Taffeta," *Renaissance Quarterly* 47 (1994): 330-50; William E. Wallace, "Michel Angelus Bonarotus Patritius Florentinus," in *Innovation and Tradition: Essays*

on Renaissance Art and Culture, ed. Dag T. Andersson and Roy Eriksen (Rome, 2000), 60–74, and Wallace, *Michelangelo*, chap. 2.

55. Lionello Puppi, "Michelangelo e Tiziano," in *Tiziano nel quarto centenario della sua morte* (Venice, 1977), 159–72, and Patricia Meilman, *Titian and the Altarpiece in Renaissance Venice* (Cambridge, 2000), 87–88.

56. On Sansovino and Michelangelo, see William E. Wallace, *Michelangelo at San Lorenzo: The Genius as Entrepreneur* (Cambridge, 1994), 10–11.

57. "Michelagnolo, andato a Venezia, è ricevuto e visitato dal doge Andrea Gritti e da molti gentiluomini; egli è offerto stipendio, se si resolve abitare quivi; il quale, essente da ogni obbligo, fa per il medesimo Gritti il disegno del ponte di Rialto." Ugo Procacci, *La Casa Buonarroti a Firenze* (Milan, 1967), 220.

58. Confirmed in a marginal note by Tiberio Calcagni: "Fu vero e ne haveva già fatto un modello, mi disse" (Elam, "'Che ultima mano,'" xliii). Vasari—"disegno rarissimo d'invenzione e d'ornamento" (Vasari-Bettarini, 6:62)—echoes Condivi: "a bridge . . . in a new style and form, never seen before" (Condivi-Bull, 58). See also James Ackerman, *The Architecture of Michelangelo, Catalogue* (London, 1961), 138.

59. Francisco de Hollanda, *Diálogos em Roma (1538): Conversations on Art with Michelangelo Buonarroti*, ed. Grazia Dolores Folliero-Metz (Heidelberg, 1998), 88. For the high *traghetto* fee, see David Chambers and Brian Pullan, eds., *Venice: A Documentary History, 1450–1630* (Toronto, 2001), 286.

60. As described by Il Lasca in *Le Cene*, for which, see John Addington Symonds, *The Life of Michelangelo*, 2 vols. (New York, 1893), 2:349.

61. Wivel, *Michelangelo and Sebastiano*, cat. nos. 8, 9.

62. On the in situ experience of the *Assunta* in the architectural setting of the Frari, see David Rosand, *Painting in Cinquecento Venice: Titian, Veronese, Tintoretto* (New Haven, 1982), 52–58.

63. "La grandeza e terribilità di Michel'Agnolo" (Roskill, ed., *Dolce's "Aretino"*, 186–87); see also Rosand, *Painting in Cinquecento Venice*, 52.

64. On the in situ experience of the *Pesaro Madonna*, see Rosand, *Painting in Cinquecento Venice*, 58–62.

65. Meilmann, *Titian and the Altarpiece*, 87–88. Tribolo's praise of the painting is found in the letter of Pietro Aretino to Tribolo; see *Aretino: Selected Letters*, trans. George Bull (Harmondsworth, UK, 1976), 120–21.

66. Vasari-Bull, 450.

67. "E par, che si senta gridare" (Roskill, ed., *Dolce's "Aretino"*, 190–91). In the style of Vasari, Norman Land offers an evocative, albeit imaginary, positive reaction of Michelangelo to Titian's *Peter Martyr* and other works in Venice and Rome. See Norman Land, "Titian, Michelangelo, and Vasari," in *Reading Vasari*, ed. Anne B. Barriault, Andrew Ladis, Norman E. Land, and Jeryldene M. Wood (Athens, GA, 2005), 211–21.

68. *Aretino: Selected Letters*, 120.

69. Roskill, ed., *Dolce's "Aretino"*, 146–47.

70. *Carteggio*, 3:284–85.

71. *Carteggio indiretto*, 1:330 and 331.

72. *Carteggio indiretto*, 1:255 and 258. See William E. Wallace, "An Unpublished Michelangelo Document," *Burlington Magazine*, 129 (1987): 181–84.

73. Condivi-Bull, 45.

74. Condivi-Bull, 48.

75. Vasari-Bettarini, 6:63; Vasari-Bull, 372. See also Condivi-Bull, 48.

76. *Carteggio*, 3:290. See Charles M. Rosenberg, "Alfonso I d'Este, Michelangelo and the Man who Bought Pigs," in *Revaluing Renaissance Art*, ed. Gabriele Neher and Rupert Shepherd (Aldershot, 2000), 89–100; and Wallace, "Michelangelo's *Leda*."

77. Letter from Benvenuto della Volpaia to Michelangelo, Novemeber 26, 1531 (*Carteggio*, 3:348–49): "E anchora mi domandò partiqularmente della Leda di pictura, che di costà n'à 'inteso assai."

78. See William E. Wallace, "Il 'Noli me Tangere' di Michelangelo: Tra sacra e profane," *Arte Cristiana* 76 (1988): 443–50; Michael Hirst and Gadula Mayr, "Michelangelo, Pontormo und das 'Noli me Tangere' für Vittoria Colonna," in *Vittoria Colonna: Dichterin und Muse Michelangelos*, ed. Sylvia Ferino-Pagden (Vienna, 1997), 335–44. Also relevant are: Jeryldene M. Wood, "Vittoria Colonna's *Mary Magdalen*," in *Visions of Holiness: Art and Devotion in Renaissance Italy* (Athens, GA, 2001), 195–212; Marjorie Och, "Vittoria Colonna and the Commission for a *Mary Magdalene* by Titian," in *Beyond Isabella: Secular Women Patrons of Art in Renaissance Italy*, ed. Sheryl E. Reiss and David G. Wilkins (Kirksville, MO, 2001), 194–223, and Andrea Donati, *Vittoria Colonna e l'eredità degli 'Spirituali'* (Foligno, 2023), 69–73.

79. Jonathan Katz Nelson and Franca Falletti, eds., *Venere e amore: Venus and Love; Michelangelo e la nuova bellezza ideale: Michelangelo and the New*

Ideal of Beauty (Florence, 2002). See also Fredrika H. Jacobs, "Aretino and Michelangelo, Dolce and Titian: *Femmina, Masculo, Grazie*," *Art Bulletin* 82 (2000): 51–67; Rebekah Compton, "'Omnia Vincit Amor': The Sovereignty of Love in Tuscan Poetry and Michelangelo's 'Venus and Cupid,'" *Mediaevalia* 33 (2012): 229–60, and Roberto Bellucci and Cecilia Frosinini, "The Replicas after the *Venus and Cupid* Cartoon by Michelangelo," in *La Peinture Ancienne et ses Procédés: Copies, Répliques, Pastiches*, ed. Hélène Verougstraete and Jacqueline Couvert (Leuven, 2006), 51–58.

80. Vasari-Bettarini, 6:381; Joannides, "Titian and Michelangelo," 137; Goffen, *Renaissance Rivals*, 331–32; Barnes, *Michelangelo in Print*, 169. Vasari's visit to Venice is evocatively described in the first pages of Bruce Cole's published lecture, "Titian and the Idea of Originality in the Renaissance," in *The Craft of Art: Originality and Industry in the Italian Renaissance and Baroque Workshop*, ed. Andrew Ladis and Carolyn Wood (Athens, GA, 1995), 86–112.

81. Giorgio Vasari, *Lives of the Painters, Sculptors and Architects*, trans. Gaston du C. de Vere, 2 vols. (New York, 1996), 2:1034; see also Juergen Schulz, "Vasari in Venice," *Burlington Magazine* 103, no. 705 (1961): 500–509/511, and Barbara Agosti, *Giorgio Vasari: Luoghi e tempi delle Vite* (Rome, 2021), esp. 54–58. Among other commissions, Vasari worked with Pietro Aretino to produce scenery for the comedy, "La Talanta." On their friendship, see Enrico Mattioda, "Giorgio Vasari e Pietro Aretino," in *Giorgio Vasari tra parola e imagine*, ed. Alessandro Masi and Chiara Barbato (Rome, 2014), 135–48, and Elena Carrara, "Aretino e Vasari," in *"Pietro Pictore Arretino": Una parola complice per l'arte del Rinascimento*, ed. Anna Bisceglia, Matteo Ceriana, and Paolo Procaccioli (Venice, 2020), 181–91.

82. Giorgio Vasari, *Der literarische Nachlass Giorgio Vasaris herausgegeben und mit kritischem Apparate versehen von Karl Frey*, 2 vols. (Munich, 1923), 1:35. I thank Maria Ruvoldt for this reference.

83. Michelangelo's development of new types, style, and purposes of drawing in the 1520/30s is one of the major themes of my PhD dissertation: William E. Wallace, "Studies in Michelangelo's Finished Drawings, 1527–1534" (PhD diss., Columbia University, 1983).

84. Contemporaries noted Michelangelo's emphasis on individual figures and gestures rather than compositions; see Cammy Brothers, *Michelangelo, Drawing, and the Invention of Architecture* (New Haven, 2008), 40–41, and nn.

67–69; and Joost Pieter Keizer, "Michelangelo, Drawing, and the Subject of Art," *Art Bulletin* 93 (2011): 304–24.

85. A. E. Popp, *Die Medici-Kapelle Michelangelos* (Munich, 1922), 126–40 and plates 9, 12, 13. Joannides suggested possible bronze or terracotta reliefs to adorn the lunettes; see Paul E. A. Joannides, "Michelangelo's Medici Chapel: Some New Suggestions," *Burlington Magazine* 114 (1972): 547.

86. *Carteggio*, 4:169, 105.

87. See Maria Ruvoldt, "Michelangelo's Open Secrets," in *Visual Cultures of Secrecy in Early Modern Europe*, ed. Timothy McCall, Sean Roberts, and Giancarlo Fiorenza (Kirksville, MO, 2013), 122, and Maria Ruvoldt, *Michelangelo's Gifts: Art, Love, and Politics in Renaissance Italy*, forthcoming (Cambridge University Press).

88. Fabrizio Mancinelli, "Michelangelo's Last Judgment: Technique and Restoration," *Michelangelo: The Last Judgment; A Glorious Restoration* (New York, 1997), 162.

89. On the cinematic character of the Pauline frescoes, see William E. Wallace, "Narrative and Religious Expression in Michelangelo's Pauline Chapel," *Artibus et Historiae* 19 (1989): 107–21.

Part II: 1545–1576

1. Harold E. Wethey, *The Paintings of Titian*, vol. 2, *The Portraits* (London, 1971), cat. no. 72 (hereafter Wethey, *Titian: Portraits*); Humfrey, cat. no. 136. For Titian's portraits of the Farnese and their many versions and copies, see Andrea Donati, "Tiziano e Paolo III nel 1543: Il primo viaggio alla corte Farnese e le sue ripercussioni artistiche," *Archivio della Società Romana di Storia Patria* 146 (2023): 193–243.

2. On Alessandro Farnese, see Clare Robertson. *'Il Gran Cardinale': Alessandro Farnese, Patron of the Arts* (New Haven, 1992).

3. Vasari-Bull, 454.

4. ". . . Acciò mettesse mano a fare di nuovo il ritratto di papa Paulo" (Vasari-Bettarini, 6:164), trans. Vasari-Bull, 454. I have modified the translation slightly.

5. Wethey, *Titian: Portraits*, cat. no. 76; Humfrey, cat. no. 147.

6. *Carteggio*, 4:182. I have simplified and paraphrased the convoluted locution. On Titian's campaign to secure a benefice for Pomponio, see Roberto

Zapperi, "Tiziano e i Farnese: Aspetti economici del rapporto di committenza," *Bolletino d'Arte* 66 (1991): 39-48.

7. *Carteggio*, 4:181-82.

8. On Michelangelo aristocratic persona, see Wallace, *Michelangelo*, chap. 2 and passim; and Wallace, "Michel Angelus Bonarotus."

9. Condivi-Bull, 67, and Giovanni Papini, *Michelangelo: His Life and His Era*, trans. Loretta Murnane (New York, 1952), 411. Caro, originally from the Marche, was married to Condivi's daughter, and was also a friend of Titian.

10. Vasari-Bull, 378. For the relationship of Michelangelo and Pope Paul, see William E. Wallace, *Michelangelo, God's Architect: The Story of His Final Years and Greatest Masterpiece* (Princeton, 2019), chap. 3 and passim.

11. Lucilla Bardeschi Ciulich, ed., *I Contratti di Michelangelo* (Florence, 2005), 278-80 (October 1549). See also Horst Bredekamp, "Zwei Souveräne: Paul III. und Michelangelo. Das 'Motu proprio' vom Oktober 1549," in *Sankt Peter in Rom 1506-2006*, ed. George Satzinger and Sebastian Schütze (Munich, 2008), 147-57.

12. *Carteggio*, 4:299 and *Carteggio*, 4:270. On the sharing of food, especially fruits, see Carole M. Counihan, *The Anthropology of Food and Body: Gender, Meaning and Power* (London, 1999); Allen J. Grieco, *Food, Social Politics and the Order of Nature in Renaissance Italy* (Florence, 2019); and Wallace, *Michelangelo, God's Architect*, 59-60.

13. Wethey, *Titian: Portraits*, cat. nos. 73 and 29, respectively; Humfrey, cat. nos. 145, 146.

14. Vasari-Bull, 454-55; the picture is presumably lost (Humfrey, cat. no. 163).

15. Vasari-Bull, 371, and Roskill, ed., *Dolce's "Aretino"*, 108-9.

16. See Wallace, *Michelangelo*, chap. 2 and passim, and Wallace, "Michel Angelus Bonarotus."

17. Vasari-Bettarini, 6:164.

18. ". . . Il Buonarruoto lo comendò assai, dicendo che molto gli piaceva il colorito suo e la maniera, ma che era un peccato che a Vinezia non s'imparasse da principio a disegnare bene" (Vasari-Bettarini, 6:164). Paul Joannides acknowledged that Michelangelo was mostly positive in his praise of Titian, especially given that there were few artists of whom it could be said that their work "much pleased him" (Joannides, "Titian and Michelangelo," 122). Carlo

Ridolfi repeated Vasari's anecdote, excised Michelangelo's criticism, and instead emphasized his commendation: "Michelangelo praised it as a singular work, affirming that it was impossible to use colors better" (Ridolfi, *The Life of Titian*, 93). For Michelangelo's negative criticism of other artists, oftentimes expressed with biting humor, see Wallace, "Michelangelo Ha Ha," 238–39.

19. Barnes, *Michelangelo in Print*, 169.

20. Vasari-Bettarini, 6:381; Goffen, *Renaissance Rivals*, 331–32; and Joannides, "Titian and Michelangelo," 137.

21. Condivi-Bull, 66–67.

22. Gabriello Pacccagli in Paris, writing on behalf of King Francis I to Michelangelo "in Roma o dove sia": "el quale Re parlò con tanta gratia e amore di voi, che quasi mi parve cosa incredibile . . ." and ". . . el magiore desiderio che de havere ogni quantunche pichola cosa del vostro" (*Carteggio*, 2:151).

23. Paul E. A. Joannides, "Michelangelo's Lost Hercules," *Burlington Magazine* 119 (1977):550–54; Paul E. A. Joannides, "A Supplement to Michelangelo's Lost Hercules," *Burlington Magazine* 123 (1981): 20–23; and Janet Cox-Rearick, *The Collection of Francis I: Royal Treasures* (New York, 1995), 302–13.

24. *Carteggio*, 4:184 (July 1544).

25. February 8, 1546 (*Carteggio*, 4:229). English translation from Cox-Rearick, *Collection of Francis I*, 295.

26. *Carteggio*, 4:229. See Cox-Rearick, *Collection of Francis I*, 313–14, and Walter Cupperi, "'Giving Away the Moulds Will Cause No Damage to His Majesty's Casts'—New Documents on the Vienna *Jüngling* and the Sixteenth-Century Dissemination of Casts after the Antique in the Holy Roman Empire," in *Plaster Casts: Making, Collecting and Displaying from Classical Antiquity to the Present*, ed. Eckart Marchand and Rune Frederiksen (Berlin, 2010), 81–98, with further references.

27. *Carteggio*, 4:237; trans. Ramsden, 2:61.

28. Wethey, *Titian: Portraits*, cat. no. 37; Humfrey, cat. no. 121.

29. Wethey, *Titian: Portraits*, cat. no. 5.

30. Since 1540, Primaticcio had been supervising the making of molds of a dozen of Rome's most famous classical statues—e.g., *Laocoön* and *Apollo Belvedere*—as well as two modern sculptures by Michelangelo: the *Pietà* and the *Risen Christ*, both intended to adorn the King's chapel at Fontainebleau (*Carteggio*, 4:229). The *Pietà* was dispatched to France, but the death of Francis I

in March 1547 interrupted the large-scale enterprise, which is probably why the *Risen Christ* never was sent to France. The languishing mold—made during Titian's sojourn in Rome—likely served to create the full-size plaster cast acquired by Titian. I thank Charles Hope, C. D. Dickerson, and Martha Dunkleman for discussing this curious incident with me. See Erica Tietze-Conrat, "Titian as a Letter Writer," *Art Bulletin* 26 (1944): 120–21; Joannides, "Titian and Michelangelo," 138; Cox-Rearick, *Collection of Francis I*, 313–14, and Victoria Avery, "Alessandro Vittoria: The Michelangelo of Venice," in *Reactions to the Master: Michelangelo Effect on Art and Artists in the Sixteenth Century*, ed. Francis Ames-Lewis and Paul Joannides (Aldershot, UK, 2003), 158, and Cupperi, "Giving Away the Moulds," 81–82.

31. On Ippolito de' Medici, see Guido Rebecchini, '*Un altro Lorenzo': Ippolito de' Medici tra Firenze e Roma (1511–1535)* (Venice, 2010).

32. Vasari-Bull, 419; Rebecchini, *Ippolito de' Medici*, 259. The gift, according to Vasari, included ten mules and the fodder and groom required for their upkeep, which seems exaggerated. It is certainly true, however, that Michelangelo owned and loved horses; see Wallace, "Miscellanae Curiositae Michelangelae," 336–39, and Deborah Parker, "Ovidian Influences and Figural Obsessions in Michelangelo's *Fall of Phaethon* Drawings," *I Tatti Studies* 24, no. 2 (2021): 401–26.

33. *Carteggio*, 4:49. See Ruvoldt, "Michelangelo's Open Secrets," and her forthcoming book, *Michelangelo's Gifts*. I would like to thank Maria Ruvoldt for many conversations regarding this fascinating moment in Michelangelo's effort to remain private even as he recognized the importance of being more in the public sphere, as Raphael and Titian had successfully negotiated.

34. Wethey, *Titian: Portraits*, cat. no. 65; Humfrey, cat. no. 98.

35. "Queste parole li trafisse el core." As reported by Sebastiano del Piombo to Michelangelo in a letter of July 22, 1531 (*Carteggio*, 3:316–17).

36. Wethey, *Titian: Portraits*, cat. no. 89; Humfrey, cat. no. 109.

37. See Wethey, *Titian: Portraits*, cat. nos. X-86 and X-87.

38. For the incident, see Wallace, *Michelangelo*, 315–16. Unfortunately, among the myriad of copies—most attributed to Marcello Venusti—Guidobaldo's paintings have never been securely identified.

39. Wethey, *Titian: Portraits*, cat. no. 10; Humfrey, cat. no. 127.

40. For the multiple ties linking Titian's *Mary Magdalene* and Michelangelo's *Noli me Tangere* with the patrons Alfonso d'Avalos and Vittoria Colonna, see Hirst and Mayr, "Michelangelo, Pontormo und das 'Noli me Tangere,'" 335–44; Och, "Vittoria Colonna," 194–223; Wood, "Vittoria Colonna's *Mary Magdalen*," 195–212; Barbara Agosti, "Vittoria Colonna e il culto della Maddalena (tra Tiziano e Michelangelo)," in *Vittoria Colonna e Michelangelo*, ed. Pina Ragionieri (Florence, 2005), 71–78; and Donati, *Vittoria Colonna*, 69–73.

41. Kenneth Gouwens, "Female Virtue and the Embodiment of Beauty: Vittoria Colonna in Paolo Giovio's *Notable Men and Women*," *Renaissance Quarterly* 68 (2015): 55.

42. See especially Maria Forcellino, *Michelangelo, Vittoria Colonna e gli "spirituali": Religiosità e vita artistica a Roma negli anni Quaranta* (Rome, 2009); Abigail Brundin, *Vittoria Colonna and the Spiritual Poetics of the Italian Reformation* (Aldershot, UK, 2008); Sarah Rolfe Prodan, *Michelangelo's Christian Mysticism: Spirituality, Poetry, and Art in Sixteenth-Century Italy* (Cambridge, 2014), and Donati, *Vittoria Colonna*, passim.

43. Hollanda, *Diálogos em Roma (1538)*, 87–88.

44. An earlier instance of Michelangelo's engagement with the Magdalene is found in the *Entombment of Christ* (National Gallery of London) where she figures as the youthful kneeling figure in the foreground. For the exceptional prominence that Michelangelo gives to the Magdalene in his own grave marker, see William E. Wallace, "Michelangelo, Tiberio Calcagni, and the Florentine *Pietà*," *Artibus et Historiae* 42 (2000): 81–99; and for Vittoria Colonna's investment in Mary Magdelene, see Agosti, "Vittoria Colonna"; Brundin, *Vittoria Colonna*, passim; and Donati, *Vittoria Colonna*, 69–73 and passim.

45. Wethey, *Titian: Portraits*, cat. no. 101; Humfrey, cat. no. 135.

46. For Michelangelo and his family's longtime ties to the Strozzi, see William E. Wallace, "Manoeuvering for Patronage: Michelangelo's Dagger," *Renaissance Studies* 11 (1997): 20–26; Ruvoldt, "Michelangelo's *Slaves*"; and Vincenzo Sorrentino, *A Patron Family Between Renaissance Florence, Rome, and Naples: The Del Riccio in the Shadow of Michelangelo* (New York, 2022).

47. *Carteggio*, 4:182n3; *Carteggio*, 4:183–84n1.

48. *Carteggio*, 4:186.

49. David Quint, "The Modern Copy: Dante, Ariosto and Michelangelo's Sistine Ceiling," *I Tatti Studies* 18, no. 2 (2015): 397–427.

50. Paul F. Norton, "The Lost 'Sleeping Cupid' of Michelangelo," *Art Bulletin*, 39 (1957): 251–57, and Clifford M. Brown, "'Lo insaciabile desiderio nostro de cose antique': New Documents on Isabella d'Este's Collection of Antiquities," in *Cultural Aspects of the Italian Renaissance: Essays in Honor of P. O. Kristeller* (Manchester, UK, 1976), 324–53.

51. Wethey, *Titian: Portraits*, cat. no. 49; Humfrey, cat. no. 83; Barnes, *Michelangelo in Print*, 41.

52. Chambers and Pullan, eds., *Venice: A Documentary History*, 180 (1540). The circle of friends described here is tightened when we add the further voice of Annibale Caro, who was a friend of both Michelangelo and Titian. In a letter from Rome to Pietro Aretino in Venice, October 22, 1545, Caro sent greetings to his friends Aretino, Titian, and Sansovino; see Charles Hope, *Titian: Sources and Documents* 6 vols. (London, 2023), 3:806 (doc. no. 54510220).

53. Thomas Martin, "Michelangelo's *Brutus* and the Rise of the Classicizing Portrait Bust in Sixteenth-Century Italy," *Artibus et Historiae* 27 (1993): 67–83.

54. Wethey, *Titian: Portraits*, cat. no. 30; Humfrey, cat. no. 151.

55. Which the artist lost on the death of Pier Luigi in 1547 (*Carteggio*, 4:276). On the Po ferry, see Ramsden, 2:266–68.

56. Wethey, *Titian: Portraits*, cat. no. 31; Humfrey, cat. no. 134. On Ranuccio, see Gigliola Fragnito, "Farnese, Ranuccio," *Dizionario Biografico degli Italiani* (Rome, 2014), 98–107. Ranuccio Farnese—not Alessandro Farnese, as is generally stated—was the owner of the faithful copy of Michelangelo's *Last Judgment* painted by Marcello Venusti in 1549; see Andrea Donati, "Marcello Venusti, Michelangelo and the Legacy of Sebastiano del Piombo," in *Sebastiano Compass and the Mirror*, ed. Mathias Wivel (Turnhout, 2021), 323.

57. On Michelangelo and Beccadelli, see Giuseppe Alberigo, "Beccadelli, Ludovico," in *Dizionario Biografico degli Italiani*, vol. 7 (Rome, 1970), 407–13; and Wallace, *Michelangelo, God's Architect*, 160–63.

58. James M. Saslow, *The Poetry of Michelangelo: An Annotated Translation* (New Haven, 1991), no. 300.

59. Wethey, *Titian: Portraits*, cat. no. 13; Humfrey, cat. no. 201.

60. Wethey, *Titian: Portraits*, cat. no. 108; Humfrey, cat. no. 132.

61. See Vittoria Romani, "Sul carteggio Aretino-Michelangelo," in *"Inchiostro per colore": Arte e artisti in Pietro Aretino*, ed. A Bisceglia, M. Ceriana,

P. Procaccioli (Rome, 2019), 201–17; and Marco Faini and Paola Ugolini, eds., *A Companion to Pietro Aretino* (Leiden, 2021).

62. ". . . Ma sete ben vui da vero unico sopra lui et tutti gli altri. Et basta" (*Carteggio*, 3:148; Michelangelo's letter to Sebastiano only survives in draft: *Carteggio*, 3:143).

63. *Carteggio*, 4:82–84.

64. *Carteggio*, 4:182 and 216. See Bernadine Barnes, "Aretino, the Public, and the Censorship of Michelangelo's *Last Judgment*," in *Suspended License: Studies in Censorship and the Visual Arts*, ed. Elizabeth Childs (Seattle, 1997), 59–84.

65. John Shearman, *Raphael in Early Modern Sources (1483–1602)*, 2 vols. (New Haven, 2003), 2:940–41.

66. ". . . Quella bellissima nuda per il Cardinal Farnese, che fu con maraviglia piu d'una volta veduta da Michel'Agnolo" (Roskill, ed., *Dolce's "Aretino"*, 110–11).

67. Mark Twain, *Innocents Abroad* (New York, 1966), chap. 27.

68. See Roskill, ed., *Dolce's "Aretino"*, 94–95, and Sheila Hale, *Titian, His Life* (New York, 2012), 466.

69. Giorgio Vasari, *Lives of the Painters, Sculptors and Architects*, trans. Gaston du C. de Vere, 2 vols. (New York, 1996), 1:811. An anecdote related by Federico Zuccari (c. 1540–1609) adds that Titian, not believing that some putti by Baldassare Peruzzi were painted, had to convince himself by touching them. See Federico Zuccari, *L'idea de' pittori, scultori e architetti* [1607], ed. Detlef Heikamp (Florence, 1961), 248.

70. Wethey, *Titian: Portraits,* cat. no. 55; and Loren Partridge and Randolf Starn, *A Renaissance Likeness: Art and Culture in Raphael's Julius II* (Berkeley, 1980). Humfrey suggests the picture "is plausibly attributed to Titian" (Humfrey, cat. no. 149). For notices of the painting in Sta. Maria del Popolo, see Shearman, *Raphael in Early Modern Sources*, 1:171–72 (doc. 1513/13), 1:846–47 (doc. 1529/1), 2:944–45 (doc. 1545/8), 2:1398–1401 (doc. 1595/1) (I thank Livio Pestilli for these references).

71. Pietro Bembo to Girolamo Quartesi, October 10, 1545; see Hope, *Titian: Sources and Documents*, 3:806 (doc. no. 54510100); and Joannides, "On Some Borrowings."

72. Leonard Barkan, *Unearthing the Past: Archaeology and Aesthetics in the Making of Renaissance Culture* (New Haven, 1999), 11–13. Titian certainly

admired other antiquities, for example, the recently discovered Toro Farnese; see Alastair Smart, "Titian and the *Toro Farnese*," *Apollo* 85 (1967): 420–31.

73. Wethey, *Titian: Religious Paintings*, cat. no. 1; Humfrey, cat. no. 250.

74. Versions in the Fitzwilliam Museum, Cambridge, and Metropolitan Museum, New York: Wethey, *Titian: Mythological and Historical Paintings*, cat. nos. 45, 46; Humfrey, cat. nos. 237, 238).

75. *Carteggio*, 4:151; trans. Ramsden, 2:27.

76. Condivi-Bull, 53.

77. Wethey, *Titian: Portraits*, cat. no. 50; Humfrey, cat. no. 154.

78. "Una soma di pronti di gesso et un'altra di vestimenti et alter sue robbe"; see Hope, *Titian: Sources and Documents*, 3:843–44 (doc. no. 54605250); see also doc. no. 55906170 and n3. One soma = 135.6 kg (c. 300 lbs), most of which weight was probably the full-size gesso cast of the *Risen Christ*. I thank Charles Hope and Livio Pestilli for discussing this document with me.

79. For this commission, see Morton Steen Hansen, *In Michelangelo's Mirror: Perino del Vaga, Daniele da Volterra, Pellegrino Tibaldi* (University Park, PA, 2013), 80; Andrea Donati, *Tiziano: Indagini sulla pittura* (Rome, 2016), 107–49; and Andrea Donati, "Painting on Stone in Rome in the Sixteenth Century," *Burlington Magazine* 165 (2023): 742–45. If Titian got wind of this painting after his return to Venice, one might surmise that it helped spur him to paint a similarly composed, stunningly violent, and sexually charged *Tarquin and Lucretia* (Wethey, *Titian: Mythological and Historical Paintings*, cat. no 34; Humfrey, cat. no. 275).

80. Simona Capelli, "Marcello Venusti: Un valtellinese pittore a Roma," *Studi di storia dell'arte* 12 (2001): 17–48; and William E. Wallace, "Michelangelo and Marcello Venusti: A Case of Multiple Authorship," in *Reactions to the Master: Michelangelo's Effect on Art and Artists in the Sixteenth Century*, ed. Francis Ames-Lewis and Paul Joannides (Aldershot, UK, 2003), 137–56.

81. *Carteggio*, 5:120–22.

82. Wallace, "Michelangelo and Venusti," 153. On the novelty and importance of color and iconography in creating images that "inspire devotion and encourage contemplation of the divine," see the sensitive and insightful discussion of Michelangelo's collaboration with Marcello Venusti in Emily Fenichel, *Michelangelo's Art of Devotion in the Age of Reform* (New York, 2023), esp. 42–63.

83. Wethey, *Titian: Religious Paintings*, cat no. 10.

84. "Cosa nuova" (Vasari-Bull, 420; Wallace, "Michelangelo and Venusti," 139–43). The altarpiece is no longer extant, but it was so much admired that it survives in at least six small-scale copies. See Donati, "Marcello Venusti," 323. Christopher Nygren notes that Titian's Roman sojourn prompted his appreciation for the "serial production of images," which was one notable result of Michelangelo's collaboration with Marcello Venusti; see Christopher J. Nygren, *Titian's Icons: Tradition, Charisma, and Devotion in Renaissance Italy* (University Park, PA, 2020), 109–11.

85. ". . . Una tavola alla Pace, sotto le figure di Rafaello." Letter of Leonardo Sellaio in Rome to Michelangelo in Florence, December 15, 1520 (*Carteggio*, 2:266). See Michael Hirst, "The Chigi Chapel in S. Maria della Pace," *Journal of the Warburg and Courtauld Institutes* 24 (1961): 161–85.

86. Wallace, "Michelangelo and Marcello Venusti: A Case of Multiple Authorship," 145–46. Much neglected and still difficult of access, the altarpiece was conserved and cleaned in spring 2018.

87. The preference is for narrative scenes, especially those that occur in a series (the life of the Virgin or of a saint), although there are also devotional images, especially the Crucifixion and the face of Christ. My thanks to Bernadine Barnes for this information.

88. Emily Fenichel nicely characterizes the Michelangelo and Venusti collaboration as producing works of "clear iconography, a relatively simple composition, and a legible message," that is, "a fundamental reevaluation of religious art in public spaces and the pursuit of a new direction for public religious art in Counter-Reformation Rome" (Fenichel, *Michelangelo's Art of Devotion*, 57 and 42).

89. Hale, *Titian*, 473.

90. Hale, *Titian*, 482; and Zapperi, "Tiziano e i Farnese."

91. Wethey, *Titian: Religious Paintings*, cat. no. 11; Humfrey, cat. no. 259. See William E. Wallace, "Titian Looks at Michelangelo Looking at Titian," *Source: Notes in the History of Art* 22 (2003): 13–18.

92. "Similar Venetian representations of the *Anunziata* are difficult to find." See Daniela Bohde, "Titian's Three-Altar Project in the Venetian Church of San Salvador: Strategies of Self-Representation by Members of the Scuola Grande di San Rocco," *Renaissance Studies* 15 (2001): 450–72.

93. Hope, *Titian: Sources and Documents*, 3:764 (doc. no. 54503100).

94. Vasari-Bull, 462.

95. In Paola Barocchi's modern critical edition, the life of Titian runs a scant nineteen pages while the life of Michelangelo is one hundred and forty pages long; however, this includes the 1550 life as well (Vasari-Bettarini, 6:155-74 versus 6:3-141). In George Bull's English translation of Vasari, Michelangelo's life is 118 pages versus 20 pages for the life of Titian (Vasai-Bull, 325-462).

96. Mario Fanti, "Le postille carraccesche alle *Vite* del Vasari: Il testo originale," *Il Carrobbio* 5 (1979): 148-64; Charles Dempsey, "The Carracci's Postille to Vasari's *Lives*," *Art Bulletin* (1986): 72-76; and José Riello, "Challenging the Concept of Naturalism between the Sixteenth and Seventeenth Centuries: Annibale Carracci and El Greco as Readers of Vasari's *Vite*," *I Tatti Studies* 27, no. 1 (2024): 117-18. See also, Vittoria Romani, "Su Vasari e i pittori veneziani," in *Giorgio Vasari e il cantiere delle Vite del del 1550*, ed. B. Agosti, S. Ginzburg, A. Nova (Venice, 2013), 105-19, and Agosti, *Giorgio Vasari: Luoghi e tempi*, 100-101.

97. Wethey, *Titian: Religious Paintings*, cat no. 44; Humfrey, cat. no. 282. In support of the hypothesis that the picture was painted for personal reasons is the fact that the quickly and roughly painted *Judith* was painted over a different composition altogether, perhaps a portrait of Charles V (Humfrey, 356). Also suggestive is the fact that the earliest provenance—albeit from 1786—places the picture in a Florentine private collection (Wethey, *Titian: Religious Paintings*) Did Titian send it to Florence as part of his campaign to be enrolled in the Florentine Accademia del Disegno?

98. I thank Julie James for this suggestion. One might also consider Titian's paintings of Salomé with the head of Holofernes, a couple of which resemble Michelangelo portraits; for example, see Humfrey, cat. nos. 213 and 256. Titian's late painting *The Flaying of Marsyas* (Humfrey, cat. no. 289) might be considered as part of this *damnatio memoriae* campaign: the god Apollo triumphs over presumptive Marsyas. Titian, the "New Apelles"—who signed the picture and may have included himself as witness to the gruesome scene—is, like Apollo, the ultimate winner of an artistic contest against an adversary who was associated with and partly identified as a grotesque faun (see Paul Barolsky, *Michelangelo's Nose*). *The Flaying of Marsyas* may also implicitly reference the *Last Judgment* given that Marsyas prefigures St. Bartholomew whose flayed skin is generally considered a self-portrait of Michelangelo; see Beat Wyss, "*The Last Judgment* as Artistic Process: *The Flaying of Marsyas* in

the Sistine Chapel," *RES: Anthropology and Aesthetics* 28 (1995): 62–77, and Bernadine Barnes, "Skin, Bones, and Dust: Self-Portraits in Michelangelo's *Last Judgment*," *Sixteenth Century Journal* 35 (2004): 969–86. From reading Vasari or Lodovico Domenichi's *facezie* (Venice, 1548), if not from personal experience of seeing the *Last Judgment* fresco himself, Titian was aware that Michelangelo, by placing Biagio da Cesena in hell, similarly had wielded art as critical weapon and rejoinder; see Norman E. Land, "A Concise History of the Tale of Michelangelo and Biagio da Cesena," *Source: Notes in the History of Art* 32 (2013): 15–19; and Leo Steinberg, "A Corner of the *Last Judgment*," *Daedalus* 109 (1980): 211–16.

Titian may have taken a further swipe at Vasari and Michelangelo in designing the "Ape Laocoön" that Niccolò Boldrini turned into a woodcut caricature shortly after Vasari's visit to Venice in 1565/66. Leonard Barkan calls Titian "the fitting competitor" who employs parody as rapier in his contest with Michelangelo carried out in the fields of antiquity, emulation, and imitation. See Barkan, *Unearthing the Past*, 13–17. I thank Caitlin Petty for drawing my attention to Barkan's discussion of the Titian / Boldrini woodcut.

99. For the exequies of Michelangelo, see Rudolf and Margot Wittkower, *The Divine Michelangelo: The Florentine Academy's Homage on His Death in 1564; A Facsimile edition of "Esequie del Divino Michelangelo Buonarroti," Florence 1564* (London, 1964). See also Smithers, *The Cults of Raphael and Michelangelo*, 179–80 and passim.

100. Moyer, *The Intellectual World of Sixteenth-Century Florence*, 255–56.

101. Wethey, *Titian: Religious Paintings*, cat. no. 86; Humfrey, cat. no. 294.

102. See Jodi Cranston, *The Muddied Mirror. Materiality and Figuration in Titian's Later Paintings* (University Park, PA, 2010).

Conclusion

1. Vasari-Bull, 456.

2. *Relazione del Centenario di Michelangiolo Buonarroti nel Settembre del 1875 in Firenze* (Florence, 1876); and Stefano Corsi and Carlo Sisi, *Michelangelo nell'Ottocento: Il centenario del 1875* (Florence, 1994). See also Franca Falletti, ed., *The Accademia, Michelangelo, the Nineteenth Century* (Livorno, 1997); and Lene Østermark-Johansen, *Sweetness and Strength: The Reception of Michelangelo in Late Victorian England* (Aldershot, UK, 1999).

3. Rosand, *Painting in Cinquecento Venice*, 75. When Carlo Ridolfi published *Le maraviglie dell'Arte* in 1648, he appended a lengthy description of the funeral of Titian, which was never carried out due to plague. Ridolfi's purpose was to raise Titian's prestige by describing esequies equal to those accorded to Michelangelo. See Ridolfi, *The Life of Titian*, 138–45.

4. On the vicissitudes of the Titian monument, see Smithers, *The Cults of Raphael and Michelangelo*, 214–17, and Maria H. Loh, *Still Lives: Death, Desire, and the Portrait of the Old Master* (Princeton, 2015), 206, 220–25.

Index

Note: Page numbers in italic type indicate illustrations.

Illustration Credits

© Aavindraa / Creative Commons Wikimedia CC0 (Fig. 1)

© Image provided by Aberdeen City Council (Archives, Gallery & Museums Collection), Scotland (Fig. 3)

© Alamy (Plates 4, 5, 26, 28, 31, 38, 48; Figs. 4, 48)

© Alonso de Mendoza / Creative Commons Wikimedia CC0 (Fig. 31)

© Archaeodontosaurus / Creative Commons Wikimedia CC BY-SA 4.0 (Figs. 12, 24, 27, 32, 41)

© Art Resource (Plates 2, 14, 18, 19, 20, 25, 35, 36, 41, 42, 46; Figs. 2, 7, 8, 10, 11, 16, 25, 30, 32, 39, 40, 41, 49)

© Bridgeman Images (Plate 7; Fig. 37)

© Dcoetzee / Creative Commons Wikimedia CC0 (Plate 6)

© Detroit Institute of Arts (Plate 47)

© Eric Denker, Washington, DC (Plates 15, 16, 17)

© FDRMRZUSA / Creative Commons Wikimedia CC0 (Plates 24, 27)

© Gallerie Nazionali di Arte Antica, Roma (MiC)—Bibliotheca Hertziana, Istituto Max Planck per la storia dell'arte / Enrico Fontolan (Plate 44)

© Houghton Library, Harvard University (Fig. 13)

© JarektUploadBot / Creative Commons Wikimedia CC0 (Plate 1)

© Livio Pestilli, Rome (Plate 22)

© The Metropolitan Museum of Art (Plate 39; Figs. 18, 21, 28, 42)

© The Morgan Library & Museum, New York (Plate 43)

© Museo del Prado, Madrid (Plates 9, 10, 30, 33, 37)

© The National Gallery, London (Plates 11, 13; Figs. 6, 26)

© Courtesy National Gallery of Art, Washington, DC (Plates 8, 23, 40)

© Odecalchi / Creative Commons Wikimedia CC0 (Fig. 23)

© Patrick Hathaway (Venice Map, Rome Map)

© Photo by author (Plates 34, 45; Figs. 5, 14, 15, 17, 20, 22, 29, 33, 43, 45, 46)

© Πυλαιμένης / Creative Commons Wikimedia CC0 (Fig. 36)

© Ralph Liebermann, Williamstown, MA (Figs. 19, 34, 35)

© Royal Collection Enterprises Limited 2024 / Royal Collection Trust, London (Plate 21)

© Sailko / Creative Commons Wikimedia CC0 (Fig. 9)

© Sailko / Creative Commons Wikimedia CC BY-SA 4.0 (Plate 12)

© Staatliche Museen zu Berlin, Gemäldegalerie / Christoph Schmidt (Plate 32)

© Stv26 / Creative Commons Wikimedia CC0 (Plate 3)

© Tetraktys / Creative Commons Wikimedia CC BY 3.0 (Fig. 47)

© Victoria and Albert Museum, London (Fig. 44)

© Zenodot Verlagsgesellschaft mbH / Creative Commons Wikimedia GFDL (Plate 29)

© 1a2b3c? / Creative Commons Wikimedia CC0 (Fig. 38)